T0348640

Guerilla Capitalism:
The state in the market in Vietnam

CHANDOS
ASIAN STUDIES SERIES:
CONTEMPORARY ISSUES AND TRENDS

Series Editor: Professor Chris Rowley,
Cass Business School, City University, UK
(email: c.rowley@city.ac.uk)

Chandos Publishing is pleased to publish this major Series of books entitled *Asian Studies: Contemporary Issues and Trends*. The Series Editor is Professor Chris Rowley, Cass Business School, City University, UK.

Asia has clearly undergone some major transformations in recent years and books in the Series examine this transformation from a number of perspectives: economic, management, social, political and cultural. We seek authors from a broad range of areas and disciplinary interests: covering, for example, business/management, political science, social science, history, sociology, gender studies, ethnography, economics and international relations, etc.

Importantly, the Series examines both current developments and possible future trends. The Series is aimed at an international market of academics and professionals working in the area. The books have been specially commissioned from leading authors. The objective is to provide the reader with an authoritative view of current thinking.

New authors: we would be delighted to hear from you if you have an idea for a book. We are interested in both shorter, practically orientated publications (45,000+ words) and longer, theoretical monographs (75,000–100,000 words). Our books can be single, joint or multi-author volumes. If you have an idea for a book, please contact the publishers or Professor Chris Rowley, the Series Editor.

Dr Glyn Jones
Chandos Publishing
Email: gjones@chandospublishing.com
www.chandospublishing.com

Professor Chris Rowley
Cass Business School, City University
Email: c.rowley@city.ac.uk
www.cass.city.ac.uk/faculty/c.rowley

Chandos Publishing: Chandos Publishing is an imprint of Woodhead Publishing Limited. The aim of Chandos Publishing is to publish books of the highest possible standard: books that are both intellectually stimulating and innovative.

We are delighted and proud to count our authors from such well-known international organisations as the Asian Institute of Technology, Tsinghua University, Kookmin University, Kobe University, Kyoto Sangyo University, London School of Economics, University of Oxford, Michigan State University, Getty Research Library, University of Texas at Austin, University of South Australia, University of Newcastle, Australia, University of Melbourne, ILO, Max-Planck Institute, Duke University and the leading law firm Clifford Chance.

A key feature of Chandos Publishing's activities is the service it offers its authors and customers. Chandos Publishing recognises that its authors are at the core of its publishing ethos, and authors are treated in a friendly, efficient and timely manner. Chandos Publishing's books are marketed on an international basis, via its range of overseas agents and representatives.

Professor Chris Rowley: Dr Rowley, BA, MA (Warwick), DPhil (Nuffield College, Oxford) is Subject Group leader and the inaugural Professor of Human Resource Management at Cass Business School, City University, London, UK. He is the founding Director of the new, multi-disciplinary and internationally networked *Centre for Research on Asian Management* and Editor of the leading journal *Asia Pacific Business Review* (www.tandf.co.uk/journals/titles/13602381.asp). He is well known and highly regarded in the area, with visiting appointments at leading Asian universities and top journal Editorial Boards in the US and UK. He has given a range of talks and lectures to universities and companies internationally with research and consultancy experience with unions, business and government and his previous employment includes varied work in both the public and private sectors. Professor Rowley researches in a range of areas, including international and comparative human resource management and Asia Pacific management and business. He has been awarded grants from the British Academy, an ESRC AIM International Study Fellowship and gained a 5-year RCUK Fellowship in Asian Business and Management. He acts as a reviewer for many funding bodies, as well as for numerous journals and publishers. Professor Rowley publishes very widely, including in leading US and UK journals, with over 100 articles, 80 book chapters and other contributions and 20 edited and sole authored books.

Bulk orders: some organisations buy a number of copies of our books. If you are interested in doing this, we would be pleased to discuss a discount. Please email info@chandospublishing.com or telephone +44 (0) 1223 891358.

Guerilla Capitalism: The state in the market in Vietnam

LAN NGUYEN

EDITED BY

Charlotte Butler
Research Studies Manager
Euro-Asia and Comparative Research Centre, INSEAD

Chandos Publishing
Oxford · Cambridge · New Delhi

Chandos Publishing
TBAC Business Centre
Avenue 4
Station Lane
Witney
Oxford OX28 4BN
UK
Tel: +44 (0) 1993 848726
Email: info@chandospublishing.com

Chandos Publishing is an imprint of Woodhead Publishing Limited

Woodhead Publishing Limited
Abington Hall
Granta Park
Great Abington
Cambridge CB21 6AH
UK
www.woodheadpublishing.com

First published in 2009

ISBN:
978 1 84334 550 3

© L. Nguyen, 2009

British Library Cataloguing-in-Publication Data.
A catalogue record for this book is available from the British Library.

Produced from electronic copy supplied by the author.
Printed in the UK and USA.

Printed in the UK by 4edge Limited - www.4edge.co.uk

To David who has changed the way I see the world

CONTENTS

List of figures and tables   xi

Preface   xiii

About the author   xv

Acknowledgements   xvii

Introduction   1

CHAPTER 1: THE ANALYTICAL BACKGROUND   **5**

   1.1. The soft budget constraint   5
   1.2. Principal / agent theory   7
   1.3. Boisot and Child's C-space framework   9
   1.4. Hofstede's culture dimensions   11
   1.5. Institutional theory   15
      1.5.1. Williamson's transaction cost theory of organisations   15
      1.5.2. Institutional theory of economic organisations in East Asia   16
      1.5.3. North's institutional matrix   18

CHAPTER 2: THE THEORETICAL FRAMEWORK   **21**

   2.1. Theoretical framework and research issues   21
   2.2. Formal and informal   22
   2.3. Assumptions about human behaviour   26

CHAPTER 3: RESEARCH METHODOLOGY   **29**

   3.1. Methodology   29
      3.1.1. Philosophical grounds   29
      3.1.2. Contextualism   31
      3.1.3. Theoretical sensitivity   33
   Data sources and data collection methods   34
      3.2.2. Data on the rules of the game   37
      3.2.3. Data on the players – three case studies   37

CHAPTER 4: AN OVERVIEW OF VIETNAMESE HISTORY AND CULTURE   **40**

   4.1. Overview of Vietnamese history   41
      4.1.1. Overview   41
      4.1.2. Vietnam and the Chinese connection   42
   4.2. Overview of Vietnamese culture and society   43
      4.2.1. Confucianism   44
      4.2.2. The family and the village in Vietnam.   51

4.2.3. Buddhism   59
4.2.4. Taoism   62
4.2.5. Forms of cognition   63
4.2.6. Confucianism in Vietnam, China and Japan   66

**CHAPTER 5: AN OVERVIEW OF THE VIETNAMESE ECONOMY IN TRANSITION
AND THE REFORM OF STATE-OWNED ENTERPRISES**   72

5.1 The legacy of French colonialism   73
5.2. The Soviet-style development model 1955-1980   75
    5.2.1. The model   75
    5.2.2. The failure of the Soviet-style model   77
5.3. The reforms   78
    5.3.1. 'Fence breaking'   79
    5.3.2. The formal stage – 'making prices matter'   79
    5.3.3. The post-stage of SOE reform in Vietnam – 'the governance structure
    and internal management'   82
5.4. The Vietnamese economy – reform process and the position of SOEs in 2002   85
    5.4.1. General   85
    5.4.2. State-owned enterprises   86
    5.4.3. The private sector   88
    5.4.4. Foreign investment sector   89
5.5. The reform process in Vietnam – 'adjustment to a given world'   90

**CHAPTER 6: THE INSTITUTIONAL MATRIX AND TYPICAL FORM OF CAPITALISM
IN VIETNAM**   92

6.1. The formal laws and institutions in Vietnam   92
    6.1.1. Lack of codification   93
    6.1.2. Incomplete legal systems   94
    6.1.3. Weak and lacking law enforcement   95
    6.1.4. Banking and the stock market   96
6.2. Informal norms in economic transactions   98
    6.2.1. Trade and the city   99
    6.2.2. Limited trust and honesty in economic transactions   101
    6.2.3. Opportunism and corruption in current business practice   104
6.3. Guerilla capitalism   107
    6.3.1. Pattern of firms   108
    6.3.2. The internal structure of the firm   110

CHAPTER 7: AUTHORITY RELATIONS WITHIN VIETNAMESE SOES   113

7.1. Research process and assessment methods   113
7.2. The Aston data of centralisation of decision making   114
    7.2.1. The shoe enterprise   115
    7.2. 2. The garment enterprise   115
    7.2.3. The light bulb enterprise   116
    7.2.4. Overall   116
    7.2.5. Comparison with China   117
7.3. The Central Domain   117
    7.3.1. Limitations of the Aston Studies' assessment method   117
    7.3.2. The Central Domain   118
    7.3.3. Formalisation and centralisation   121
    7.3.4. Party, trade union and management – all in one piece   123

CHAPTER 8: THE INDUSTRIAL GOVERNANCE OF SOES   **127**

8.1. The governance structure – a formal framework   128
     8.1.1. Central SOEs   128
     8.1.2. Local SOEs   129
     8.1.3. State corporations   130
8.2. The nature of the relationship between the enterprise and the
higher hierarchical levels   132
     8.2.1. Formal administrative relationships   132
     8.2.2. Centralisation and patrimony   133

CHAPTER 9: THE MANAGEMENT PROBLEMS OF THE VIETNAMESE SOES   **136**

9.1. Other people's money – the 'bonus' problem   138
     9.1.1. Qualitative evidence   138
     9.1.2. Quantitative evidence   139
     9.1.3. Private vs public   141
9.2. The shoe enterprise   143
     9.2.1. Research strategy   143
     9.2.2. The formal structure of the enterprise   144
     9.2.3. The organisation of sales   146
     9.2.4. The general agent (GA) and the exercise of power   149
     9.2.5. Sources of power   151
9.3. Additional evidence from the shoe enterprise and from the garment and
the light bulb enterprises   153
     9.3.1. Additional qualitative evidence from the shoe enterprise   153
     9.3.2. Qualitative evidence from the other two cases   155
     9.3.3. Quantitative evidence   157
9.4. Other people's money: reconsidered   158

DISCUSSION   **160**

Action and structure   160
Transactions   163

**CHAPTER 10: EMBEDDED MATERIALISM – THE LIMITATION OF THE INCENTIVE
STRUCTURE IN VIETNAMESE SOES**   **164**

10.1. Marx's labour theory of value   165
10.2. Payment practice in the Vietnamese SOEs   166
     10.2.1. The salary budget   167
     10.2.2. Other regulations on payment   168
10.3. Embedded materialism, incentive structures and the problems of
Vietnamese SOEs   170

CHAPTER 11: POLICY IMPLICATIONS   **176**

11.1. Privatisation / equitisation   176
11.2. Further reform of the SOEs   178
     11.2.1 Autonomy   178
     11.2.2. 'Normalisation' and the role of the market   180

SUMMARY AND CONCLUSIONS   **184**

   1. Summary   184
   2. Contribution of the research   185
   3. Limitations   188

   4. Further research   188

   Appendix 1: list of decisions or responsibilities investigated
   (a replication of the Aston Studies)   190

   Appendix 2: Questionnaire I – perceptions about management in SOEs   192

   Appendix 3: Questionnaire II - the 'bonus' phenomenon in economic transactions
   in Vietnam   194

   Appendix 4: General information about the sample in the study of economic
   transactions (Questionnaire III)   196

BIBLIOGRAPHY   **197**
INDEX   **218**

TABLE OF FIGURES

Figure 1.1. Typology of transaction-governance structures   10

Figure 1.2. The Codification-Diffusion Curve of transaction-governance structures   11

Figure 1.3. The market failure framework   15

Table 2.1. Varying emphases: three pillars of institutions   23

Figure 2.1. The research framework - a conceptual model   27

Figure 3.1. The research strategy   34

Table 3.1. A general profile of the three SOEs in 1998   38

Figure 4.1. Cultural determinants of individual Vietnamese values and institutions –
                a conceptual structure   44

Table 5.1. The legacy of French colonialism: Vietnam in 1930s   74

Figure 5.1. The operating mechanism of a factory during the Soviet-style economy   76

Figure 5.2. Stages to capitalism   79

Table 5.2. Industrial output growth: annual rate of growth (%)   80

Table 5.3. Growth and inflation of the Vietnamese economy 1986-2000   86

Table 5.4. Contribution of SOEs to the government's revenue   87

Table 5.5. Share of GDP by sector ownership (%)   87

Table 5.6. Financial status of weak SOEs   88

Table 5.7. GDP growth by sector ownership (%)   89

Figure 5.3. Reform in Vietnam – 'adjustment to a given world'   91

Figure 6.1 The characteristics of the Vietnamese institutional matrix   108

Figure 7.1. Distribution of decisions by hierarchical level – shoe enterprise   115

Figure 7.2. Distribution of decisions by hierarchical level – garment enterprise   115

Figure 7.3. Distribution of decisions by hierarchical level – light bulb enterprise   116

Table 7.1. Distribution of decisions by hierarchical levels.   116

Figure 7.4. Distribution of decisions by hierarchical level in Chinese and Vietnamese SOEs   117

Figure 8.1. The administrative framework in Vietnamese central SOEs   128

Figure 8.2. The administrative framework in Vietnamese local SOEs   129

Figure 8.3. The administrative framework in the Vietnamese Decision-91
                state industrial corporations   130

Figure 8.4. Formal structure of a Decision-91 corporation   132

Table 9.1. The frequency with which private buyers and SOE buyers requested a bonus   142

Figure 9.1. The formal structure of the shoe enterprise   146

Figure 9. 2. The enterprise structure – 'important areas'   147

Figure 9.3. A formal hierarchical structure – the sales context   148

Table 9.2. Perceptions of opportunistic behaviour   157

Table 10.1. Salary of a middle manager and a worker in 1999 (in VND)   170

Preface

For several decades first INSEAD's Euro-Asia Centre and then its successor, the Euro-Asia and Comparative Research Centre, have focussed on the study of the countries of Pacific Asia, conducting and encouraging empirical and theoretical work on the topic of their varying business systems. A number of monographs, textbooks, research papers and case studies have resulted and the present volume is a continuation of that effort. In this case the work of Charlotte Butler at the Centre has been crucial.

This time the topic is the emergent business system of Vietnam, a matter of significant curiosity to many outside observers as they attempt to compare it with its giant neighbour China, and try to estimate its attractiveness as a field of investment, its likely future trajectory, and the nature of its distinct response to its own culture and history. The specific field of study is the state sector, and here we see evidence of the Asian tendency in development to retain a strong government connection into the economy, albeit in different ways country by country. This description of the Vietnam case also illustrates the wider national context for a full picture of the transitions being undertaken. The author' preference for qualitative research releases refreshing insights into local reality that supplement the more standard data sets also in use.

I first met Lan Nguyen in the MBA classroom in Hanoi, when I was a professor at the University of Hong Kong, and it gives me special pleasure to see this book as an outcome of his continued pursuit of knowledge, and his wish to impart to a wider audience what he has learned about the revival of his great country as it emerges from its sad history into its new role on the world stage.

Gordon Redding
Director, Euro-Asia and Comparative Research Centre, INSEAD.

About the author

Dr. Lan Nguyen is currently working for the International Finance Corporation (IFC) in Vietnam where he leads a technical assistance programme that aims at improving the regulatory environment for business and corporate governance practices there. Prior to that, Dr. Nguyen lectured at Vietnam's National Economics University Business School where he taught economics, business law, and project management. He has carried out extensive research on business environment issues in Vietnam.

Acknowledgements

This work would have never been brought to the reader without the support of INSEAD's Euro-Asia and Comparative Research Centre. I would like to address my special thanks to Gordon Redding and Charlotte Butler at the Centre for their great encouragement and support in getting this work published. I would like to express sincere gratitude to Charlotte Butler specifically for her efforts in helping turn my tedious Ph.D. thesis into this monograph. I am also deeply indebted to Anthony O'Connor for the time he spent working to ready the book for print.

My study could not have been completed without the help of my two supervisors, David Richards and Stephen Linstead. I should like to thank them for their support and encouragement. David helped me to 'enter' the Western world both physically and mentally. He taught me how to write an e-mail, how to correspond in English with Western recipients and to how to play the Western intellectual game with regard to social science. When I first went to England to study, I had a 'magical' image of the world in my mind, believing that there was only one way to see it and that everything could be understood through numbers and formulae. David proved to me that there are multiple realities and different ways to see the world so that, the closer I came to finishing my studies, the more I realised that social science was a kind of religion, a matter of belief and disbelief. For me, to study 'Western' social sciences was, in fact, to practice a new religion and in this, David was a patient and whole-hearted missionary who successfully converted me (I believe) to another denomination. I shall never forget him.

Throughout my research for this work, I also relied on the advice and encouragement of a number of people. Among those I would like to thank are Peter Blunt and Merrick Jones at the Northern Territory University in Australia, Paul Cook and Collin Kirkpatrick at the University of Manchester who gave me much advice and warm support while I was there, and Nancy Napier for her support when I was doing my fieldwork in Vietnam. In addition, my research was also inspired by the work of many authors, but I need to give a special thank to Gordon Redding, John Child and Max Boisot for their influential and inspirational work on management in China and transitional economies.

I was lucky enough to be one of those who benefited from an aid project funded by SIDA (Swedish International Development Agency). The project financed my MBA and partially my Ph.D. The Vietnamese proverb *an qua nho ke trong cay* means 'when one eats the fruit, one must remember the person(s) who grew the tree'. I must not, therefore, forget the Swedish taxpayers who always were, and still are, very generous to Vietnamese people. In the SIDA project, we were very lucky to have Suzanne Hosley as the project manager. I am deeply indebted to her for her support and encouragement. She constantly supported and encouraged my research and though she was always very busy, never failed to answer a single question during my time overseas. She was really special.

I would like to thank the director of the three Vietnamese enterprises who allowed me to conduct my research in their companies, an unusual way of doing research in Vietnam. Special thanks must also go to the managers of the enterprises. They were kind enough to join the interview process but, since they were promised anonymity, regretfully cannot be thanked by name. Their help was greatly appreciated.

I would like to thank my research colleagues: Adel, Catherine, Cinzia, Gulia, James, Mandy, Marietta, Michael, Monica, Tomo, Tony, for their warmth, support and encouragement. Special thanks go to Michael and Gulia for their support and encouragement; my ideas were sharpened through talking to them.

Last but not least, I would like to thank my wife for her support, understanding and patience throughout my study.

Introduction

This monograph focuses on the business environment and behaviour of state owned enterprises (SOEs) in a transitional country, Vietnam, a country well known to the world through war but still little understood when it comes to business and management. Like China and other former socialist countries in Eastern Europe, Vietnam first pursued the Soviet-style development model, characterised by the central planning of economic and social activity. Then in the early 1980s, the country began a transitional process towards a market economy. As a result, especially after 1986 when a radical reform programme (called doi moi in Vietnamese) was implemented, the Vietnamese economy grew rapidly and the living conditions of the Vietnamese people improved significantly.

Today Vietnam is following the capitalist path to development, despite there being a reluctance to admit it. Although the country has recently made notable economic progress, its transition process is far from over. The economy is still burdened with a large and inefficient state sector and the institutional systems associated with a market economy remain, to a great extent, underdeveloped. Given that Vietnam is the world's 13th most populous country, with a population of about 80 million and a rich pool of natural and human resources, there has been growing interest among international investors, institutions, and organisations in the country's potential economic development. This study aims to provide the various audiences interested in Vietnam with hitherto unavailable information on the country's business environment in general, and the behaviour of its dominant type of businesses, the SOEs in particular.

Although this research is mainly concerned with the behaviour of Vietnamese SOEs, it does not consider them independent of their environment. As current social science theory would argue, since organisations in general and SOEs in particular are embedded in their broad societal context; they are not the same everywhere. This research is, therefore, designed to study first, the Vietnamese business environment and then its SOEs with reference to their environment.

In fact, 'environment' is perhaps too weak a concept, since there are many different kinds and numerous definitions of what it means. In the case of the Vietnamese SOEs, any concept of their environment must take into account two important factors and consider how they have interacted to shape the behaviour of the enterprises operating within that environment. The first, the informal environment, is constituted by Vietnamese history and culture while the second, the formal context, is defined by the nature of the economic transition process occurring in the country. This study incorporates these two factors into a model of analysis by first constructing an 'ideal type' of business in Vietnam, and then interpreting SOE behaviour with reference to this ideal and the particular characteristics of the transitional process. The 'ideal type' is thus a construct for the purpose of comparison and explanation, a way to capture the key characteristics of Vietnamese culture and history and their bearing on business organisations operating in that specific context. By comparing them with an 'ideal type', certain aspects of the SOEs become 'known'. SOE behaviour, and in particular some of the problems associated with them, can be explained by combining the 'ideal type' method with an analysis of the particular features of the reform process in Vietnam.

The major questions tackled in this study are:

What are the major characteristics of Vietnamese culture and history, and what bearing have they had on the form of business organisation and management practice in Vietnam? More specifically, given its historical, cultural and institutional background, what would be the 'ideal type' of business organisation operating in Vietnam?

What are the key differences between SOEs and the 'ideal type' (in terms of ownership and governance, for example) and how can SOE behaviour in general and some of their particular problems, be explained by reference to these differences?

What are the current limitations and difficulties of SOE reform in Vietnam, and how do these limitations account for and exacerbate some of the problems within the SOEs?

What policies should the Vietnamese government adopt in order to overcome problems associated with the SOEs, and to improve their performance?

The study is divided into three parts. Part 1 consists of three chapters and is concerned with theories and methods. Its objective is to review various theories concerning the present topic. A brief review of the literature is given in *Chapter 1*. In fact, very little has been written about management and organisational behaviour in Vietnam and so this review focuses on the theories and research that appeared most relevant. These include the soft budget constraint (SBC) theory, agency theory, Hofstede's culture dimensions, Boisot and Child's C-space, and several versions of institutional theory.

Chapter 2 is concerned with the theoretical framework of the study. It further elaborates the two broad research questions referred to above, and lays out the rationale for the chosen theoretical framework. North's concept of institutions is chosen as the theoretical tool to establish the pattern of the firm in the Vietnamese institutional environment, and the internal structure of the 'ideal' firm is drawn from, or conceptualised as, a consequence of the Vietnamese culture. *Chapter 3* concerns the study's methodology and methods. Since this research was concerned with interpreting and building theories rather than testing hypotheses and theories quantitatively, I chose an *overall* qualitative methodology and an interpretative approach for this study. The data used were drawn from multiple sources ranging from proverbs and stories to direct interviews, observations and questionnaires.

Part 2 is concerned with the process of building the ideal type, the typical firm associated with the cultural and institutional environment in Vietnam. It too consists of three chapters. *Chapter 4* covers Vietnamese history and culture and demonstrates how and why the Vietnamese share many cultural traits with the Chinese, Confucianism being the dominant value system. This fact allows management and organisational studies literature written about China to be incorporated into the study. *Chapter 5* presents a history of the Vietnamese economy and more importantly, the country's recent economic reform process, and provides the context for the later chapters about institutions and the organisational behaviour of the Vietnamese SOEs. *Chapter 6* describes the institutional framework in Vietnam and the type of capitalism associated with it. The current Vietnamese institutional matrix presented in the chapter is characterised by insecure property rights and high or inefficient transaction costs. This framework, the chapter argues, is associated with a special form of capitalism, 'guerilla capitalism' in which business firms (the ideal type) are characterised as small-scale, with little fixed capital, short-term orientation, family controlled and managed. Throughout the process of building the ideal type, a comparative methodology was used that took evidence about Chinese and Japanese culture, family and trade, and compared and contrasted it with that of Vietnam.

Part 3 consists of five chapters and is directly concerned with SOE behaviour. *Chapter 7* deals with authority relations within the state enterprises, the major characteristics of which are patrimonial and *over-centralised* since the firm's director, who to some extent resembles the family head, makes almost all management decisions. *Chapter 8* looks at the industrial governance of SOEs. It demonstrates how they are still, to a great extent, dependent on government officials since important decisions, especially those concerning finance and investment are made by government officials. *Chapter 9* presents the findings of the research into the problems of managing SOEs, notably the ubiquity of opportunism. This chapter presents an in-depth case study, the shoe enterprise, in which the son of the director used his power to obtain his own ends.

The explanation for the problem of opportunism offered here rests on the difference between SOEs and the ideal type, the family business. SOEs are not owned by the family, but by the 'ambiguous' owner, the state, yet whenever there is a conflict of interest, the family is always placed above everything else. A discussion section follows that is aimed at reconciling action and structure within the Vietnamese SOE context to confirm the ideal type thesis of capitalism in Vietnam. Chapter 10 presents and analyses what we call 'embedded materialism'. It argues that Marx's labour theory of value, with its emphasis on materialism, was the building block of the old system in Vietnam, and still exercises a great influence. The current 'rules of the game' (i.e. payment policy and incentive systems) applying to SOEs are still heavily material-oriented. This embedded materialism either accounts for, or exacerbates, some of the problems presented in Chapter 9. Based upon these research findings and analysis throughout the study, Chapter 11 offers several suggestions as to how to overcome some of the problems associated with SOEs and so improve their performance.

The final section summarises the key points of the research and its major theoretical contributions. It also highlights some of the limitations of the present study and indicates some directions for future research.

Part 1: Theories and methods

Chapter 1: The analytical background

Since 1989, the year that marked the collapse of the socialist system, there has been a rapid growth in literature on management and organisation studies in transitional countries and not surprisingly, SOEs have been a major target. Most of the literature, however, is about the economic reforms advocated and financed by financial and donor institutions such as the International Monetary Fund (IMF), the World Bank (WB) and the Asian Development Bank (ADB). Consequently, the focus has been on the implementation and effectiveness of structural adjustment programmes in general, and privatisation in particular. These sources of research and literature are undoubtedly practical in their focus but not really 'academic' in the strict meaning of the term. Only a few studies have been concerned with explaining and interpreting the behaviour of SOEs in transitional countries, and not a single one has focused on management behaviour in the SOEs of Vietnam, a country notorious through war but about which little is known in a business and economic development context.

This chapter reviews the major theories and studies that are most closely related to research on the behaviour of the Vietnamese SOEs. It also points out the relevance and limitations of each theory in explaining the social phenomena under investigation.

1.1. The soft budget constraint

One of the influential theories concerning state enterprises in the former socialist and now transitional countries is the theory developed by Janos Kornai called 'soft budget constraint' (SBC). Kornai (1980) extended the term 'budget constraint' from the theory of the household in microeconomics to the context of the firm. SBC refers to the situation in which a "strict relationship between expenditure and earnings has been relaxed, because excess expenditure over earnings will be paid by some other institution, typically by the state" (Kornai, 1990, p.21). More importantly, according to Kornai, the "decision maker expects such external financial assistance with high probability and this probability is firmly built into his behaviour" (p.21). The consequence is that firms in a SBC situation will not try to improve their performance because "they feel that when they cannot pay the bills, someone else will step in and bail them out" (p.27).

Kornai also pointed out a number of ways in which SBC can occur. Examples are what he termed 'soft' subsidy, 'soft' taxation and 'soft' credit. 'Soft' here means negotiable or subject to bargaining. Soft taxation, for example, occurs when "the fulfilment of tax obligations is not strictly enforced; there are leaks, *ad hoc* exemptions, postponement" (p.22-23). Since it was introduced, SBC has been widely recognised as a major source of inefficiency in various economic systems, especially the former socialist economies (Li and Lang, 1998). Kornai's work on the SBC in transitional countries focuses on the vertical relationship between the government and the enterprise. His explanation of SBC centres on bureaucratic paternalism, the government agent as a superior and the enterprise as a subordinate. The superior has to protect the subordinate and the subordinate takes advantage of this paternalism and repeatedly makes financial losses (Li and Lang, 1998). Price decisions are an example. Kornai (1990, 1998) argued that the assumption that decision makers are price responsive is far from self-evident in the socialist economies in which the price and cost responsiveness of decision makers is quite weak.

SBC provides a useful framework to explain the inefficiency of enterprises in socialist economies. It has certainly influenced the practice of enterprise reform programmes in traditional countries. In Vietnam, for example, foreign donors and Vietnamese policy makers talked about measures to 'harden' the budget constraint. Various World Bank and IMF reports also use the term SBC or hard budget constraint. SBC was certainly relevant to explain firm behaviour in the Soviet-style economies and, to some extent, in transitional economies at the early stage of transition when 'everybody is equal' was still, to a great extent, the order of the day. It would not be very difficult to imagine that nobody will try hard knowing that their labour will not be rewarded.

The explanatory power of SBC theory, which treated SBC as the major source of inefficiency or poor financial performance of enterprises in mixed and socialist economies at the post-stage of transition is, however, limited. It is true that bailing out, relaxed taxation and other means of subsidy are still common in many countries, especially developing and transitional countries. In Vietnam, for example, the government is still 'soft' towards SOEs. But it could be that because SOEs cannot survive on their own, the government believes it has to support them. The government, for some reason, cannot let them or does not want them to die away since they were already 'born'. The situation could be referred as 'path dependence'. This is true. Despite the fact that under new financial regulations, employees of the Vietnamese SOEs can only become better off if their enterprises perform well, many enterprises are still making a loss and the government has to subsidise them. SBC theorists implicitly conceptualised that the firm was a 'naughty boy', always expecting financial support from the father so the father should be tough on him. This conception is too simplistic and misleading. Firstly, the firm is not a passive instrument, it is a social organisation with people with values and interests who are not always lazy and looking for 'someone else to pay their bills'. Secondly, the relationship between the firm and the government is often more complicated than the simple dyadic conception of the SBC theorists. In reality, it is not always a matter of 'give' and 'take' (e.g. the government always gives and the firms always takes). Like other economists, SBC theorists, employed an *as if* reasoning. If, for example, the

6

government acts like the American government which is 'hard' and 'fair' to the firm, then the firm will 'stand on its own feet' and prosper. This 'as if' reasoning clearly fails to capture the complexity of the reality of social phenomena.

1.2. Principal / agent theory

Agency theory can offer some insights into the management behaviour of SOEs in Vietnam, since the heart of the enterprise reform programme is, by and large, about incentive structure, authority delegation and decentralisation (see Chapter 5). This primarily involves the relation between two parties: the government (principal) and the enterprise (agent).

Agency theory is rooted in one of the oldest problems of political philosophy, that of understanding the relation between the 'master' who is given socially legitimate control over certain actions and the 'servant' who controls the information on which the 'master' acts (Cyert and March, 1992). Berle and Means (1932) introduced the theory to the context of the modern firm where ownership and management is separated. The theory has developed substantially since the 1960s and 1970s (Eisenhardt, 1989) and became centrally concerned with the relationship between two contracting parties. Jensen and Mickling (1976) define an agency relationship as "a contract under which one or more persons (the principal(s)) engage another person (the agent) to perform some service on their behalf which involves delegating some decision-making authority to the agent" (p.333). The theory assumes that both the principal and the agent are utility maximizers with different interests, and that because of information asymmetry the agent will not always act in the best interests of the principal. The principal can limit the divergence of interest by establishing appropriate incentives for the agent and by incurring costs termed *agency costs* (Jensen and Mickling, 1976).

Agency costs include: (1) monitoring expenditure by the principal to limit any aberrant activities of the agent; (2) bonding expenditure by the agent to ensure that he will not take certain actions that could harm the principal; and (3) residual loss: the US dollar equivalent of the reduction in welfare experienced by the principal due to the divergence between the agent's decisions and those decisions which would maximise the welfare of the principal (Jensen and Mickling, 1976). In the management literature, the principal-agent relation is more or less prototypic of the relation between shareholders (principals) and management (agents). The formation, as Cyert and March (1992) point out, is a classic one of employment contract. The theory addresses the information problems associated with such contracts. The focus of the theory is "on determining the most efficient contract governing the principal-agent relationship given assumptions about people (e.g. self-interest, bounded rationality, risk aversion), organisation (e.g. goal conflict amongst members), and information (e.g. information is a commodity which can be purchased)" (Eisenhardt, 1989, p.58). The theory also seeks to identify an incentive system that can motivate and ensure that the agents will act in line with the principal's interest.

Agency theory is controversial. Proponents argue either that it is a 'powerful' organisational theory (Jensen, 1983) or that it offers "unique insight into information systems, outcome uncertainty, incentive and risk" (Eisenhardt, 1989, p.57). Opponents argue that agency theory rests only on a narrow assumption of human behaviour. Donaldson pointed out that agency theory depicts managers as "inherently tending to act in opportunistic, self-serving, guileful, and lazy ways-at cost to their employers", and that it lacks concepts for acknowledging a more positive view of management motives and behaviour (Donaldson, 1990, p.343). More emotionally, Perrow (1986) considered the theory as dehumanising and even "dangerous" (p.235). I argue that every theory can provide certain insights into the phenomena under investigation. The problem is that organisation theorists often tend to try to apply a certain theory to every organisation in every setting. It is the context of the social phenomena under investigation that matters.   It is true that by overemphasising agency costs, agency theory ignored the broad cultural, social and political background in which social actors find themselves. Agency theory, however, undoubtedly offers insights into certain contexts in which interests are, to a great degree, in conflict.

In the context of the present study, the Vietnamese SOEs are under the ownership of the state. There is a kind of principal-agent relationship here between government bureaux and the management of SOEs. The state agency (relevant ministries and bureaux) could be regarded as the principal and the state enterprise or its management team as the agent. Agency theory would predict that the poor performance of many Vietnamese SOEs (see Chapter 5) is due to the lack of control exerted by the government over the enterprise. It is true that there are many *principal-agent problems* (e.g. who actually owns the enterprise) involved in the management of the Vietnamese SOEs (see Chapter 5). Cheating, self-serving and other opportunistic behaviours are not uncommon in the Vietnamese SOEs (see Chapter 9). Agency theory offers insights into these problems since undoubtedly they result from a lack of control by a principal somewhere. The problems are, however, beyond the explanatory framework which agency theory would allow.

Firstly, the Vietnamese government bureaux (the principal) are quite different from the shareholders of Western corporations. The government bodies and officials are not the *real* owners of the enterprise (e.g. they are not profit-claimers). Also, Vietnamese SOEs, under new regulations, are entitled to claim part of the enterprise's profit. The enterprise employees, therefore, share the ownership with the government. 'People's ownership' is still very much the case in the context of Vietnamese SOEs. It is not clear, therefore, who is the agent and who is the principal in Vietnamese SOEs. The same situation is found in Chinese SOEs. From their study, Boisot and Child (1996) pointed out that the ownership of the Chinese SOEs is "intangible" (p.620). Secondly, as we have mentioned, the essential tenet of agency theory is the employment contract. In Western countries, the legal system is well developed. The administration system is a rational-legal one in which formal contracts assume great importance. Management behaviour, therefore, may be explained by a theory that takes contracts as its core. In Vietnam, as we shall see in

8

the later chapters, businesses are characterised by a low level of formalisation. Formal employment contracts of a Western kind are foreign to the Vietnamese.

In summary, agency theory offers insight into agency problems that are common in the Vietnamese SOEs. This theory alone, however, is inadequate to explain the management behaviour of the Vietnamese SOEs. It is, therefore, as recommended by Eisenhardt (1989), necessary to incorporate the agency perspective in a broader framework.

1.3. Boisot and Child's C-space framework

Given the fact that Vietnam and China share many cultural, political and economic development aspects (see chapter 4) the literature on Chinese SOEs is worth discussing here. One important source of literature about management in China, especially the management behaviour of the Chinese SOEs, is that of Max Boisot and John Child and their Chinese students. Boisot and Child both worked for the China-European Community Management Institute (CEMI) in Beijing, China. First Boisot and then Child were dean and director there for nearly a decade. They taught the first groups of Chinese MBA students, which gave them a unique opportunity to study management in China during their time there. They have accordingly published extensively about management in China. One of their contributions to the literature on the transition process in transitional countries in general, and in China in particular, is the concept of culture space or C-space (C stands for culture) (Boisot, 1986, 1987, 1994 and 1995; Boisot and Child, 1988, 1996 and 1999; and Child 1990, 1994). The C-space is a two dimensional space. The two dimensions are information related: *codification* and *diffusion*. The space posits information environments for transaction.

Boisot and Child (1988) identified four 'ideal' types of transaction-governance structures associated with different combinations of codification and diffusion. The four transaction-governance structure types they termed: *fief*, *clan*, *bureaucracy*, and *market* (see Figure 1.1 and 1.2). The 'market' type of environment is found in Western developed countries where information regarding business transactions is well codified and widely diffused. Transactions are impersonal.

In their numerous publications, Boisot and Child pointed out that given the country's cultural background, the transaction environment in China is characterised by a 'fief' type. Information regarding business transactions is, to a great extent, uncodified and undiffused. Transactions are characterised by (1) personal trust, (2) high uncertainty and (3) 'small-number bargaining'. The transition in China is in fact the process of moving up from the 'fief' to the 'market' quadrant of the C-space. Given the tenacious nature of culture, the transitional process from 'fief' to 'market' would take a long time and entail considerable effort.

9

Figure 1.1. Typology of transaction-governance structures

<table>
<tr><td rowspan="2" style="writing-mode:vertical">Codified information</td><td>B- Bureaucracies

Information diffusion limited and under central control

Relationships impersonal and hierarchical

Submission to super-ordinate goals

Hierarchical co-ordination

No necessary to share values and beliefs</td><td>C- Markets

Information widely diffused, no control

Relationships impersonal and competitive

No super-ordinate goals-each one for himself

Horizontal co-ordination through self-regulation

No necessary to share values and beliefs</td></tr>
</table>

	B- Bureaucracies	C- Markets
Codified information	Information diffusion limited and under central control Relationships impersonal and hierarchical Submission to super-ordinate goals Hierarchical co-ordination No necessary to share values and beliefs	Information widely diffused, no control Relationships impersonal and competitive No super-ordinate goals-each one for himself Horizontal co-ordination through self-regulation No necessary to share values and beliefs
Uncodified information	**A- Fiefs** Information diffusion limited by lack of codification to face to face relationships Relationships personal and hierarchical (feudal/charismatic) Submission to super-ordinate goals Hierarchical co-ordination Necessary to share values and beliefs	**D- Clans** Information diffused but still limited by lack of codification to face to face relationships Relationships personal and non-hierarchical Goals are shared through a process of negotiation Horizontal co-ordination through negotiation Necessary to share values and beliefs

       Undiffused information   Diffused information

Source: Boisot and Child (1988, p.509)

Boisot and Child also used the C-space to explain the internal management and structure of the Chinese SOEs. They reconciled the two dimensions: codification and diffusion of information in the C-space framework with formalisation and centralisation (Child, 1990 and Boisot, 1994). They pointed out that Chinese SOEs are characterised by high centralisation and a low level of formalisation. They operate in the "fief" area of the C-space. Boisot and Child (1990) also pointed out that the "fief" area is only suitable for small family businesses. This partly explains the phenomenon of widespread opportunism in the SOE sector in China, as SOEs are not small family businesses.

Figure 1.2. The Codification-Diffusion Curve of transaction-governance
structures

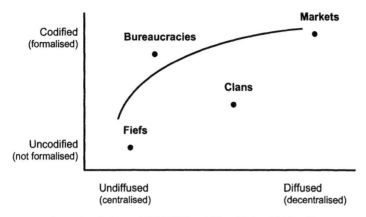

Source: *Adapted from Boisot and Child (1988, p.510) and Boisot (1994, p.41)*

C-space is a unique tool to explain both the internal working of SOEs and the transitional process in China as a whole. The framework can also help explain the challenges faced by China in that country's transitional process to a market economy in a comprehensive way, as well as providing a framework for practical solutions.

In summary, Boisot and Child provided a unique tool that can be used to explain both the processes and problems of economic transition in former socialist countries in general, and in China in particular. Given the fact that Vietnam shares many cultural characteristics and institutional arrangements with China, the C-space concept and other work of Boisot and Child on management and transition process in China provide useful insights into, and vocabulary for the study of, the behaviour of SOEs and economic transition in Vietnam.

1.4. Hofstede's culture dimensions

For many anthropologists and sociologists, culture is undoubtedly the major source of explanation of the difference among different societies in many social aspects: management, economics, politics, and other institutions. The major part of the work of great social thinkers such as Weber and Durkheim concerns culture. However, until recently culture has not received much attention in organisation studies. Culture is not even mentioned in the index, or only briefly covered in such well-regarded review books of organisation theories as that of Pfeffer (1982 and 1997) and Perrow (1986). Hickson and Pugh (1995) pointed out that only two out of the 62 "great writers on organisations" (selected by them) really study "culture in its own right in order to better to understand its consequences." (p.8). The two writers, according to Hickson and Pugh, are Ouchi (a Japanese-American) and Hofstede (a Dutchman).

Following Hofstede's study (Hofstede 1980), there has recently been an increase in literature that links national cultures to management and organisations (see, for example, Hampden -Turner and Trompenaars, 1993; Hofstede, 1991; and Triandis, 1994). Given the success of East Asian economies in recent years and the increasing number of multinational corporations, there has also been a growing literature on management and economic organisations in the outside Western world. The structure and functioning of the South Korean *chaebol*, the Japanese large corporation and the Chinese family business have been most frequently studied and compared (Redding 1993; Whitley, 1992, 1994 and 1999; and Orru, Biggart and Hamilton, 1997). Although these studies employed different approaches and arrived at slightly different explanations, cultural values are increasingly seen as important variables in determining an organisation's effectiveness (Richards, 1991). Although culture is considered an important source of explanation of management and organisations, different studies have, however, treated culture differently. In this section, we focus our analysis on Hofstede's study, which is considered as both important and influential.

Hofstede's five cultural dimensions provide a simple, but useful framework for comparison cultural values across the global. These five dimensions are:

1. Individualism versus collectivism;
2. Large versus small power distance;
3. Strong versus weak uncertainty avoidance;
4. Masculinity versus femininity;
5. Confucian dynamism (later called the long-term orientation dimension).

Hofstede's original study concerned comparative work-related values of a sample of 40 countries. The value systems of these 40 countries were drawn from a questionnaire survey of employees of a single multinational: IBM (Hofstede, 1980). The original study concerned only the first four dimensions above while the fifth was added later. Countries were placed within these dimensions. Hofstede used this system of values to explain differences between countries in many aspects: management, organisations, economic growth, development and political theories.

Hofstede's studies have undoubtedly been influential. The five cultural dimensions have been used in many organisational and management studies. Cultural dimensions have widely accepted as an important explanation source of the differences in organisational structure and management practice in different countries. Organisations in high power distance cultures, for example, are often more centralised than those in low power distance ones. Although Hofstede's culture dimensions allow us to explain certain aspects of social phenomena, it is important to note that, like many other concepts and theories, culture dimensions cannot explain every social aspect. Hofstede himself, for example, tried to explain almost all aspects of society through the tool of the five culture dimensions (see Hofstede, 1980, 1991). Since culture is crucial in the approach of the present research, it is necessary to present briefly our own comment on Hofstede's study of culture dimensions.

There have been a number of studies using the point scale from Hofstede's study quantitatively as independent variables from other dependent macro variables such as economic growth, GDP per head or even corruption. We argue that such research is both naïve and misleading and that the dimensions should be used *qualitatively* (e.g. small, medium and high) rather than quantitatively. This is mainly because of the problems associated with the research methodology used in the original Hofstede's study. Assuming that if we asked Vietnamese employees working in joint-ventures such as IBM to fill in Hofstede's questionnaires and used the score to compare with other countries in Hofstede's original sample, we would obtain a very distorted picture. Vietnam is a poor country with very high unemployment rate, people who get a job at IBM subsidiaries would be the lucky or even relatively 'high status' people in society. This fact really counts in answering a too general question: How long do you think you will continue working for this company? Secondly, one should note that there are different meanings or forms of the same dimensions. Confucianism, for example, is not the same in different societies (see Chapter 4). Collectivism is another example. From their comparative management study between Hong Kong and Japan, Kirkbride and Tang (1994) pointed out that:

"In Japan, the key collectivity is usually work-based, with high levels of organisational allegiance. In contrast, HK collectivism is usually family-based." (p106).

Taiwan and South Korea are ranked closely in all five of Hofstede's culture dimensions. They are almost identical in two dimensions: power distance (Korea 60, Taiwan 58) and individualism (Korea 18, Taiwan 17) (Hofstede, 1991). But the organisational structure and behaviour of the dominant business forms in the two countries (the *chaebol* in Korea and family businesses in Taiwan) are, to a great extent, different (Orru, Biggart and Hamilton, 1997; and Whitley, 1992).

The above examples show that it is necessary to supplement culture dimensions with additional understanding of the society under investigation.

One study which links culture dimensions directly and quantitatively to other social variables is that by Hofstede and his colleague Michael Bond. Hofstede and Bond (1988) made a direct link between their Confucian dynamism dimension and economic growth. Since Vietnam is a neo-Confucian country with high Confucian dynamism or Chinese values (see Chapter 4), it is worth discussing Hofstede and Bond's research here. Hofstede and Bond found that there was a strong correlation between Confucian dynamism scores and economic growth and they contended that high Confucian dynamism *causes* high economic growth. Hofstede and Bond could be right to draw that conclusion since Chinese values such as hard-work, thriftiness and/or high saving appeared to be associated with economic achievement. The point is that their conclusion could be misleading since they did not take into account or incorporate other factors in their modelling. We accept that there are no *perfect* social theories or models, but it is clear that Hofstede and Bond missed important points.

Hofstede and Bond did not take into account the development levels of different countries in their sample. Developed countries in Hofstede and Bond's sample had already reached a high stage of development. How could these countries have an economic growth rate of, say 8-10% annually for a period of 20 years, like some developing countries? Also, modernised or developed countries, as Anthony Giddens points out, are very future oriented (Giddens, 1990). In those countries, institutions have developed to the extent that individuals can count on them. Currency and banking and social security systems were well developed and reliable. These factors can partly explain why people in such countries such as the UK, the USA and Canada ranked low in Hofstede's "long-term orientation". By contrast, in countries like Vietnam and China, people do not trust the government and formal institutions such as the banking system. This has created the urge to keep money "under the bed" to secure the future. Under such conditions, saving and thriftiness do not necessary lead to economic growth. The following example supports our point. In the last two years, Chinese and Vietnamese governments have tried to encourage people to spend. They have allowed more holidays and cut working hours to encourage people to spend more time and money on holidays to boost the demand side and thus economic growth (The Economist, 2000). Keynes's "paradox of thriftiness" has actually been relearned. In addition, hard work and thriftiness can bear fruit only if harnessed to the right ideas and directed to the right ends (Armour, 1995). Governments can play an important role in releasing the potential resources of growth, a point clearly supported by the obvious differences in the development level between North and South Korea and between overseas and mainland China. The following quotation from Yeh and Lawrence (1995) sums this up:

> "Failure to incorporate other factors that affect economic growth into the analysis... confuses the reader. If cultural values are not sufficient conditions for explaining economic growth... then how is the reader to interpret the regression model that includes only these factors but excludes other potentially necessary conditions for economic growth? Further, the primary cultural dimensions that these researchers (Hofstede and Bond) find to be associated with economic growth, Hofstede's individualism and Confucian dynamism, appear to be related to other factors which are generally considered to play a role in determining economic growth. The omission of these factors indicates possible model mis-specification and potentially misleading results." [p.7][*]

Cultural values are undoubtedly important sources of explanation for economic performance, but economic performance is not reducible to cultural values.

The above analyses of Hofstede's culture dimensions and Hofstede and Bond's Confucian thesis demonstrate that in order to understand and explain social phenomena such as economic growth, organisation structure or functioning and management practice, one should also take into account other political, historical and institutional aspects of the country under investigation. We need more languages

---

[*] The page number in the square brackets "[..]" indicates a reference to an EBSCO page (electronic source).

than five cultural dimensions to 'read' social 'texts' like organisation behaviour or economic growth.

1.5. Institutional theory

There are many different versions of institutional theory. This section briefly reviews those versions that are closest to the present research topic.

1.5.1. Williamson's transaction cost theory of organisations

An economist, Williamson naturally approached organisations from an economic viewpoint. Economic approaches to organisation behaviour are generally ignored by organisational theorists and sociologists, so Williamson's work is a special case. Williamson is actually on Hickson and Pugh's (1995) list of 62 "great writers on organisation", whose writings about organisations have drawn attention (and often criticism) from theorists in various disciplines.

Williamson developed his theory from the idea, originated by Ronald Coarse (1937) that organisations exist because there are positive transaction costs. Organisations exist because they can mediate to obtain lower costs associated with transactions or transaction costs. Williamson (1975) extended the transaction cost thesis to what he called the "market failure framework". This framework is built on two human behavioural assumptions: bounded rationality and opportunism. The framework consists of two pairs of relationship: bounded rationality – uncertainty/ complexity and opportunism – small numbers (see Figure 1.3).

Figure 1.3. The market failure framework

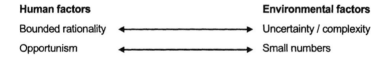

Human factors	**Environmental factors**
Bounded rationality ⟷	Uncertainty / complexity
Opportunism ⟷	Small numbers

According to this framework, the market will fail when bounded rationality couples with complexity/uncertainty or opportunism couples with the small numbers condition[*]. Under such conditions, the market mechanism becomes less efficient than a bureaucracy because "each party will opportunistically claim higher costs or poor quality, whichever is in his or her interest. In order to maintain such an exchange each party will have to go to considerable expense to audit the costs or performance of the other." (Ouchi 1980, p.133).

According to this perspective, under the condition of high transaction costs firms will decide to 'make' instead of 'buy' to avoid transaction costs. This line of reasoning is, to a large extent, also shared by Chandler in his *The Visible Hand* (1977).

---

[*] Small numbers refer to the market situations where there are only a small number of players (e.g. suppliers) or bilateral monopoly.

This transaction cost perspective takes efficiency as the core element in determining the nature of organisations. Transaction cost economics assumes that there are conflict interests within and between organisations and that participants will lie, cheat, shirk and steal in their own self-interest if they can (Cyert and March, 1992). Williamson's stylised analyses are the conditions under which a firm will be financed through debt, rather than equity and the M-form hypothesis (Williamson, 1975 and 1991).

Williamson's market failure framework and transaction cost theory of organisation have been severely criticised by organisation theorists, sociologists, anthropologists and economists (see, for example, Perrow, 1986; Pfeffer, 1982 and 1997; Granovetter, 1985; Dore, 1983; and Orru, Biggart and Hamilton, 1997; Douglas, 1986; and North, 1990). The criticisms centred on Williamson's narrow assumptions of human behaviour and the assumption of the rational firm. Criticisms of Williamson's work are many, and this continued attention indicates that 'his work must have something to say'. Williamson's work, I argue, served as an "ideal type" and has "provocative power". It may not be 'true', but it provides a certain vocabulary for useful discourse. People have criticised Williamson's theory in order to build or strengthen their own theory. Granovetter's "embeddedness" perspective was certainly inspired or clarified through the author's criticism of Williamson's market and hierarchy dichotomy. With regard to Williamson's work, we agree that transaction costs are one important type of the cost of doing business. Organisations cannot ignore transaction costs. However, since transaction costs are associated with human behaviour (e.g. trust) and legal systems, they need to be placed in a broader framework. We will return to this point when we discuss the "embeddedness" thesis in Chapter 6.

1.5.2. Institutional theory of economic organisations in East Asia
Given the fact that Vietnam shares the Chinese-connection culture with other East Asian countries, the source of literature on economic organisations in East Asian successful economies is worth reviewing here. The various works on East Asian economic organisations (see especially Redding and Whitley, 1990; Whitley, 1992; and Hamilton, Biggart and Orru, 1997) have one thing in common: they all sought an institutional explanation for the structural pattern of economic organisations and the economic successes of East Asian countries. The important contribution of this source of literature is that they have taken the institutional, historical and political factors (e.g. family structure and government-business relations) seriously and attempted to understand the organisation's relationship to them. Economic firms are seen as 'embedded' in their societal context. Different levels and 'types' of trust rooted from the family and the village, for example, are considered important variables to the forms and functioning of different types of business organisations in different societies. The role of the state is emphasised.

Redding and Whitley (1990) and Whitley (1992), for example, make detailed comparative analyses of the dominant forms of businesses in Japan, Korea, Taiwan

16

and Hong Kong. They specify major characteristics for each type of business (Chinese family businesses in Hong Kong and Taiwan, Korean *chaebol* and large Japanese corporations) and argue that these characteristics are associated with the societal contexts in which they have become established. They identify five main interconnected characteristics of the societal context which have 'determined' those forms of businesses:

1. Authority patterns;
2. Trust relations;
3. Nature of the state elite;
4. Basis of societal elite;
5. Inheritance system.

Chinese family businesses, for example, "have sprung from an environment of patrimonial authority, general but not specific mistrust, aloof government, a free entrepreneurial environment, and traditions of equal inheritance" (Redding and Whitley, 1990, p.101). The Korean chaebol, however, have emerged from an environment which "is also patrimonial, less fraught with mistrust, has a similarly Confucian moral-based government, but highly interventionist, a somewhat free entrepreneurial environment, and a modified version of equal inheritance" (ibid.). The environment of large Japanese corporations is characterised by a feudal rather than patrimonial pattern of authority, high trust across the society, aloof but influential government, and an inheritance system based on primogeniture.

In a similar spirit, Orru, Biggart and Hamilton, in their various papers, also take into account important societal factors in their explanation of the structure and success of the dominant forms of businesses in East Asian societies (see, Orru, Biggart & Hamilton, 1997). Hamilton and Biggart argue that both cultural and economic explanations of the forms and success of businesses in East Asia are important, but neither deals directly with organisations themselves. They point out that the market explanation focuses on immediate factors (e.g. efficiency; demand and supply; and competition conditions) and the cultural explanation on distant ones (e.g. broad cultural values). They offer an authority approach which concentrates on "principles of domination" as an alternative explanation. They argue that organisational structure is situational determined, and, therefore, the most appropriate form of analysis is one that "taps the historical dimension".

The authority approach is clearly related, but not reducible to culture. It also incorporates historical, political and economic elements into the analysis. They point out that different patterns of organisation in different East Asian societies (Japan, South Korea and Taiwan) are associated with different authority patterns in these societies (Hamilton and Biggart, 1988). Japanese firms, for example, enact a communitarian ideal or logic related to a feudal society and the collective traditions and inter-family collaboration of the Tokugawa village. The Korean firms enact a patrimonial principle partly inherited from patterns of authority and subordination prevalent in pre-modern Korea, and to some extent, Japanese colonialism. Chinese family businesses enact a patrilineal logic partly derived from Imperial China, where village cohesion was weak, and from the particle inheritance system, and so on. The economic success of these East Asian countries is because:

> "...they have created organisational arrangements and management practices that give them a competitive advantage. Japan, South Korea and Taiwan all pursue business strategies that suit their social arrangements – their cultures, their traditional ways of organising and managing, and their government structures. Not one of these nations attempts to do everything, and none has attempted to imitate the West. Instead, each has focused on industries and processes in which it has a particular social advantage" (Orru, Biggart & Hamilton, 1997, pp.103 –104).

In summary, an important contribution of this source of literature on economic organisations and economies in East Asia is that it attempts to place the firm in a broad societal context. It takes into consideration various societal factors including cultural values, history and government in explaining the form and the success of economic organisations in different societies. It provides a *general* approach in studying different forms of businesses which have emerged in different societies at a general macro level.

1.5.3. North's institutional matrix

Douglass North's contribution to new institution economics earned him a Nobel Prize in Economics in 1993. Unlike Williamson and many other institution economic theorists, North took historical and cultural factors into his analysis of organisations and economy. From his study of economic history, North (1990) pointed out that despite the fact that there has been a huge and successful development of technology and a high level of modernisation in the Western world, there are still many economies with a persistently poor performance over long periods of time. He identified institutions as the major source of explanation, arguing that institutions determine economic performance and that institutional change is incremental (North, 1990). According to North, institutions are "the rules of the game in a society or, more formally, are the humanly devised constraints that shape human interaction." (North 1990, p.3). He also makes a distinction between the formal and informal aspects of institutions.

> "Institution constraints include both what individuals are prohibited from doing and, sometimes, under what conditions some individuals are permitted to undertake certain activities. As defined here, they therefore are the framework within which human interaction takes place. They are perfectly analogous to the rules of the game in a competitive team sport. That is they consist of formal written rules as well as typically unwritten codes of conduct that underlie and supplement formal rules, such as not deliberately injuring a key player on the opposing team. And as this analogy would imply, the rules and informal codes are sometimes violated and punishment is enacted. Therefore, an essential part of the functioning of institutions is the costliness of ascertaining violations and the severity of punishment." (p.4)

Formal rules, according to North (1990), include "political (and judicial) rules, economic rules, and contracts. The hierarchy of such rules, from constitutions, to statute and common laws, to specific bylaws, and finally to individual contracts defines constraints, from general rules to particular specification" (p.47). North also made a distinction between political and economic rules:

> "Political rules broadly define the hierarchical structure of the polity, its basic decision structure, and the explicit characteristics of agenda control. Economic rules define property rights, that is the bundle of rights over the use and the income to be derived from property and the ability to alienate an asset or a resource. Contracts contain the provisions specific to a particular agreement in exchange."(p.47)

Formal rules define what one can and cannot do legally. They structure human activities in a society. Formal rules are important. History has proved that there has been a significant difference in economic performance between countries with the same cultural background but which followed different paths of development. The huge difference in economic performance between former socialist and Western European countries is an obvious example.

Informal norms are embodied in customs and traditions and in all other interpretations of the social world that have passed the 'test of time'. Formal rules can change overnight, but cultural norms are tenacious. North (1990) argues that the tenacious survival ability of cultural norms is the key factor to explain the nature of the incremental change of institutions, and thus the economic performance of different countries.

Formal rules and informal norms are all socially devised or constructed. Their differences are matters of degree (North, 1990). Formal rules can only work effectively (e.g. produce intended results) if they are in line with informal norms. There have been many examples where the same set of formal rules did not work out the same in different societies with different cultural backgrounds.

North's theory of institutions is constructed from a theory of human behaviour (through formal and informal constraints) combined with a theory of transaction costs. In order for economic exchanges to take place, a certain degree of human co-operation is needed. Even in simple transactional situations, a certain level of trust and honesty is needed. Laws and third-party enforcement are necessary to facilitate more complex transactions.

Formal rules and informal norms form an institutional matrix or a set of 'rules of the game' which structure economic exchange constrained by transaction costs and property rights. Firms are the *players*. North (1994) argues that firms come into existence to take advantage of profitable opportunities. The opportunities are provided by the institutional framework. That is, "if the institutional framework rewards piracy then piratical organisations will come into existence; and if the institutional framework rewards productive activities then organisations-firms will come into existence to engage in productive activities" (p.361). North pointed out that the costs per exchange in third world countries are much greater than in an advanced industrial economy – and sometimes no exchange occurs because costs are too high. This is because the institutional structure in the third world lacks formal structure and/or its enforcement that ensures efficient markets.

North's concept of institutions incorporates not only economic but also political and cultural factors making his treatment of transaction costs different from Williamson's. Transaction costs are dependent factors rooted in the 'background' (the institutional constraints) and in turn, transaction costs constrain economic exchange. Williamson treated transaction costs as an exogenous independent variable. North's theory of institutions is not a theory of the firm, but the theory can explain patterns of firms in a particular institutional setting.

Chapter 2: The theoretical framework

2.1. Theoretical framework and research issues

Many in the West would argue that the collapse of the socialist system in the late 1980s marked the 'triumph of capitalism'. It is a matter of fact that for now, capitalism is widely considered the best method of human organisation and seems to be spreading to every corner of the world. Capitalism is not merely an alternative way of resource allocation but a way of life, in which individuals and organisations interact with each other in pursuit of their private ends. As globalisation increases, it seems that a country or society can no longer act alone or do things on their own. Vietnam is no exception, the country is undoubtedly following the capitalist path of development despite some reluctance to admit it.

Capitalism, on the one hand, has its own laws. When it reaches a certain level of development, capitalism absorbs other institutions into its own image. On the other one hand, capitalism is not the same everywhere. Given the fact that the world is becoming more and more integrated, a country or society that does not know how to 'do' capitalism, or whose cultural background does not 'suit' the development of capitalism is likely to be exploited by and dependent on (both economically and politically) more 'advanced' societies. In order to operate effectively, capitalism requires certain cultural traits and a certain level of institutional development, for example the existence of a banking system and stock market, and the enunciation of laws concerning transactions and private property.

The review of literature in the last chapter pointed out that different forms of capitalism have emerged in different societies with different historical, institutional and cultural background (Boisot and Child, 1996; Redding , 1993; Orru, Biggart and Hamilton, 1997; Whitley, 1992; and North, 1990). In other words, the market and capitalism are embedded in the broad social environment. This 'embeddedness' perspective suggests that studies of economic organisations should, and for certain purposes *must,* refer to the broad societal context in which the organisation is embedded. In this context, the present study does not intend to conceptualise the Vietnamese SOEs independent of their social environment, rather they are seen as embedded in it.

There is a theoretical puzzle in approaching the Vietnamese SOEs since, unlike the South Korean *chaebol*, large Japanese corporations or the small family businesses that characterise Taiwan and Hong Kong, the Vietnamese SOEs were not 'born' rationally or naturally but were more or less, products of social events (see Chapter 5). Therefore, unlike the other business forms referred to previously, they should not be treated as the inevitably dominant form of capitalism 'emerging' from, or the 'product' of the social environment, or as deeply 'embedded' in it. Vietnamese SOEs are Vietnamese economic organisations run by Vietnamese people operating in a Vietnamese context. The people working in the SOEs are 'embedded' in their social environment. Any theoretical framework that attempts to capture the complexity of the Vietnamese SOEs must take the above facts into consideration.

The present research follows Weber's 'ideal type' methodology, beginning first with the construction of the 'ideal type', the typical business form most likely to emerge from the Vietnamese social environment. It next compares and 'reads' the SOEs based on the language of the ideal type. The two broad research questions asked are:

1. Given its particular historical, cultural and institutional background, what is the typical form of capitalism (type of business firms and their behaviour) most likely to emerge in Vietnam?
2. What are the differences between the Vietnamese SOEs and those ideal types, and how can these differences explain their behaviour?

In other words, Vietnamese SOE behaviour is interpreted with reference to the language of the ideal type.

The first question is crucial since it sets the framework and the language for the answer to the second. In fact, this research follows North's (1990) institutional framework (the matrix of formal rules and informal norms) to draw and explain the general pattern of business firms in the Vietnamese institutional setting. We, then extend the analysis of the informal norms to the analysis of the internal structure of the firm to complete our project of building an explanation of the form of capitalism in Vietnam.

From our review, we concluded that North's institutional matrix was the most appropriate to the context of the present study. His theory of institutions incorporates not only economic, but also historical, cultural and political factors into the explanation framework. The section below gives a rationale for choosing North's institutional matrix as the study's theoretical framework.

2.2. Formal and informal

This monograph argues that the categorisation of formal rules and informal norms in the analysis of institutions allows history, culture and politics to play their part. Theoretically, the classification between formal rules and informal norms is not uncontroversial, it is the context of the social phenomena and the particular formal rules and informal norms the theorist is describing that matter. With regard to the present research, I argue that the classification is theoretically plausible and important. The arguments and examples below should clarify this point.

The analysis of formal and informal aspects of institutions takes into account different aspects of human action. It is often the case that institutional sociologists tend to stress informal norms, whereas institutional economists tend to place more weight on formal rules or regulations. Scott (1995) identified three 'pillars' of institutions: "Institutions consist of cognitive, normative, and regulative structures and activities that provide stability and meaning to social behaviour. Institutions are transported by various carriers – cultures, structures, and routines – and they operate at multiple levels of jurisdiction" (p.33).

This concept of institutions characterises institutions as multifaceted systems. Institutions incorporate both symbolic systems – normative and cognitive elements – and regulative processes. The emphases of the three pillars are given in the table below.

Table 2.1. Varying emphases: three pillars of institutions

	Regulative	Normative	Cognitive
Basic of compliance	Expedience	Social obligation	Taken for granted
Mechanism	Coercive	Normative	Mimetic
Logic	Instrumentality	Appropriateness	Orthodoxy
Indicators	Rules, laws, sanctions	Certification, accreditation	Prevalence, isomorphism
Basis of legitimacy	Legally sanctioned	Morally governed	Culturally supported, conceptually correct

Source: Scott (1995, p.34)

Scott also pointed out that the emphasis on different pillars stems from the object of study. The study of economic systems and institutions often emphasises the regulative aspects. The emphasis should be relative to problems on which the observer focuses his or her attention. In the present research, in order to understand economic behaviour in a country in transition, we must pay attention to the formal rules. North's conception of the institutional matrix incorporated all three institutional 'pillars' in Scott's framework. Formal rules resemble regulative and informal norms resemble normative and cognitive aspects of institutions. Formal rules may change overnight while informal norms are more stable. Formal rules are policy variables.

Formal rules, on the one hand, do not come out of a vacuum, and cannot be effective if they are not supported by cultural norms. A certain set of rules may work well in one culture, but not in another. Formal rules may vary, but within a 'boundary-maintaining' system. Parsons (1951) defined a boundary-maintaining system as follows:

> "The definition of a system as boundary-maintaining is a way of saying that, relative to its environment, that is to fluctuations in the factors of environment, it maintains

certain constancies of pattern, whether these constancies be static or moving. These elements of constancy of pattern must constitute a fundamental point of reference for the analysis of process in the system. From a certain point of view these processes are to be defined as the processes of maintenance of the constant pattern." (p.482).

In the context of Confucian values, for example, Parsons (1951) pointed out that instrumental orientations must be "kept under control or strongly inhibited" in a Confucian society (p.197). The 'code of propriety' is more ritualised than instrumental, therefore the development and enforcement of formal rules and laws must be limited in comparison to the situation in Western societies. The literature on management and business systems in the 'post-Confucian' East Asian countries confirmed Max Weber's thesis of the patrimonalism of a Confucian state and Parsons's 'boundary-maintaining' system (Hamilton et al, 1997; Whitely, 1992; and Redding, 1993). Whitley (1992) found that East Asian economies were dominated by the state, since the state was the only agency capable of co-ordinating large-scale economic development. Legal systems are weakly developed and subordinated to the state elite. Banking and financial systems are dominated by the state and businesses too, to a larger degree, are subordinate to and dependent on the state. Whitley (1992) also pointed out that the differences between institutional systems in East Asian and western societies are:

> A weak legal system and its subordination to the state elite;
> Businesses, to a large degree, dependent on and subordinated to the state;
> Banking and financial systems dominated by the state.

These characteristics are 're-achieved' over time since they are the products of the symbolic interaction processes (see, for example, Blumer 1962; Mead, 1934; and Rose, 1962). They form a 'boundary' to the formal rules in Confucian society.

On the other hand, formal rules have their own rights. Politics has its own logic as demonstrated by the following arguments and examples.

At the philosophical level, it could be argued that any classification of social phenomena is underpinned by certain philosophical assumptions of social world. According to Hegel, only the whole is true, therefore any moment, part or phase must be partially untrue. In order to try to understand and explain social phenomena, we "cannot avoid evaluating and criticising societies' own self-understanding" (Sayer, 1984, p.41). Sayer pointed out that, for example, "any attempt to explain the present economic recession would have to make a critical evaluation of the (formal and informal) theories which have not only described but informed the actions of politicians, institutions and other individuals" (ibid). We believe that social science is not value-free. In other words, we take the critical theory perspective in our view of social science. We argue that critical elements in understanding social phenomena cannot be avoided. To make the distinction between formal rules and informal norms concerning transactions is to acknowledge that government and politics matter. Politics has its own logic and place in society.

24

There have been many examples of situations where formal rules can make a significant difference. It is reasonable to claim that Japan, Korea, Taiwan, China and Vietnam belong to the same broad category of social system- the 'post-Confucian' social system. But these countries diverged significantly in the development path they followed and consequently, in economic performance. The most obvious example is perhaps the different paths followed by North and South Korea and the huge differences in economic performance as a result. Such facts support the claim that formal rules matter. An 'efficient' set of rules and its enforcement mechanism create incentives for businesses to invest in the productive activities. Whitley (1992) and Orru, Biggart & Hamilton (1997) provided detailed comparative analyses of the relationship between government and businesses in Japan, South Korea and Taiwan. They concluded that governments from these countries played an important role in promoting different kinds of businesses. The economic success of South Korea could not have been possible without the commitment to economic growth of the military government led by Park Chung Hee and his successor, Chun Doo Hwan. Until the early 1960s, Korea was a typical developing country with high unemployment and poverty (Yoo and Moon, 1999). After leading the successful coup in 1961, Park determined to lead the country toward economic growth. As Jones and Sakong (1980) put it:

"Economic growth under private enterprise being well understood as the dominant system goal, officials can seldom afford to act in a manner that seriously obstructs that goal." (quoted in Whitley, 1992, p.150).

The 'rules of the game' favoured the development and growth of the *chaebol*.

"The opportunities for personal gain that such discretionary command affords bureaucratic and political elites have here been substantially offset by the strong commitment to national growth and the highly centralised command system that ensures such commitment is implemented through monitoring performance. While corruption does occur in post-1961 Korea (Kim, 1979), it is limited by the overriding objective of economic development which provides a relatively straightforward measure of success. The existence of a competing regime in North Korea, and the need to justify military domination in a society where the military have traditionally had little prestige, has encouraged the institutionalisation of growth as the prime goal and restricted the extent to which elites could appropriate surpluses (Haggard, 1988; Wade, 1988)" (in Whitley, 1992, p.150).

The South Korean case provides evidence to support the view that a dictatorship government can boost economic growth by providing the rules and, more importantly, committing to the rules that direct businesses to productive activities.

In Singapore, prime minister Lee Kuan Yew, played an important role in the country's success. An 'efficient' system of rules coupled with a 'strongman' can change economic performance significantly.

The above examples demonstrate that politics can turn things around. It is beyond the scope of this work and the ability of the author to discuss politics at a deeper level. The study of politics, especially policies, formal rules and enforcement that a country employs, is interrelated with the study of culture, but may not, and should not be, reducible to it. The study of formal rules helps us understand diversity among societies which share a broad cultural background. In the context of the present study, we cannot ignore the political features and their expression in formal rules in Vietnam, a country in transition and run by the Communist Party.

2.3. Assumptions about human behaviour

Another reason to believe that North's institutional framework captures reality better than other versions of institutional theory is its more realistic assumptions about human behaviour. At the macro-level, by incorporating cultural norms into the model, North correctly abandoned the efficiency assumption of human institutions. This concept of institutions is shared by many writers including Max Weber, Talcott Parsons, Mary Douglas and Anthony Giddens. At the firm level, North shares with Max Weber the assumption that "participants in market economies reach decisions based on rational means end calculation of interests." (Hamilton and Feenstra, 1997, p.63). The assumption about competition and scarce resources is thus retained. This assumption is explicit in the treatment of high transaction costs and insecure property rights as constraints to firm growth and economic development. Redding in his "*The spirit of Chinese capitalism*" also shares this conception. He points out that insecure property rights and inefficient transaction costs are amongst the major impediments to economic development in Mainland China (Redding, 1993).

This concept of institutions is different from some versions of the so-called institutional theory of organisation in the organisation study literature (see, for example, Powell and DiMaggio, 1983 and Zucker, 1988). Powell and DiMaggio's (1983) article about institutional isomorphism has been influential and widely cited in organisation study literature. This version of an institutional theory of organisation denies the reality of purposeful, interest-driven and conflictual behaviour by a human actor. The assumption of rational action, as Granovetter (1985) pointed out, "must be always be problematic, it is a good working hypothesis that should not easily be abandoned" (p.506). Any social theory which abandons the assumption of rational action is limited in its explanatory scope to certain settings. It is certainly true of the institutional theory of organisation. DiMaggio (1988) admitted that:

> "Institutional theory may suffice to explain most organisational phenomena in certain kinds of fields – those that are highly institutionalised and have a weak technical base (such as banks but not computer-software designers) or those in which the legitimacy of member organisations is largely based in traditional authority (such as established churches but not scientific research institutes or those that play too trivial a role in the allocation of resource to attract much political behaviour (such as funeral parlours but not long-distance trucking company). (p.6).

DiMaggio also pointed out that "without more explicit attention to interest and agency of the kind that institutional rhetoric has thus far obstructed, institutional theorists will be unable to develop predictive and persuasive accounts of the origins, reproduction, and erosion of institutionalised practices and organisational forms" (p.11).

With regard to the source of literature on economic organisations in East Asia, Whitley (1992); Hamilton *et al* (1990); and Orru, Biggart and Hamilton (1997) acknowledged the importance of efficiency. At the end of a paper, Hamilton *et al* (1990), pointed out that there is a lack of theories, which they called "macro-organisational theories", which can better explain economic organisations in East Asia:

> "What is needed, then, are macro-organisational theories of economies. Certainly efficiency in the allocation of resources and the state's control of business are both important parts of such theories, but these factors are not singular in nature, universal in character and unambiguous in practice. These factors reflect their social location...Such organisational theories should not create, in a Parsonian fashion, an abstract world of pattern variables, but rather should concentrate on real worlds of human activity and of distinctive cultural meanings. Although many diverse analytic traditions provide beginnings for such theories, these macro-organisational theories remain promising tasks for the future." (p126).

North's theory of institutions certainly provides a framework for such a macro-theory of organisations.

North's theory, however, as mentioned earlier, is not itself a theory of organisation. It explains the typical pattern of economic organisations in each particular institutional setting, but not the internal structure of the firm. To complete the project of building the form of capitalism in the Vietnamese environment we combine North's institutional framework with the 'embeddedness' perspective to explain not only the pattern, but also the internal structure of the Vietnamese 'ideal' firm. The framework that guided the present research is summarised below (Figure 2.1).

Figure 2.1. The research framework - a conceptual model

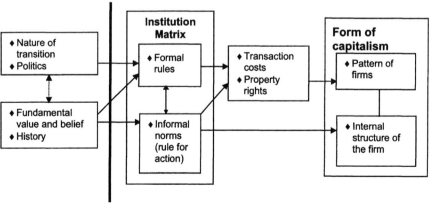

With regard to the process of constructing the typical form of capitalism in Vietnam, two major analytical tasks will be undertaken by this work. The first is an analysis of the nature of the institution matrix, including both the formal and informal side. The second task is to link it to the form and structure of the firm (the ideal firm) which is conceptually demonstrated on the right hand side of the bold vertical line in Figure 2.1 above. The institutional framework determines the pattern of the firm through its incentive structure. The incentive structure is materialised through transaction costs and property rights. That is, for example, an institution matrix with an incentive structure characterised by high transaction costs and insecure property rights is likely to produce small-scale businesses. The institutional matrix (especially the informal side) also partly determines the internal structure of the firm. That is, for example, a low or bounded trust culture is often associated with family business. We will discuss how the Vietnamese institution matrix determines the patterns and structure of the firm in Chapter 6.

The nature of the Vietnamese institutional framework (the first task) is drawn from factors given on the left-hand side of the bold vertical line in Figure 2.1. There are two broad categories of factor. One is the deep-rooted values and beliefs and practices which have been carried out and survived the test of time (the background). The other concerns the 'matters at hand' (the proximate), the nature of transition to a market economy, and the temporary political ideology in Vietnam. This task will be carried out in Part 2 of this work. SOE behaviour will then be analysed and interpreted with reference to the ideal type.

Chapter 3: Research methodology

"People who write about methodology often forget that it is a matter of strategy, not of morals. There are neither good nor bad methods but only methods that are more or less effective under particular circumstances in reaching objectives on the way to a distant goal." (George C. Homans, 1949, p.330).

"Every data-gathering class – interviews, questionnaires, observation, performance records, physical evidence – is potentially biased and has specific to it certain validity threats. Ideally, we should like to converge data from several different data classes, as well as converge with multiple variants from within a single class." (Eugene J. Webb, 1966, p35).

(Both in Pettigrew, 1973, p.52.)

Methodologically, the present research employed an overall qualitative approach with data collection and analyses, guided by the principles articulated in the above two quotations.

This chapter presents the rationale and general methodological approach to this research, including the philosophical assumptions and practical awareness underlying the methodology and methods used. More detailed descriptions and discussions of different research processes, methods used and their justifications are provided in chapters that directly concern particular research issues under investigation. The 'Aston Studies' instruments and data generation methods, for example, are discussed in Chapter 7 on the authority relationships within SOEs. The methods used to uncover the use of power in the shoe enterprise are discussed in Chapter 9 concerning the management problems of the Vietnamese SOEs. This arrangement allows us to discuss and assess different research methods in greater depth with direct reference to the contexts in which they are used.

3.1. Methodology

3.1.1. Philosophical grounds

There have been many debates among scholars on the ontological, epistemological and methodological issues in social sciences (see, for example, Burrell and Morgan, 1979). The selection of methodology in carrying out a particular research project depends on the research questions, resources, and more importantly, the researcher's assumptions about the nature of social science. It is not accidental, for example, that researchers who subscribe to symbolic interactionism are more likely to choose an ethnographic methodology.

I subscribe to the view that reality is socially constructed. This view is not new. It goes back to Hegel and Marx (Douglas, 1973). The theme was subsequently developed by Alfred Schutz, and later by Peter Berger and Thomas Luckmann (1966). Society is viewed in this perspective as balanced in a dialectic between objective givenness and subjective meanings, with social reality having an essential component of consciousness (Berger, Berger and Kellner, 1973). It is not the ontological structure of the objects, but the meaning of our experiences that constitutes reality. Durkheim and Mauss (1963) pointed out that things are not simply arranged by humans, but that the social relations of men provided the prototype for the logical relationship between things. Yin-yang, for example, is a way that the traditional Vietnamese and Chinese classified and gave meaning to things. Different societies and social groups construct their own reality, their own way of classifying and interpreting the social world and therefore could be significantly different from one another. Ample empirical cultural and anthropological studies have supported this view (see, for example, Evans-Pritchard, 1937 and Douglas, 1973). The view that reality is socially constructed means that the social sciences, if indeed they aim at explaining social reality, "must include a reference to the subjective meaning an action has for the actor" (Schutz, 1973, p.21). In other words, "all scientific explanations of the social world *can* and for certain purposes *must*, refer to the subjective meaning of the action of human beings from which social reality originates," (ibid., original emphasis). In a broad sense, one should or must refer to the context of the social phenomenon under investigation.

Consequently, a qualitative methodology was chosen for the present study. It is important here to note the difference between the two terms 'method' and 'methodology'. The term 'method' will be used to refer to different techniques to collect and analyse data in order to explain the phenomena under investigation, whereas, 'methodology' is a way of thinking about and approaching social reality (Strauss and Corbin, 1998).

Since qualitative research is "many things to many people" (Denzin & Lincoln, 1998, p.8) and often confusing (Strauss & Cobin, 1998), it is important to clarify what is meant by 'qualitative methodology' or 'qualitative research' in the present study. The term 'qualitative methodology' or 'qualitative research' is used here to denote that the present research is concerned with explaining and interpreting social phenomena rather than testing and predicting theories and hypotheses quantitatively. Unlike most quantitative research, we do not seek to discover *universal* laws or statements which *always* hold true. We are not concerned with complex statistical measures and methods to either confirm or reject *universal* hypotheses and laws.

This is not to deny the importance of survey and questionnaire methods. Qualitative research, as Denzin and Lincoln (1998) pointed out, has no distinct set of methods that are entirely its own. Qualitative researchers use various data sources and data analysis methods including semiotics, narratives, content, discourse, archival, phonemic analysis, historical method and also statistics. (Denzin & Lincoln, 1998). Qualitative methods are not limited to observations and interviews. The emphasis is not placed on how data are analysed and used. Interviews and observations, for example, are often associated with qualitative research, but this does not always mean that research that uses observation and interviews techniques is qualitative research. If the researchers code data from interviews and observations in a manner that allows them to be statistically analysed and tested, they are, in effect, quantifying qualitative data (Strauss and Corbin, 1998). The 'Aston Studies' of organisation studies are an illustrative example of quantitative research (Bryan, 1988) which used quantified qualitative data. Similarly, quantitative data (e.g. questionnaires and statistics) may be used to generate and verify theory in qualitative research.

Bearing the above philosophical assumptions in mind, in designing the present research we did not set out to discover *universal* laws that *always* hold true, but to explain the phenomenon under study in their context. While agreeing with the view that there are no universal laws that always hold true, we do not deny that there are common structural features in a society or culture formed and reproduced through *symbolic interaction processes* (Blumer 1962; Mead, 1934; and Rose, 1962). These common features can be identified through the study of, for example, shared symbols like religions and languages, especially proverbs and expressions. There are also common features which can be known through surveys and questionnaires. We are not opposed to the idea of causality in social sciences, but we argue that causality must be placed within a phenomenological context.

Given the above views and the nature of the research questions, nevertheless in designing the present research we did not employ a strict version of qualitative research such as ethnomethodology, which focuses solely on actions as opposed to structure and uses observation and conversation analyses as the sole methods. The present research uses various sources of data and data collection and analysis methods including historical analysis, document analysis, cultural studies, interviews, observations and questionnaires. The two major reasons for characterising this study as qualitative research are that: (1) the Vietnamese SOEs are studied in their context. We have 'placed' SOEs within their cultural background (i.e. Vietnamese cultural values) and historical context (i.e. the analysis of the embedded materialism in Chapter 10). In addition, throughout the analysis we have frequently made reference to the inside view of the actors involved through interviewed data and 'tailored' questionnaires; (2) We did not follow a pre-designed framework from the start of the research. The theoretical framework of the research has 'emerged' during the research process. The researcher of the present project has worked as what Denzin and Lincoln (1998) would call a 'bricoleur', who uses the tools of his own methodological trade, deploying whatever methods or empirical materials as are at hand. These two major points are briefly discussed below.

3.1.2. Contextualism
The purpose of constructing an ideal type or "its function is the comparison with empirical reality in order to establish its divergences or similarities, to describe them... and to understand and explain them causally." (ibid p43). An ideal type is,

therefore, a tool for comparison and explanation. It is a means rather than an end. Following Weber's ideal type methodology we have constructed an ideal type, a business model abstracted from various Vietnamese societal characteristics. Drawing from various sources and various societal aspects (i.e., cultural values, history of development, institutions), we have constructed an 'ideal' business type in Vietnam as small family-owned and managed businesses (see Chapter 6). The ideal type method has allowed us to capture the general *context* of the business environment in Vietnam and allowed us to explain the behaviour of the Vietnamese SOEs. Many researchers would agree that one should or must study a social phenomenon in its context. In the present study, for example, a study of Vietnamese SOE behaviour must take into consideration the Vietnamese culture, history, institutions and so on. The question is how - how to contextually analyse and explain the social phenomenon under investigations. Weber's 'ideal type' concept offered an answer. The 'ideal type' method applied in present research has allowed us to bring divergent societal aspects into analysis. The ideal type of businesses in Vietnam is not studied as an end in itself, but as a means through which various aspects of the 'real' object of study, SOEs, could be compared, analysed and explained.

In addition to the ideal type approach presented above, we have also provided a detailed analysis of the legacy of the Vietnamese SOEs (see Chapter 10). While the ideal type approach has allowed us to capture the general context at the macro-level, the detailed analysis of the legacy of the Vietnamese SOEs deals with context at the micro-level. We argue that a study of SOEs must refer to both the general Vietnamese social context and their own particular history. This method has allowed me to approach the phenomenon under investigation from specific to general, general to specific and back to the general.

It is not uncommon for context to be paid insufficient attention or ignored by western researchers in their studies of social phenomena in non-western societies. The research comparing decision making and organisational democracy between British corporations and Chinese SOEs carried out by Frank Heller is one example (Heller, 1993). Frank Heller took part in research concerning industrial relations practices focusing on organisational democracy: the Industrial Democracy in Europe Research (IDE) which was a comparative quantitative study of 154 organisations (9000 respondents) in twelve European countries (carried out in the late 1970s and 1980). He also participated in another research project called DIO (Decisions in Organisations): a quantitative study of seven organisations in three countries: The Netherlands, Yugoslavia and Britain. (Heller et al 1981, 1988). Almost the same set of questionnaires and analytical framework used in these two research projects were then used to compare decision making and organisational democracy in ten British companies and eleven Chinese SOEs in his 1993 research (Heller and Wang, 1993). The implicit assumption of this research is that the configurations of British and Chinese state-owned enterprises are similar: the defined role of trade unions, of middle managers and of banks and industrial bureaux are the same. The findings of this kind of research are not only superficial but can also be misleading, since they fail to take into account the significant and undoubted differences between the structure and the context of the two kinds of enterprises in the two countries. The concept and practice of trade unions in China are significantly different from those in Western countries (see e.g. Child and Lu, 1990).

3.1.3. Theoretical sensitivity
The organisational and management behaviour of SOEs in transitional countries in general, and particularly in Vietnam, is a relatively new topic. The boundaries between SOEs and their broader societal context have, to a great extent, not been 'evidenced'.

In addition, as noted in the analytical background chapter, there is very little research of a Western kind into management in Vietnam. This fact, together with the changing nature of socio-economic environment and the lack of reliable statistical data in transitional countries makes it difficult to form comprehensive frameworks or reliable data generating instruments without spending a significant amount of time observing and interviewing people. The problem of getting data and the difficulty of doing research in Vietnam is well documented by Vietnamese and foreign researchers (see, for example, Fforde and de Vylder, 1996; Malesky et al, 1998; and Richards, Ha, Harvie and Nguyen, 2002).

Having taken on board all the above and the view of social studies presented in Section 3.1.1, this research did not begin with a pre-determined model or theoretical framework, but followed Strauss and Cobin's advice that a researcher should not "begin a project with a pre-conceived theory in mind... Rather, the researcher begins with an area of study and allows the theory to emerge from the data." (Strauss and Corbin 1998, p.12). The advantage of this approach is that "theory derived from data is more likely to resemble the 'reality' than is theory derived by putting together a series of concepts based on experience or solely through speculation (how one thinks things ought to work)" (ibid.).

The present research, therefore, was not designed in the traditional way by which data collection follows a pre-conception theoretical framework. Instead, data collection, research design, data analysis, interpretation and theoretical generation were inter-related and inter-played during the research process. The research strategy of the present study is illustrated in Figure 3.1 below.

Figure 3.1. The research strategy

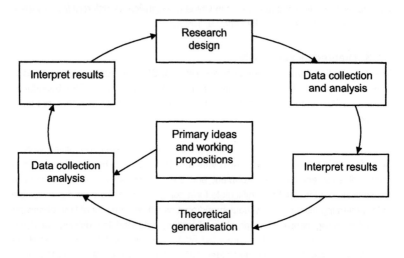

The research strategy illustrated above worked well in the present study. The first version of the research proposal was an investigation of Total Quality Management (TQM) in the Vietnamese SOEs. One of the primary ideas was that Vietnamese SOEs were unable to compete in the market because of their poor quality products. In order to improve the product quality, TQM appeared an attractive method but during the research process, I discovered that the reality was much more complicated. There are more important things to say about the Vietnamese SOEs than the language of management techniques can offer. Several other theoretical frameworks (e.g. agency theory and decision making approach) were considered during the research process. The chosen theoretical framework presented in Chapter 2 actually emerged during the research process and the writing up period of this work.

Data sources and data collection methods

The interplay of different types of data

The methods used in the present research were guided by the two quotations at the beginning of the chapter. The research drew on a variety of data sources ranging from law codes in traditional Vietnamese society to the most recent laws and regulations concerning business practice in Vietnam, and the author's own experience since childhood. It was also based on in-depth interviews of SOE managers and government officials.

The major source of *primary* data came from the investigation of three case studies (three SOEs). The data collection techniques employed include: observation, interview, questionnaires (Questionnaire I) and company document analysis.

A second questionnaire (Questionnaire II) was designed to find out the nature of economic transactions in Vietnam, supplemented by interviews and observations.

Various government documents were used, including laws, regulations, statistics and discussions and comments on the official Vietnamese newspapers and reports, and secondary data about Vietnam from the World Bank, IMF and other published sources.

The author also drew on his own knowledge of Vietnamese society through folklore, folk songs, proverbs, poems and other stories.

Observations and interviews were generally recorded by notes taken during the process or (if allowed) recorded on tape. When the research was concerned with sensitive issues, the researcher tried to memorise key points and record them immediately after the interview. Certain types of data, for example, on the general perception of employees about the management of their company, were acquired through a questionnaire, which was considered the best method. *Questionnaires, however, were not designed at the beginning of the research but during the data collection process when the researcher felt the need to do so.*

The two questionnaires used in the study were designed and used after the researcher had gained a certain degree of knowledge about the subject under investigation. Although questionnaires were used to collect data, only descriptive statistics were used to test their significance. The quantitative data in this case were used to explain or characterise the phenomenon under investigation rather than to confirm or disprove a *universal* hypothesis or law. This way of using questionnaires and quantitative data is unusual, but was considered appropriate by a number of qualitative methodology experts such as Strauss and Cobin (1998) and Bryan (1988).

Questionnaires (quantitative data), observations and interviews (qualitative data) and documents (archival data) were, to use Strauss and Corbin's (1998) term, "interplayed" during the research process. In general, the data generation methods were used flexibly and sensitively in respect to the social context in which the data were produced. At the end of the research process, the researcher found that the research was actually, again to use Strauss and Corbin's (1998) phrase, a "messy affair". The present research confirmed Strauss and Corbin's observation that "research rarely proceeds completely as planned" (p.32). The approach to the case studies is one obvious example:

I planned to spend a considerable amount of time in each enterprise to play an observation role. The actual observation process, however, did not work out in this way. "It is very strange if you sit here in the company, people think that you are trying to investigate something." said a manager in the shoe enterprise (one of the three cases studied). The word 'investigate' in the above quotation means to uncover any wrongdoing or illegal practices. It is unusual for a researcher to play an observation role in a Vietnamese enterprise. The idea of outside consultancy is new and hardly ever practised in Vietnam. Perceptions about social research are also very different from the West. When I arrived at the enterprises, managers expected to give me only statistical data about the firm. They believe that *scientific* research is associated with numbers, especially financial performance. Researchers should not expect to be given a chair or office space in Vietnamese companies, but to work and act as an observer.

Having become aware of this, the author changed his strategy following Yin's (1994) advice that when carrying out case study research, the researcher should be adaptive and flexible. I tried to find other ways of obtaining data and at the same time, tried to observe as much as I could when the opportunity arose. I visited the firm once or twice a week between July and December (1999). I deliberately did not visit the same department frequently, so that the workers would not believe that I was investigating some wrongdoing. I gradually developed relationships with managers there, having lunch and dinner with them on several occasions. As far as possible, I tried to observe and talk to people informally. At the same time other data collection methods, such as the use of questionnaires, were being considered and designed.

After two months of investigation into the first case study, the shoe enterprise, I became clearer about the area I aimed to explore and started to investigate the other two cases, where again, the observation role proved difficult. The first case was studied in greater depth than the other two due to the fact that the researcher had good contacts with some of the people there who were either friends or former students.

Triangulation and validity

Triangulation refers to the use of multiple methods and data sources in the study of the same phenomenon (Strauss and Cobin, 1998; Denzin & Lincoln, 1998; Bryan, 1988; and Denzin, 1978). Triangulation can overcome the potential bias resulting from the use of a single method or single source of data in a study. Triangulation can, therefore, increase the validity and reliability of the research (Strauss and Cobin, 1998; Yin, 1994 and Denzin, 1978). The present research used triangulation in this way, using different data sources and methods in the study of the same phenomena. In the study of Vietnamese culture, for example, I used various methods including historical analysis (i.e. the Vietnamese history and its bearing on culture), comparison (i.e., comparing Vietnamese and Chinese culture) and language and discourse analysis (i.e. folklore and expressions).

Another example is the study of the structure of Vietnamese SOEs. This study used data from different sources including interviews with managers and government regulations and policies. The study of opportunistic behaviour used interviews, questionnaires and data from newspapers and government reports. Different methods and data were used that were either supplementary or confirmatory.

36

Since the two major research questions were about the rules of the game (institutional matrix) in Vietnam and the players (SOEs), the rest of the chapter briefly discusses the sources of data collected about these two broad issues.

3.2.2. Data on the rules of the game

The rules of the game, or institutional matrix, was 'built' from various material sources including observations, interviews, secondary sources, laws, folklore, proverbs, mores, and stories. Multiple sources of evidence were used to validate arguments and propositions. The observation and interview data, for example, were far from representative or sufficient enough to qualify certain propositions. However, they were supplemented by other sources of evidence, for example proverbs.

In constructing the 'rules of the game', I also followed the historical methodology. 'Ways of doing' are carried over time or institutionalised by means of symbolic interaction processes, expressed in laws, folklore, mores and the like. As Schutz (1973) points out:

> "The more (these) interlocked behaviour patterns are standardised and
> institutionalised, that is, the more their typicality is socially approved by laws,
> folkways, mores, and habits, the greater is their usefulness in common-sense and
> scientific thinking as a scheme of interpretation of human behaviour" (in Douglas,
> 1973, p.19-20).

Formal laws, folklore, proverbs, mores and so on were, therefore, considered as one of the major sources of evidence. In additional, a considerable number of the materials used came from secondary sources such as various Vietnamese newspapers and other studies about Vietnamese society such as those of Hickey (1967) about village life, McMillan and Woodruff (1999a and 1999b) on trading relations and Phan Van Thuyet (1996) on legal systems.

In the study of the specific 'rules of the game' applied directly to the SOEs, including the nature of the industrial governance (i.e. embedded materialism and payment policy presented in Chapter 10), I collected and analysed a fair number of government documents of reports, regulations and policies concerning the management of SOEs. Some of the documents studied have never been published in any language other than Vietnamese. In addition to documents, a number of government officials were interviewed to get a greater insight into the issues.

3.2.3. Data on the players – three case studies

The three SOEs chosen for study were the shoe enterprise, the garment enterprise and the light bulb enterprise. All three are located in the Hanoi area where most important enterprises are found. Another selection criterion for the cases was that the enterprise must be *stable*, meaning that it was not in the process of being privatised, merged, sold, on the edge of bankruptcy or of entering a joint-venture. Following the government reform policy, many SOEs are now on target for ownership change. Since radical changes are often associated with many technical problems and psychological effects, limiting the choice to those 'stable' SOEs made the research process both manageable and controllable.

All three enterprises were established in the late 1950s with the help of technology from China. Their initial objective was to serve the army during the American-Vietnam War. A general profile of the three enterprises in the year 1998 is given in Table 3.2. Two of the enterprises (shoe enterprise and garment enterprise) are in two key export industries (footwear and garment/ textiles). Vietnam is no different from many other developing countries, its main export products are raw natural resources and labour-intensive products, including garments and footwear. The shoe enterprise specialises in manufacturing canvas shoes. A large portion of its revenue (63.2% in 1998) comes from export. The garment enterprise specialises in manufacturing a variety of garment products. About 80% (81.7% in 1998) of its revenue comes from export. Despite this reliance on exports, neither enterprise has been able to sell its products directly into foreign markets but are subcontractors for foreign companies or agents. The light bulb enterprise manufactures various kinds of lamps, light bulbs and vacuum flasks. The light bulb enterprise is the only company manufacturing vacuum flasks in the northern and central parts of Vietnam.

Table 3.1. A general profile of the three SOEs in 1998

Enterprise	Number of employees	Revenue (million VND)	Profit before tax (million VND)
Shoe enterprise	1,614	127, 883	1,309
Garment enterprise	3,018	110,103	10,667
Light bulb enterprise	1,292	108,674	6,667

(USD1 ≅ VND1, 400 in 1998)

The case study method appeared appropriate to the context of the present research, but the question, as always, is how valid are the interpretation and the theories generated from a few case studies. This is an important question, since the research is not only concerned with the interpretation of a few cases, but also intends to say more about management and organisation behaviour in Vietnam in general. It is true that one cannot generalise from one or few cases, especially in the quantitative sense of the word.

We can, however, learn a lot from one or two cases. It is also important to note that the author's main concern in doing this research concerned concepts and their relationships through cases and not 'cases' in its literal meaning. Since science is socially constructed, it is common that many concepts and their relationships used in a case analysis are already well developed in the literature. The more abstract a

38

concept, the greater is its explanatory and generalised power. In addition, as Sartre (1981) pointed out, no individual or case is just an individual or a case. Any case will necessarily bear the trace of the more general social processes.

Part 2: Vietnam's history, culture, economy, institutions and form of capitalism

Chapter 4: An overview of Vietnamese history and culture

This chapter presents key aspects of Vietnamese history and culture that are directly related to any analysis of institutions and organisations. Vietnam has been popularly known to the world through its wars against France and the US. Over the years, the voluminous books written about the country have been chiefly concerned with these wars and, to some extent, with the Vietnamese political culture. Only a few studies have been directly concerned with Vietnamese culture and society. These include Jamieson (1993), Woodside (1971), and Hickey (1967). Each of these studies, however, revealed only one particular aspect of Vietnamese culture and society. Woodside (1971) for example, compared Vietnamese and Chinese institutions in the early nineteenth century; Jamieson (1993) looked at certain aspects of Vietnamese society through its literature and Hickey (1967) presented an ethnographic study of a southern Vietnamese village. No study of Vietnamese culture has been systematically concerned with cultural aspects that are directly linked to management, organisations and institutions in Vietnam.

The purpose of this chapter is to provide a synthesis of those aspects of Vietnamese culture in order to form a basis for the analysis of management, organisations and institutions. The materials for this chapter were taken partly from secondary sources, and partly from the author's own observations and reflections as an insider. As a Vietnamese, the author had unique advantages such as: easy to access Vietnamese materials; the cultural experience that comes with knowing the language (e.g. proverbs, folklore and stories) and the real world experience of the culture throughout his life.

There are many different ways to define and approach culture. One popular reference for students of comparative management and organisational studies are Hofstede's culture dimensions which allow a comparison of specific national attributes amongst different counties. However such studies, as Child (1981) pointed out, "treated culture as a residual factor which is presumed to account for national variations which have neither been postulated before the research nor explained after its completion." (p.306). This chapter is concerned with cultural patterns and values that are deep rooted in history and have survived the test of time. Culture is considered both as "conditioning elements of future action" and as "products of action" (Kroeber and Kluckhohn,1952: 181). A study of culture should, as Child (1981) pointed out, "isolate as well as account for dominant values in a society by reference to the historical development of its political, social, economic and other institutions, and also by reference to the manner in which key events and crises have been handled within the country" (p.329). In the case of Vietnam, a study of its culture should enrich our understanding and explain, for example, how the country handled reform after the collapse of the socialist system, why the Communist Party is still in control in Vietnam and China but not in Eastern Europe, and why Vietnam and China employed the 'gradual' rather than 'shock therapy' approach to economic reform used in Eastern Europe and so on.

It is also important to note that the present study is not a study of culture *per se*, but uses culture as a reference point in the analysis of management, organisations and institutions. Therefore, it makes use of the language and findings taken from comparative cultural studies.

4.1. Overview of Vietnamese history

4.1.1. Overview

Vietnam is a Southeast Asian country with a long history. The early Vietnamese shared many traits with people in other countries in Southeast Asia, a region believed to have seen the dawn of human history and civilisations (Molyneux, 1995; Woodside, 1971; Tran Ngoc Them, 1997). The history of Vietnam is a history of continuous resistance to foreign invasion, especially the Chinese. Unlike many developing countries, Vietnam has had experience of centralised administrative systems for at least two thousand years, if not far longer (Fforde and de Vylder, 1996, p.47). For over two thousand years, Vietnam along with Korea, Japan and China was a member of what might be called the East Asian classical civilisation (Woodside, 1971, p.7). The first known kingdom of Vietnam, Van Lang, existed over 2,500 years ago and was ruled by the Hung kings. The last Hung king is believed to have committed suicide in 257 BC after being defeated by a neighbouring chieftain from the North, and a new kingdom of Aulac emerged with the help of a Golden Turtle spirit (Jamieson, 1993, p.7). Vietnam became a Chinese colony in 111 BC. Before Chinese rule, Vietnam and other parts of Southeast Asia had reached a certain level of civilisation (characterised by the Dong Son culture which knew the art of bronze casting and had an old written language) and had some influence to the North (China) (Ha Van Tan, 1983 and Tran Ngoc Them, 1997). A rich variety of artefacts have been found – big bronze drums, lamps, bells, pearls and elaborately decorated pottery – dated between 3,000 and 4,000 years ago, which suggest a prosperous and lively society (Molyneux, 1995). The high level of civilisation achieved during this period led to the formation of a cohesive society, able to resist and fight against powerful invaders and keep its identity during the next two thousand years. Following invasion, from the first century BC to the tenth century Vietnam fell under the rule of the Chinese empire and consequently, was heavily influenced by Chinese culture and institutions.

The Vietnamese gained independence from Chinese rule in A.D. 939 and thereafter enjoyed a period of independent development during which it was ruled by two dynasties: Ly (1009-1225) and Tran (1225-1400). Between 1407 and 1427, Vietnam once again fell under Chinese rule until their expulsion by a great leader Le Loi who established the Le dynasty in 1428. Vietnam enjoyed the first period of the Le dynasty, especially the thirty seven year reign (1460-1497) of another great king Le Thanh Tong. Afterwards, however, the dynasty fell into decline and whilst it retained control, for the next three centuries recession and internal conflicts sapped the wealth and energy of the country. One of the features of this period was the expansion and standardisation of the Vietnamese writing system *(Nom)* which was transcribed from the Chinese.

The later decades of the eighteenth century were dominated by the Tay Son rebellion. The Tay Son era is poorly understood in Vietnamese history (Jamieson, 1993). The Tay Son, however, are widely regarded as progressive and open-minded and were responsible for making *Nom* the official writing system. The Nguyen dynasty began in 1802 and was responsible for making Confucianism the foundation of the national culture. Almost all institutional arrangements from examinations to legal systems were copied from the Chinese Ch'ing dynasty.

From the later half of the nineteenth century until 1975, Vietnam suffered occupation first by France and then by the US. During the Vietnam civil war (dates) millions of people died through hunger or in American bombing raids. The victory of the North left a united Vietnam under the rule of the Communist Party. Since 1986, the government has initiated an open-door policy and implemented some radical reforms aimed at establishing a market economy. Although the country has made significant strides in economic development, it is still one of the poorest countries in the world.

4.1.2. Vietnam and the Chinese connection
Geographically located to the south of China and having been ruled by the Chinese Empire for a thousand years, during which time genes, languages and other cultural aspects interacted, Vietnam is undoubtedly influenced by Chinese culture. Woodside (1971) pointed out that:

> "...Over this span of nine hundred years, the Vietnamese people received a comprehensive initiation into the scholarship, political theories, familial organisation patterns, bureaucratic practices, and even the religious orientations of Chinese culture.... Furthermore, Chinese rule gave the Vietnamese people - through the imposition of Chinese social, bureaucratic, and familial forms - a cohesion that guaranteed their permanence, on the eastern edge of a sub-continent where impermanent states were the rule rather than the exception." (p.7).

Under Chinese rule, every significant local aristocratic group in Vietnamese society was wiped out, leading some Vietnamese historians to argue against any qualitative difference between Chinese and Vietnamese culture (Woodside, 1971, p7). One Vietnamese historian has argued that when Vietnam gained independence from China "it was merely an instance of a fruit ripening and dropping from its mother tree in order to begin a related but geographically separate life." (Woodside, 1971, p.8).

Even during the thousand years of independence from 939, Vietnam remained heavily influenced by the Chinese, for example the government had to continue paying tribute to the Chinese. The Vietnamese were always threatened by their huge and unfriendly neighbour, and over the years the Chinese made a number of attempts to colonise Vietnam (in 981, 1075-1077, the 1250's and the1280's 1406-1427, and 1788) (Woodside, 1971, p.20). During the second era of Chinese rule (1407-1427), the Chinese destroyed almost all Vietnam's cultural heritage and books (Tran Ngoc Them, 1997). Ideas, institutions and other aspects of Chinese life continued to influence Vietnam through language, books and direct interaction. Woodside (1971) made a direct comparison between the civil government of the Nguyen dynasty in Vietnam and the Ch'ing dynasty in China in the first half of the nineteenth century. From this it is clear that there were more similarities than differences between the two countries. The Vietnamese law code of the early 1800s was a copy of the Chinese Qing dynasty law code (Woodside, 1998, p.196).

So it is no accident that modern Vietnam and China share many unique characteristics in their political, economic and social systems. Today, both claim to be socialist countries, are both ruled by the Communist Party, and both are following a market-socialism path to modernisation. Without much effort, one can easily observe that many Vietnamese economic and social policies were inspired by, or actually followed (with some minor modifications) those of China. The Vietnamese Foreign Investment Laws, for example, are very similar to the Chinese Foreign Investment Laws (Cohen, 1990).

All this demonstrates the strength of the connection between Vietnam and China in terms of culture and institutions and so makes it possible to make reference to the literature on Chinese society when discussing these societal aspects. This is extremely useful given the fact that the literature on Vietnamese culture and institutions is so modest.

4.2. Overview of Vietnamese culture and society

With regard to Chinese and Chinese-connected culture and society, the most comprehensive and influential work of reference is that of Max Weber. Applying the Weber method, which stressed the important role played by beliefs and values, to Vietnamese culture can give an interpretation of the relationship. In the case of both Vietnam and China, the dominant values are those of Confucianism. The fundamental beliefs and values come into existence via the social interactions within the family, villages and other institutions which define the rules for individual action. Our analysis of the Vietnamese culture and society will follow the structure below.

Figure 4.1. Cultural determinants of individual Vietnamese values and institutions – a conceptual structure

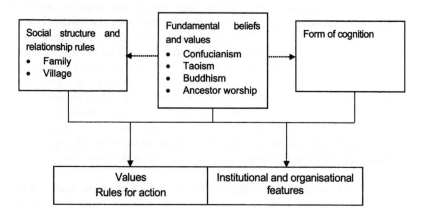

4.2.1. Confucianism

Western scholars interested in Vietnam often regard it as a Neo-Confucian society (Woodside, 1998; Jamieson, 1993; Fforde and de Vylder, 1996; and Smith, 1973), a view supported by an analysis of the fundamental principles of Confucianism and the history of Confucianism in Vietnam.

Confucianism was first introduced into Vietnam at the beginning of the first millennium (Tran Ngoc Them, 1997, p.515) and affected almost every aspect of Vietnamese culture and the social system. During the Chinese colonial period, Vietnamese scholars such as Li Cam, Li Tien and Khuong Cong Phu did well in the civil service examinations and held high positions in the government. Khuong Cong Phu, for example, was appointed a King's first minister in the Chinese government of his time, despite being Vietnamese (Tran Ngoc Them, 1997, p.516). Following independence from Chinese rule in 939 A.D there were strong anti-Chinese feelings amongst the Vietnamese. The greatness of the Ly dynasty (1009-1225), for example, rested partly on "a foundation of unprecedented moral force that was built by calling forth ... spirits of past culture heroes to bolster the efficacy and legitimacy of their rule." (Jamieson1993, p.9). However, the social structure and many other aspects of Chinese society were so firmly established that the Vietnamese could not "escape" them. In 1070 a Temple of Literature (*Van Mieu*) dedicated to Confucius was built in Thang Long (Hanoi today) (Tran Ngoc Them, 1997; Jamieson, 1993). The first Confucian examination in independent Vietnam took place in the year 1075. The examination system continued over the years until the nineteenth century when Vietnam fell under French rule.

During the period from the tenth to the nineteenth century, the practice of examinations rose and fell depending on different rulers and the degree to which Buddhism was practiced. But from the fifteenth century, and especially during the first half of the nineteenth century before the French took over, neo-Confucianism dominated Vietnamese society.

Confucianism was formed out of living conditions in traditional Chinese society. Redding (1993) pointed out that

"China has always been an agrarian state and one in which subsistence level living has been the lot of most people. In these circumstances, there is much to be said for a value system which places a constraint on the expression of individual desires and also sponsors group sharing of limited resources (Bond and Hwang 1986:215). The self sufficiency of the family unit, based on its ability to manage its affairs well, was its only insurance against disaster, and the common budgets and common property of the chia (family) formed a rational collective response to the surrounding circumstances (Cohen 1976: 11)" (p. 43-44).

Confucianism is a set of ethical principles originating in the teachings of Confucius. Born in 551 BC, Confucius lived during a time of moral chaos characterised by hunger, corruption and social unrest. He spent most of his life teaching and recording his ideas about how people should live together and how the county should be run. His ideas were further developed by his followers and compiled into five books, often called five Confucian classics.

The key ideas and concepts of Confucianism as an ethical system are:

The gentleman ideal

The 'gentleman ideal' is a key concept in Confucianism. For a Confucian ideal man, or gentleman, the first thing he needs to do is 'tu than' (cultivate himself through learning) and then follow the formula: te gia, tri quoc, binh thien ha. 'Te gia, tri quoc, binh thien ha' means a man should regulate his family first (te gia), before thinking about the government of the country (tri quoc) or peace of the world (binh thien ha). 'Tu than' means to study and behave oneself according to Confucian values and principles.

Five cardinal virtues

The five cardinal virtues of an ideal gentleman are: nhan, nghia, le, tri, tin in Vietnamese, often translated into English as: benevolence or humanity, righteousness or justice, propriety, intelligence or wisdom, and faith or truthfulness or sincerity. The two virtues which lie at the heart of the Vietnamese and Chinese character building are nhan (human) and le (jen and li in the English transcription of the Chinese). Cormady and Cormady (1983) provided an informative description of jen.

"The ideogram for jen represented a human being: jen is humanness-what makes us human. We are not fully human simply by receiving life in a human form. Rather, our humanity depends upon community, human reciprocity. Jen pointed in that direction. It connected with the Confucian golden rule of not doing to others what you would not want them to do to you. Against individualism, it implied that people have to live together hopefully, even lovingly. People have to cultivate their instinctive benevolence, their instinctive ability to put themselves in another's shoes. That cultivation was the primary educational task of Confucius and Mencius" (quoted in Redding, 1993, p.49).

Jen emphasises that individuals are not independent entities but are bound by the social context – the family, the clan, the village, and the nation. Conformity to the social group is the rule. Le (li Chinese) could be translated in English as appropriate manners or propriety. Li, as Redding (1993) pointed out, "provides the lubrication necessary to reduce social friction and it fosters the sublimating of self-indulgence in daily interaction" (p.49). A certain level of propriety characterises every culture, but in Confucian societies, propriety moved to the core of life. Propriety was a system of social codes which aimed at preserving or maintaining hierarchical orders. Le is very important in the Vietnamese society. The slogan 'tien hoc le, hau hoc van' (one needs to learn the rites or appropriate ways of conduct (le) first, before studying literature and science) is posted at the gates of many primary, secondary and high schools and even in universities in Vietnam.

There are many examples of propriety that westerners would consider insignificant but that are very important to the Vietnamese. For example, subordinates need to visit their boss after coming back from an overseas business trip, or on certain holiday occasions. Junior staff should not give opinions in certain meetings and so on. Individuals learn and practice these and many other unwritten rules about propriety all their lives. The author himself experienced criticism on several occasions on the grounds of improper conduct, for example: playing football and going to the pub with students, or not visiting the head of his department. The daily life of the Vietnamese is sometimes over-occupied with questions about propriety: what one should do and should not do. It is not, therefore, surprising that westerners are often puzzled by certain events when they interact with the Vietnamese and Chinese. Hickson and Pugh, in their Management Worldwide (1995) told a story about one of the author's experience during a Chinese dinner. He did not know that one should not eat all the food at the dish and so did not realise he was acting improperly. He believed that leaving some food on the dish was a signal that one was already full, being unaware of an unwritten rule of propriety that one should leave some food on the dish regardless of whether one is full or not. Guests who eat all the food in a dish would be considered as uncultured.

At mealtimes in Vietnam, there are distinct classifications between chu (members of the household) and khach (guests or visitors). Guests are normally expected to be polite (should not eat until full or eat all the food in the good dishes). But these classifications are neither ritual nor rational in the Western meaning of the word.

Five cardinal relationships
Above all else, Confucianism, emphasises social *order* or *hierarchy*. The five cardinal relationships are:

Parent-child
The parent-child relationship is the most important (stable, unchanging and lasting) relationship. Those who do not respect their parents are regarded as *animals*.

Ruler-subject
The ruler-subject can be seen as an extension of parent-child relationship.

Elder brother-younger brother
Elder brother-younger brother represents the inherent higher status of someone who is older, has more experience and so presumably more wisdom. Thus, the older-brother has a duty to care about his younger sibling, and the younger brother has a duty to listen to his elder. This relationship is not confined to the family, but is also extended to any senior-junior relationship.

Friend-friend
Friend-friend is the only equal relationship amongst the five cardinal relationships. It is based on mutual trust.

Husband-wife
The wife is expected to submit to the husband.

The traditional Sino-Vietnamese view of socio-political integration was built upon three bonds (tam cuong): a bureaucrat's loyalty to his emperor, a son's obedience to his father, and a wife's submission to her husband.

Confucian education
Education is highly respected in many societies in the world but is perhaps most respected most in Confucian societies. Education is, above all, important to the ideal man, the gentleman. The traditional Vietnamese class structure derived from the Confucian classics, which ranked classes hierarchically in order of importance: si-nong-cong-thuong. Scholars (si) came first, peasants (nong) second, artisans (cong) third, and merchants (thuong) fourth and last. The attitude toward education was reflected in many romantic folk songs, like: "Chang tham ruong ca ao lien. Tham vi cai but, cai nghien anh do." This translates as telling how a girl does not care about a man from a rich family with a lot of ruong ca (rice-fields) and ao lien (big gardens), but loves men with education, symbolised by cai but (pens) and cai nghien (ink). "Anh ve lo hoc chu Nhu. Chin trang em doi muoi thu emcho." tells anh (the man), "please go and learn Chinese writings and classics and em (the girl) will wait for ever", symbolised by chin trang (nine full moons) and muoi thu (ten falls).

The respect for education was such that many Vietnamese were reluctant even to step on pieces of paper with Chinese characters written on them. This attitude towards education still prevails in Vietnam today, as indicated by the country's literacy rate. Although one of the poorest countries in the world, Vietnam's literacy rate is quite high, standing at over 90%. One of the most important duties and goals of most of Vietnamese parents is to get their children educated. Low-income Vietnamese families would sacrifice almost everything for this.

It is important to note that the concept of education is culture-bound. As in China, traditional Vietnamese education concerned mainly literature and Chinese classics. The purpose was to follow, and not to question classical ideas and theories. The most respected scholars were those able to memorise and recite long verses or paragraphs from the classics. This feature of education still dominates the education system in Vietnam. In the period before reform was introduced, Marxist books and materials were translated and studied in Vietnam in the same spirit as traditional Confucian classics. Social science students had to cite Marx and officials often recited Marx's writings in their speeches, and nobody was allowed to question the ideas in the books. Western political theorists would ascribe this to communism, but in fact it was much more than that. One needs to understand the deep-rooted culture of a society to see how it handled such a social phenomenon.

There are two possible explanations for this continued positive attitude toward education. The first, rational reason, would cite the economic benefits associated with education while the second is known as the 'mystic image of the world'. Educated men, the literati, (those who passed Confucian examinations to a certain level) became government officials (quan) and enjoyed many privileges, as we will discuss in Chapter 6. The 'magic image of the world', will be discussed later in this section.

The concept 'xiao' and the institutionalisation of power
In order to understand how Confucianism worked in general and the five cardinal relationships in particular, we need to discuss the concept *hieu* (in Vietnamese) or *xiao* (in Chinese). *Hieu* is often translated into English as filial piety. This is such a key concept that Weber observed that being without filial piety is the only 'sin' in a society (China) otherwise devoid of such a concept of the transcendental (Redding, 1993, p.59). For the sake of consistency, in the following discussion we will use the term *xiao* in stead of *hieu* in Vietnamese.

Xiao is a key concept of Confucianism and ranked above all other virtues. Hamilton (1984) argued that *xiao* has prevented China from institutionalising power in the way that has occurred in Western countries. Throughout Chinese philosophy, humanity resided in roles rather than institutionalised power. The philosophical idea behind this is to let people observe and carry out their roles, and its importance goes beyond the law. Hamilton (1984) correctly pointed out the difference in meaning between *xiao* and the traditional Roman *patria potestas*, claiming that Max Weber treated the two concepts the same. *Patria potestas* means literally the father's power and it meant that the head of the family could exercise personal discretion and control although there were 'free zones' left for children. The Western system emerged from this institutionalisation of power and jurisdiction. As Redding pointed out:

"From this developed systems of jurisdiction which attempt to place boundaries around individual freedom without prescribing individual behaviour. The person is thus left with much discretion and initiative and in practice, encouraged to exercise them" (Redding, 1993, p.45).

He also pointed out that the stability and order of Western society relies on "the acceptance of the boundary constraints, and the principles they rest on, by more or less independent individuals" (p.45).

Xiao is different. It does not define a clear-cut relationship between the power and the weak, only a difference:

"As a principle of domination, xiao is an injunction: Live up to the responsibility of the role of life. Obedience to others-a son obeying a parent or a wife her husband-is to occur in the absence of commands and even in the absence of someone to command. Sons remain sons, and wives remain wives, even after their fathers and husbands die, just as the ruler always remains the Son of Heaven. Obedience is simply a part of a role and roles make up the whole. Everyone's obedience, everyone practising xiao, represents a harmony of wills. In principle, then, the act of commanding another is not an act of personal will, but rather an act of duty. Power derives from role obedience, not from jurisdiction prerogatives. Emperors have a duty to govern their subjects: parents have a duty to educate children; men have the duty to admonish their wives: and older brothers have the duty to correct their younger brothers. All must be dutiful, if disasters are not to occur." (Hamilton 1984, p.415, the author's emphasis).

There are thus always un-stated rules in every relationship. There is always a significant shared amount of tacit knowledge between two parties in any social context. *Xiao*, however, became relatively codified in certain periods of time in history, especially, in China. Like the concepts 'moral' or 'ethical', *xiao* was contextual, so open to interpretation. It was a duty of both parties and formed a dialectical relationship between the powerful and the weak. It also emphasised *reciprocity,* as a saying (or causal statement) associated with each of the five cardinal orders indicates. These are: *quan minh than trung* (which translates as if the King is fair and justified, then the subordinates will be loyal); *phu tu tu hieu* (if the father is gentle and kind, sons and daughters will be *xiao*); *phu nghia phu kinh* (if the husband is righteous, the wife will respect him); *huynh luong de de* (if the older brother is good, the younger will respect him); and *bang huu huu tin* (friends show good faith to each other mutually). There is always room for two parties to observe and act in a xiao relationship. When there is question of moral wrong, there should be correction. Everything comes from within and power results from the practice of one's role. It is a duty of the father, for example, to educate his sons, and at the same time, sons have a duty to respect their father.

However, this philosophy and way of life did not support the development of capitalism and modern science (Weber, 1951; Needham, 1956). Needham (1956) pointed out that:

"Social and world order rested, not on an ideal of authority, but on a conception of rotational responsibility...Thus the mechanical and quantitative, the forced and the external imposed, were all absent. The notion of Order excluded the notion of law." (Needham 1956, quoted by Hamilton, 1984, p.418).

Confucianism – a 'civil' religion

Confucianism consists of a set of rules of conduct concerned with how people adjust to living. Its lack of metaphysical foundations makes it an ethical doctrine rather than a theistic religion (Weber, 1951). Confucianism differs from other religions in three aspects (1) it has no deity but is based instead on rules of conduct; (2) it was not established in a way that competes with other religions; and (3) it has no large-scale institutional 'church' with priests and ceremonial and a laity (Redding, 1993, p.46).

No God

People from Confucian societies, especially from China and Vietnam where Confucianism is an orthodoxy, and followers do not consider themselves as members of a Confucian sect. In Vietnam, the official word for Confucianism is Nho Giao – Sino-Vietnamese for Ju Chiao in Chinese. Both mean 'doctrine of the literati'. Nho *giao* even sounds negative in Vietnamese, although the Confucianism life orientation is as strong as ever in Vietnam today. The choice of *Van Mieu* (the Temple of Literature, originally dedicated to Confucius) by the Vietnamese government and the Communist Party as the key place to celebrate the new millennium (year 2000) and one of the places for US President Bill Clinton to visit during his trip to Vietnam in November 2000, was a clear acknowledgement of the Confucian ethic. The spirit of the celebration was to remind people to respect tradition: respect education, family and social order.

Confucianism was seen by Weber as a "rational ethic" which aimed at reducing "tension with the world to an absolute minimum" (Weber, 1951, p. 227). He also pointed out that within Confucianism, there is an absence of tension between "nature and deity", between ethical demands and human short-comings, consciousness of sin and the need for salvation, and the lack of ethical demands raised by a supra-mundane God in opposition to convention and tradition. The Western metaphysical man and God are equivalent to *men and men* in a life oriented towards Confucianism. Men worship not God but their parents, their bosses, and their ancestors. They do things not because 'God has commanded' them, but because of 'other men'. This orientation perhaps accounts for the difference between what Vietnamese call the inner orientation of Western people and the *outer orientation* of the Chinese and Vietnamese.

Does not compete with other religions

As a *civil* religion, Confucianism did not oppose other religious ideas or systems. For Confucian men, the principle is to live in a way that makes them human. It tends to tolerate or blend with other religions in a harmonious and, to a great extent, a traditional way. This feature of Confucianism perhaps accounted for the avoidance of the worst religion-driven disorders that plagued European politics in the sixteenth and seventeenth centuries, and in several parts of the world today. In both traditional and contemporary Vietnamese homes one might find "dozens of different kinds of altars to spirits from the pantheons of Taoism, Buddhism, popular mythology, Vietnamese history, and local legends". (Jamieson 1993, p.36). In more recent decades, Ho Chi Minh, and even Marx and Lenin became worshipped on altars in many homes. The sanctification of tradition and convention, as Weber pointed out, implied toleration of magical religions and spirits.

This feature perhaps partly accounts for the lack of the development of science and rational laws that facilitated capitalism. In Vietnam, superstition and mythical elements are still very much alive today. Rumours have occasionally circulated that certain things or people (often associated with the deformed) have the power to cure the sick or help the poor. Many people then travel to see them and pray. Occasionally one can see altars with perfume sticks on big trees so if there is a big tree on the premises of a family business, it is likely that altars will have been placed in the tree because the owner believed the tree brought luck to his business.

No churches
Weber (1951) observed that "the Chinese "soul" has never been revolutionised by a prophet." (p. 142). This statement is equally true of the Vietnamese. There is not even a special word for 'religion' in Vietnamese. The Vietnamese words for 'religion', 'Confucianism', 'Buddhism' and 'Taoism' are *Ton giao*, *Nho giao*, *Phat giao*, and *Dao giao,* respectively. All these words are Sino-Vietnamese. *Giao* means a doctrine or education. A teacher or lecturer is also called *giao*. The majority of Vietnamese do not belong to any official religious sect and consequently, as Weber (1951) argued, in China (and also in Vietnam): "anything corresponding to our cure of souls was absent...there was not a trace of "church discipline", which meant in turn that the means for religious control of life were lacking" (p.225).

4.2.2. The family and the village in Vietnam.
The previous section outlined and discussed the key ideas and principles of Confucianism and to some extent, the history of Confucianism in Vietnam. It is important to note that the values of different Confucian societies may not be the same and are not necessarily the same as those Confucius spoke or wrote about. As Woodside pointed out:

> "Just as the Christian Bible might resonate differently in the minds of Scottish Calvinists, German Lutherans, or Polish Catholics, so too could such texts as the Confucian Analects be read differently by Chinese or Korean academicians or Vietnamese village teachers." (1998 p.194).

Redding (1993) also noted that Confucianism contains many interpretations within it and "that it is a live set of ideas which has developed and changed over time" (p.46). Within China, Confucianism differed according to the dynasty – there were, for example: Han, Sung and Ch'ing versions of Confucianism. The Vietnamese version of Confucianism was more like with that of the Sung dynasty (Tran Ngoc Them, 1997, p.516). Each dynasty emphasised different characteristics of the 'gentleman ideal'. Redding (1993) used the metaphor "capitalism" to emphasise the possible different interpretations of Confucianism. He wrote that "Confucianism, like capitalism, is a matter of what you do" (p.47). Although a number of countries are today labelled 'neo-Confucian', different histories and different ways of classifying social relations have resulted in differences in cultural values amongst these societies that are not trivial. The later part of this chapter will discuss the different forms of Confucianism and cultural values found in Japanese and Chinese and Vietnamese societies.

In order to understand Vietnamese culture, we must study the social contexts in which individuals interact and share values. In the case of Vietnam, this must be the family and the village. In traditional Vietnam, the family and village were the most important places, and to a great extent, the only places where social contacts occurred.

Traditionally, almost all Vietnamese lived in villages (still true today) and made their living by cultivating rice. Their lives were attached to the wet-rice fields and they almost always struggled to fulfil their basic needs. Redding (1993), Cohen (1976), and Bond and Hwang (1986) all argued that these difficult living conditions partly accounted for the development and sustenance of Confucian values. In fact, the living conditions of the Vietnamese people were even worse than those of the Chinese as, compared to China, Vietnamese society was poorer (Woodside, 1971). Jamieson (1993) gives an informative summary of the country's ecology and its bearing on culture:

> "The Red River is subject to rapid and extreme variation in water level, and both flood and drought have always occurred with ominous regularity. Epidemics and pest infestation have also been common. The Red River delta has simultaneously been one of the most densely populated and least safe regions in the world. In an uncertain and dangerous environment, hunger and social unrest have been constant threats. As a result, the local culture has emphasised the subordination of the individual to collective discipline of family and village. Both the family and the village have been relatively closed, corporate entities, self-reliant, and responsible for the action of their individual members." (pp4-5).

The cultivation of the wet rice-fields depends greatly on the weather conditions and needs extensive care, and so villagers stayed in their villages to cultivate and care for the rice fields throughout the year. Almost all social activities took place in their villages which meant that the family and the village were very important to them. The village, the wet-rice fields, the invaders and above all, the hard way of life featured in many Vietnamese arts, novels, folklore and poems. As one Vietnamese popular child poet, Tran Dang Khoa, described in a poem (later turned into a song) during the Vietnam War when he was eight years of age:

The rice of our village,
Contains the July's storms,
Contains the March's rains,

Drops of sweet,
In the June's noon,
The water's boiling,
Small fishes can't survive,
Crabs have to move to the shore,
My mum goes down to transplant rice,
The rice of our village,
In the years of American bombs.
Pours down onto the roofs of the houses…
(the author's translation)

Family and kinship

Jamieson (1993) pointed out that each individual Vietnamese family was like a "small nation" and that "the parent-child relationship was at the very core of Vietnamese culture, dominating everything else." (pp38-39). Over time, the family became a major symbolic social organisation. A study of Vietnamese history during the Nguyen dynasty of the early part of 19th century carried out by Woodside (1971) suggested that the Vietnamese bureaucracy itself "was symbolically meant to suggest a gigantic family," (p.39). The word *gia* in the Sino-Vietnamese word for nation (*quoc gia*) means family and the nation was metaphorically a big family. Filial piety within the family even influenced to the conduct of state affairs. During the Nguyen dynasty, for example the ethical attitude of a son toward his parents (filial piety) became one of the selection criteria for government posts. The prince who was seeking a loyal minister, for example, was supposed to visit households with filial sons, a feature that still holds true today. So, before anyone could qualify to be a Communist Party member, a senior communist official had to visit his or her home and "investigate" their family background. In traditional Vietnam, almost everything ranging from revenue matters to political theory and military recruitment were associated with the family. During Gia Long's rule (early nineteenth century), if soldiers defected from the army then their parents, brothers and 'lineage relatives' were immediately taken to replace them.

Family values are taught and reinforced in almost every aspect of the lives of Vietnamese people. Children are taught filial piety in their families and in their schools, whilst the dead are worshipped within the family. Each family maintains an altar for their ancestors as a reminder and to reinforce family values. They also maintain an altar where they worship *tho cong*, a deity who resides in the land of the family and who protects the family from evil.

In a world of very limited resources (subsistence level existence), the driving force of family and blood relationships could equally mean the exclusion of 'outsiders'. It was Mencius, who found difficulty in balancing the 'love of family' and 'love of man'.

> "Mencius rejected the universal 'love of man' with the comment that it would extinguish piety and justice and that it is the way of animals to have neither father nor brother." (Weber 1951, p.236).

The meaning and priority indicated by the formula for a gentlemanly ideal: *te giatri quoc-binh thien ha*, meant in practice that "the individual's desire for a bureaucratic career sprang more from a basic design for the enhancement of the reputation and the power of his family." (Woodside, 1971, p38).

There is a saying in Vietnamese: *mot giot mau dao hon ao nuoc la* (one drop of blood is more valuable than a pond of water). At the monarchical level, clan conflict was inherent in the Vietnamese tradition (Smith, 1973). Clan conflicts were also perhaps transmitted through Chinese culture. Intense conflicts (murders, the killing of infant princes) within many monarchies were documented in Chinese history books and featured in many Chinese films. The coherence and importance of blood relationships were illustrated by many Vietnamese proverbs, for example: the Vietnamese saying *mot nguoi lam quan, ca ho duoc nho* means that if someone became an official (*quan*), then his whole lineage could count on or benefit from him. The cohesion of blood relationships were also indicated by the saying: *Say cha con chu*; that if someone loses their father, they still have an uncle while *say me bu gi* means that if a baby loses his or her mother, then they can be suckled by their aunt.

Covering up and the practice of *nepotism* are facts of life in Vietnam. Even Confucius himself, according to Vietnamese sources, encouraged the practice of covering up. Tran Ngoc Them (1997) cited the following story about Confucius:

> "After listening to a story told by a district official about a person who was so 'straight' he revealed that his father had stolen sheep, Confucius responded: We are not like that, a father should cover up for his sons and vice versa." (p.506, the author's translation).

In the Vietnamese culture, covering up for family members and relatives is encouraged. Anybody who fails to cover up for a family member or relative would be considered immoral or lacking in filial piety and in short, a real disaster.

The Vietnamese household

Todd (1985) classified the different household organisations in the world into seven main categories based on three criteria dimensions: liberty/submission, equality/inequality and endogamy/ exogamy. The seven families were:

1. Absolute nuclear family;
2. Egalitarian nuclear family;
3. Authoritarian family;
4. Exogamous community family;
5. Endogamous community family;
6. Asymmetrical community family;
7. Anomic family.

Source: Todd, 1985, pp 19-31

According to Todd's classifications, the traditional Vietnamese family and to a great extent the contemporary family belong to the Exogamous community family type. The characteristics of this type of family are: (1) equality of inheritance; (2) cohabitation of married sons and their parents; and (3) no marriage between close relatives.

Todd (1985) observed that communism took place in areas where the exogamous community family type was dominant. He argued that:

> "...communism is a transference to the party state of the moral traits and regulatory mechanisms of the exogamous community family. Sapped by urbanisation, industrialisation and the spread of literacy, in short by modernisation, the exogamous community family passes on its egalitarian and authoritarian values to the new society. Individuals with equal rights are crushed by the political system in the same way that they were destroyed in the past by the extended family when it was the dominant institution of traditional Russian, Chinese, Vietnamese or Serbian society." (Todd, 1985, p.33).

Todd's hypothesis, which directly linked a family type (exogamous community family) and a political structure (communism) is undoubtedly controversial. However, the proposition that individual values and their perceptions of the world are, to a great extent, influenced by and developed from the family is widely accepted. The Vietnamese family and kinship system in general is very solid and cohesive as a unit. This does not mean, however, that within the unit (the family), people lived in a harmonious way. The classification between blood and non-blood relationships was equally applied within the family. Marriages in Vietnam as well as in other Confucian societies had to be exogamous. In Vietnam, marriages between relatives of even five generations distance were rare.

The relationship between the family (blood relationship) and the outsider (the sons' wives) was not always peaceful. The Vietnamese saying: *khac mau tanh long,* which means, literally, that dirty or unfriendly attitudes and thoughts came from blood difference, possibly originated from the family. The relationship between daughter-in-law and mother-in-law (*me chong-nang dau*) was above all the most difficult one. Vietnamese people often referred to *me chong-nang dau* when they encountered difficult relationships. The nature of this relationship was inevitably the same in China. Managers from Chinese SOEs, for example, when describing the difficult relationship between the enterprise and government bureaux dubbed the latter 'the *mother-in-law*' (Child and Boisot 1988). *Me chong-nang dau* was not the only difficult relationship. The relationship between a husband's sisters and his wife was sometimes considered as even worse than that between enemies. The Vietnamese saying: *giac ben Ngo khong bang ba co ben chong* means brutal Chinese invaders (Ngo) are even better than husband's sisters. The blood and non-blood relationship is also expressed in the saying: *thuong nhau nhu chi em gai, rai nhau nhu chi em dau*. Vietnamese symbolised human love toward each other as *thuong nhau nhu chi em gai* that literally means 'love each other like sisters'. *Thuong* means love, share, and care about each other.

For sisters-in-law, the picture was completely different. The word 'rai' in *rai nhau nhu chu em dau* (hate or dislike each other like sisters-in-law) has an opposite meaning to the word *thuong*. Living under the same roof with shared property in such an environment, it was not difficult to justify sisters-in-law trying to take advantage or compete for their own families (husbands and children). Although a daughter-in-law was supposed to treat her husband's parents as if they were her own parents, her heart was perhaps not always convinced. The Vietnamese say '*nuoc mat nang dau*' (tears of a daughter-in-law) meaning that tears from daughter-in-law (at her parent-in-law's funeral) are crocodile tears.

The traditional Vietnamese practised an inheritance system in which the father's wealth was divided equally amongst his sons. In some historical periods, daughters were also allowed to share an inheritance. Vietnamese inheritance law codes starting from sixteenth century treated women more equally and generously than those of China (Woodside, 1971). Vietnamese people always had a strong sense of equality and this, together with a strong sense of blood relationships, resulted in family relationships that were not always harmonious. The family head was thus very important in keeping the whole family living together harmoniously. People were often very proud if they were the head of a family which had four or five generations living under the same roof. The Vietnamese government during the Nguyen dynasty encouraged and reinforced the cohesion of the family. If a household with five generations was together in the same home (*ngu dai dong duong*) they were rewarded with money. This practice was probably borrowed from the Chinese Ch'ing. The intention of such government activity, as Woodside pointed out, was to honour the "discipline-dispensing family head, not a large population but rather visible social control obtained through familial methods." (Woodside 1971, p41).

The village

The village was almost a closed world in traditional Vietnamese times. Almost all social activities took place there and the sense of a village identity was as strong as a family identity. The village was a world in itself. This fact was expressed in the well-known proverb *phep vua thua le lang* (the laws of the king yield to the custom of the village). It was a "self-contained homogeneous community, jealously guarding its way of life – a little world that is autonomous and disregards (if not disdains) the outside world." (Hickey 1964, p.276). The Vietnamese village had great solidarity as a unit in opposing the outside world, but at the same time, was very competitive within it. The strong sense of blood relationships and the clear distinction between blood and non-blood relationships were perhaps the starting points, and were extended to the distinction between village and non-village members. In the traditional Vietnamese village, there was a clear distinction between *dan chinh cu* (official village members) and *dan ngu cu* (people from other places, who, for some reason, came to settle in the village). There was a clear discrimination against *dan ngu cu* (the outsiders).

> "The discrimination (toward dan ngu cu) is very fierce: dan chinh cu enjoyed full
> rights and privileges, whereas, dan ngu cu do not have any rights at all: (they) are

56

not allowed to join giap (a kind of social club, very important to the villagers), they can only build houses at the rear of the village (not very safe areas), have to do inferior jobs that dan chinh cu do not want to do...but still have to pay taxes...In order to become dan chinh cu, dan ngu cu must meet the two criteria: have settled in the village for three generations and possessed some land (rice-field)" (Tran Ngoc Them 1997, pp.210-211, the author's translation).

This hostile attitude towards *dan ngu cu* was one of the main reasons why Vietnamese stayed in their village throughout their lives. They were very afraid of moving to other places. As Tran Ngoc Them (1997) pointed out:

"People often talk about the fact that the Vietnamese were attached to their villages, to the "home of their ancestors", to "where they were born" from generation to generation as a special love of their village. In fact, that is just a consequence of the discrimination towards dan ngu cu....people were afraid of that and did not dare go somewhere else..." (p.211, the author's translation).

There were also clear distinctions between villages, as expressed in many folk songs. Examples are *trong lang nao lang ay danh, thanh lang nao lang ay tho* (to beat only the drums of one's own village, to worship only the deity of one's village), *trau ta an co dong ta* (our buffaloes eat the grass of our fields) and *ta ve ta tam ao ta, du trong du duc ao nha van hon* (we'd better take baths at our water pond regardless of whether it's clean or not).

Clearly, this hostile attitude toward 'outsiders' accounted for the *lack of trust* beyond the family and to some extent the village. In the village, there were detailed classifications of and strong competition for social status between families. Status was very important to families, and the price of status was constant vigilance, conformity to village norms, and conspicuous generosity. If people did not follow these requirements, then respectful behaviour would be withdrawn. Traditionally, the Vietnamese accepted hierarchy and cared passionately about *face* and social status.

Competition between families for social status could be very fierce:

"Village members were ranked in a strict hierarchy corresponding to named social status. The upper strata of this hierarchy were known collectively as the Council of Notables. Although the particular status and the criteria for recruitment varied, all villages had a status hierarchy with a body of notables at the top. Directly beneath the nobles were the village elders, and beneath them came other adult members of the village. Within these broad categories were many finer distinctions." (Jamieson, 1993, p.30).

The classification of the social ranks was perhaps most apparent in the village feasts:

"Seating arrangements and the distribution of portions at such feasts were prescribed down to the smallest detail in accord with relative position in the hierarchy. Status was manifested by who sat at which table, how many men would share a tray of food, who received which cut of meat." (ibid., p.31).

From the above analysis of the Vietnamese family and the village, we can conclude that Vietnamese society was characterised by three perhaps contradictory characteristics:

1. A strong sense of equality and liberty;
2. A very strong sense of kinship;
3. An acceptance of (perhaps preference for) strong social hierarchies.

These three key elements accounted for many paradoxes within Vietnamese society. Jamieson (1993) concluded that:

> "Logically contradictory principles – competition and co-operation, hierarchy and egalitarianism, conflict and solitary – were functionally complementary parts of the political economy. This duality of structure characterised the ideology and society of traditional Vietnam." (p36).

Although competition occurred between families within the village, a certain level of co-operation was necessary to keep the village identity and oppose the outside world. From an ethnographic study of a Vietnamese village, Hickey (1967) concluded that:

> "Cultural values and social behavioural patterns are shared because the inhabitants have a common tradition... It does not necessarily follow that members of village society have strong social bonds or a sense of social solidarity. These qualities are found within the village but cannot be attributed to the village." (p.278)

As Weber pointed out, social classification based on "social rank" resulted in deadly jealousy, *distrust* and hostility (Gerth and Mills, 1948). The social structure and relationships within the Vietnamese family and the village certainly encouraged a strong sense of competition, jealousy, distrust and *limited cooperation.*

Tran Ngoc Them (1997) pointed out that a typical Vietnamese negative trait was *cao bang, do ki* (one does not want others better than oneself). Jealousy and competitiveness is, of course, not unique to the Vietnamese culture or its people. But the Vietnamese social structure and institutions (family and village) encouraged jealousy and *competitiveness*. People competed strongly for social status. This is expressed in the Vietnamese saying: *tha lam dau ga hon la duoi voi* (it is better to be the head of a chicken than the tail of an elephant). This could account for the urge to *become bosses* among Vietnamese and the strong *entrepreneurial sprit* among both Vietnamese and Chinese people.

The Vietnamese tell many jokes about themselves. One popular one is that if one Vietnamese fell into a lake, he would be able to get out. But if two or three fell in, they would never be able to get out because if one tried, the others would prevent him from getting out. There is certainly a lack of co-operation and trust outside family members and close friends. These characteristics prevented the Vietnamese people from developing and maintaining large scale organisations. This issue will be discussed in the next part.

4.2.3. Buddhism

Buddhism, whose history goes back over 2500 years, developed in a large number of schools and sects, "many of them almost as far apart from each other in fundamental tenets and practices as any totally unrelated schools of thought and sects that could be imagined." (Klostermaier 1991, [p.1]). This section provides an overview of the general development and position of Buddhism in Vietnamese society.

It is believed that Buddhism was introduced into Vietnam around 168-189 A.D. (Tran Ngoc Them, 1997; Vu Duy Tu and Bechert, 1976). Buddhism came to Vietnam via two roots: India and China. In the early period, Indian Buddhism dominated but then gradually, Buddhism came to Vietnam from China and from the ninth century on, Chinese Buddhism became predominant. Buddhism exercised a great deal of influence in Vietnam, for two major reasons. Firstly, as we have seen previously, there was a continuing tendency towards the elimination of Chinese cultural elements and Buddhism was considered a replacement for borrowed Chinese culture. Secondly Buddhism, with its feminine characters (*yin*), was close to the national character of traditional Vietnam. It is believed that before the Chinese conquest, Vietnamese culture was more matriarchal-oriented, for example, some Vietnamese cultural heroes were women (the Trung sisters and Ms.Trieu). Buddha was called *But* in Vietnam, later sinicised into *Phat*. *But,* featured in much Vietnamese folklore as very kind and gentle, was a superpowerful figure who could appear anywhere to help kind, honest, poor or disadvantaged people. One of the proverbs about *But* in Vietnamese is "*hien nhu But*" which means "gentle like *But*".

Buddhism started flourishing in Vietnam following its independence from China, especially, in the Ly dynasty (1009-1225). Many Ly Kings spent a part of their lives in monasteries (Jamieson, 1993) and several large pagodas and cultural buildings were constructed during this period. However these, along with many books written by Vietnamese, were later destroyed by the Chinese when they took the country over again following the wars between 1407 and 1427 (Tran Ngoc Them, 1997). In the Tran dynasty (1225-1400), whilst Buddhism was important, Confucian elements continued to develop in official ideology and subsequently Buddhism gradually declined, especially after Confucianism became the official national cult under the Le dynasty.

Until the Tay Son period in the later decades of the eighteenth century, King Quang Trung promoted both indigenous tradition and Buddhism at the expense of the borrowed Chinese elements. Part of the *Van mieu*, for example, was damaged by the Tay Son's troops and the Trung sisters were once again revitalised as national cultural heroes of the first order. (Jamieson 1993). However, the Quang Trung period was a relatively short period in the history of Vietnam. From 1802, the Nguyen dynasty held power and made persistent efforts to make Neo-Confucianism the foundation of national culture (*ibid.*). In the immediate aftermath of the first French colonisation, Buddhism was forbidden and began to wither quickly. Although it was widely expected to disappear completely there was in fact a resurgence of it during the first half of the twentieth century in response to the confrontation with Western culture and influence. In the 1970s, Buddhism met extreme Marxism and many pagodas were destroyed. Today, the Vietnamese government is more relaxed and tolerant toward Buddhism and other religions.

Buddhism, with its focus on a faultless and a god-like being, was accessible to the average person seeking an authority figure. It certainly gained a foothold in Vietnam, although Buddhism never became the official national religion. Asked to identify themselves amongst the different religions, Vietnamese people would probably say that they are Buddhists but in fact, they are rather 'occasional' Buddhists, for Buddhism did not prove strong enough to 'break' the Vietnamese faith due to the strong position of Confucianism, and the lack of proper teaching in Vietnam. Under Confucianism), which emphasised governance and politics, Buddhism was kept under strict control. Buddhism had a more universal application than Confucianism in that it touched the faith of the poor. It identified with them against mandarin tax-gatherers, who from time to time tried to get rid of Buddhism by closing the pagodas or forbidding Buddhist texts (Molyneux, 1995, p34). The following quotation from Bechert and Vu Duy Tu (1976) sums up the general situation of Buddhism under Confucian government.

> "Monks were required to pass examinations, pay taxes and fees to the state, and appear personally at the imperial courts in order to pursue petitions. On the other hand, the influence of the hierarchy within monasticism was relatively weak and control over the keeping of monastic vows rather superficial. An opposition developed within the monastic orders between those who held high ranks, enjoyed privileges accorded them by the state, often received pensions, and were culturally under strong Chinese influence, and those whose interest was identical with that of the peasant population. Members of the lower monastic ranks in rural areas often took part in rebellions" (p.187).

The effect of the strict control it was under and the lack of proper teaching led to Buddhism being adapted and to some extent dissolved into tradition (family piety, resting on a belief in spirits). There were pagodas (*chua* in Vietnamese) in almost every traditional Vietnamese village, however, the "Buddhism of the pagoda was a form of folk religion; little of the philosophical content of Buddhist teachings was known there." (Bechert and Vu Duy Tu 1976, p.188). The word *Phat* (originally meaning Buddha) was *Vietnamised* to refer to any religious figures in the Buddhist sect.

Not only statues of *Phat* but also of *Than* and *Thanh* were present and worshipped in *chua*. The design of Vietnamese pagodas followed the pattern of '*tien Phat hau Than*', mean statutes of *Phat* were placed on the front of the pagoda and *Than* on the back. *Than and Thanh* referred to folk religious figures like the drum and local tutelary deities and also Vietnamese national and local heroes. There are *chua* that have a space for the worship of Ho Chi Minh (Tran Ngoc Them, 1997, p.486). The few monks residing in the pagodas were considered Buddhists, but the mass of the people were 'occasional Buddhists'. They went to the pagodas to pray for luck for

60

their families and asked the monks to perform rites for the dead.

Again, the metaphor *family* was extended to Buddhist institutions. The architecture of the *chua* was similar to that of a Vietnamese home. For example, a *chua* was built like a Vietnamese house with *ba gian hai trai* (three compartments or rooms with two lean-tos). There have been a number of folk songs associating and comparing the family and the *chua* or Buddhism. One of them is "*Tu dau cho bang tu nha, tho cha kinh me moi la chan tu.*" meaning that cultivating or behaving oneself at home (e.g. respecting parents) is the true way (rather than cultivating or worshipping in the pagodas). *Phat* and ancestors were sometime used interchangeably: *Phat trong nha khong tho di tho Thich-ca ngoai duong* explains 'why one does not worship *Phat* (parents and ancestors) at home, but worships Sakya in the street or outside'. *Phat* in this case are ancestors and parents. The folk songs cited above were used to teach people to respect *their parents and ancestors*.

Another difference that marks Buddhism out is that it is not a religion with a god, but remains magnetic. Redding (1993) throws light on this point:

> "Attempts to explain this "reality" are usually given in term of what is not, as it is sufficiently unworldly to defy description in worldly terms, and this mysterious nothingness, or nirvana, at the centre of things, seen nevertheless as a source of perfection and fulfilment, is the reason why Buddhism remains magnetic." (p.51).

The pervasive Buddhist values in Vietnam were non-involvement, detachment and especially mysticism (Jamieson, 1993, p.9). Today, children are still taught not to touch anything in the pagodas, especially, statutes of *Phat* and *Than*. They are told that if they do so, Phat and Than might cause them trouble.

In summary, although Buddhism gained a significant foothold in Vietnam, the dominance of Confucianism and lack of teaching limited the ability of Buddhism to become a *proper* religion there, and it was not able to 'break the faith' of the Vietnamese.

The following example about the rise of the Cao Dai and the Hoa Hao (often regarded as Buddhist sects) in the 1930s and 1940s supports this argument and at the same time, throws light on the pragmatic attitude of the Vietnamese towards religion and beliefs.

The Cao Dai established in the 1920s, had about two million followers at its peak. It had:

> "A huge building, like a pagoda, a mosque, and a cathedral all in one, with a mixture of religious statutes, such as figures representing Confucius, Lao Tze, Christ, Vishnu, and the Buddha: something for everyone, as it were." (Molyneux 1995, p.25).

The Hoa Hao, at its peak also had about two million followers. This sect was founded by Huynh Phu So who suffered chronic ill health. He stated that he had had a profound religious experience in May 1939 when his ill health was cured by faith healing. Huynh Phu So travelled the country preaching to the desperately poor that they needed no pagodas or priest, but could practice their religion at home without professional help. The teaching of the Hoa Hao emphasised on *tu on* (the four ethical values: one should bear moral debt to *first, ancestor and parents*; second the country; third, *Tam bao* Buddhas — monks devoted to Buddhist doctrines; and lastly the people (the mass). The family is the most important social association of all.

4.2.4. Taoism

Taoism, like Confucianism, rests on the concept of harmonic order in nature and society. Both Confucius and Lao-Tze shared the concept of *Tao but* Taoism differed considerably from Confucianism since it sought enlightenment in ultimate, rather than inner-worldly principles of cosmic order. *Tao* means "the eternal order of the cosmos and at the same time, its course, an identification frequently found in a metaphysics but which lacks a thorough dialectical structure." (Weber 1951, p.181). It is difficult, for example, to conceive of the concept of *Tao* since "the *Tao* which can be conceived is not the real *Tao"*.

Lao-Tze brought *Tao* into some form of god seeking the mystic. Taoists sought happiness or supreme good by severing themselves completely free from worldly interests and passionate desires until release from all activity was attained (*wu wei* or *vo vi* in Vietnamese). The important Taoist principles are inaction, simplicity and living in *harmony with nature*. Taoist philosophical principle rested on a belief in the law of unity of the two opposite forces: *yin* and *yang*. If one tried too hard to attain a certain want, the law of reverted effort would start to operate and as a result, the effect would be the exact opposite of that desired. Governance was an example given; according to Lao-tze: "governing a large state is like boiling a small fish" (Tao Te Ching). If one boils 'a small fish', one need not remove its inside organs nor stir it but simply cook it gently over a little heat. The metaphor 'governing a large state is like boiling a small fish' is itself open to interpretation but the author believes that the rulers of China and Vietnam are still greatly influenced by Taoism in the way they govern.

Taoism as a philosophy has had an influence on modern thought. Some great Western thinkers such as Carl Jung admitted to being inspired by Taoism. Needham also pointed out that:

> "The Tao is the Order of Nature, which brought all things into existence and governs their every action, not so much by force as by a kind of natural curvature in space and time...The sage is to imitate the Tao, which works unseen and does not dominate. By yielding, by not imposing his preconception on nature, he will be able to observe and understand, and so to govern and control." (Needham 1956, cited by Yang, 1951).

Taoism, however, with its contemplative mysticism and cultivation of magic turned the world into an irrational realm of spirits and demons. Mark Weber correctly concluded that Taoism supported traditionalism even more strongly than Confucianism (Weber, 1951).

Taoism was introduced into Vietnam at the end of the second century (Tran Ngoc Them, 1997). It did not exercise as much influence in Vietnam as did Buddhism (Bechert and Vu Duy Tu, 1976) and in fact was not a clear cut discipline, but blended with Buddhism, Confucianism, ancestor worship and animism to form the mental attitude of the Vietnamese people (Molyneux, 1995). Like Buddhism, Taoism as a philosophy was little understood. It was the magic feature of Taoism that attracted the Vietnamese. Tran Ngoc Them (1997) pointed out that unlike *Nho giao* (Confucianism), Taoism (*Dao giao*) got an immediate foothold with many followers shortly after being introduced. This, according to Tran Ngoc Them, was because the Vietnamese had a strong belief in magic and superstition, which was then dissolved into Taoism. Over the years, magical and superstitious practices were carried out under the name of *Dao giao* (Molyneux, 1995). Quite a few Vietnamese social scientists referred or grouped all Vietnamese ancient folk religions as *Dao giao* (Tran Ngoc Them, 1997, p.537). A number of Taoist names, said to possess super magical powers, were documented in some Vietnamese history books.

Another feature of Taoism is anchoretism, which emphasised the immutable order of harmony and tranquillity. Many Taoists lived in the woods or mountains separating themselves from the 'world' and a number of well-known officials retired from office and spent the rest of their lives in quiet places distancing themselves from the "world". Amongst them were Chu Van An, Nguyen Binh Khiem, Nguyen Cong Tru and Phan Huy Ich (Tran Ngoc Them, 1997). It was, however, political reasons rather than the quest for salvation that accounted for anchoretism in Vietnam. Politically unsuccessful literati or cultured men who were dissatisfied with the way things were and could not change it (*bat man*).

In general, Taoism as a philosophy was little appreciated in Vietnam. However, with its irrational elements, together with folk religions it did have an influence on the individual and social cognition of the Vietnamese.

4.2.5. Forms of cognition

The cognitive aspects of culture are often ignored in many cross-cultural studies of organisations. Cognition is the deepest level of culture; it is the construction of reality which takes place in people's mind and so should not be ignored in any cultural study. This section will briefly describe the cognitive aspects of the Vietnamese culture and how these may have an impact on the broad level of society: the development of science and laws, and on the micro-level of the individual and organisational behaviour.

From the analysis of religion and philosophy in the previous sections, it should not be surprising to learn that Vietnamese people 'see the world' differently from others, especially, from western people. Jamieson (1993) and Tran Ngoc Them (1997) pointed out that traditional Vietnamese viewed the world through the lens of yin-yang and other Chinese cosmological forms. Along with other cultural aspects, the Vietnamese way of 'seeing the world' was undoubtedly influenced by the Chinese. According to Redding (1980 and 1993), in a "survey of thinking", Nakamura (1964) concluded that Chinese thinking displayed five characteristics:

1. an emphasis on the perception of the concrete;
2. the non-development of abstract thought;
3. an emphasis on the particular, rather than universals;
4. practicality as a central focus;
5. a concern for reconciliation, harmony, balance.

Magic and superstitious elements are still very much part of the Vietnamese mindset. Although Confucianism, as Weber pointed out, is rational, it lacks the metaphysical foundation that can eliminate a magic image of the world. Confucianism, with its unconditional affirmation and adjustment to the world "presupposed the unbroken and continued existence of purely magical religion." (Weber 1951, p.229). It is the author's own observation, as a native Vietnamese, that superstitious and magical elements still influence the Vietnamese mind whether or not they are educated or cultured, many people believe in horoscopes and other traditional Chinese 'pigeon holes'. The influence of the *I Ching* is still alive there, and in recent years when the government began to tolerate beliefs and religions and when the 'luck' elements came as an association with a free market mechanism, it even underwent a revival.

The Vietnamese mindset exhibits a preference for thinking in terms of chance rather than causality and statistical truth. Carl Jung, in his forward to the *I Ching*, pointed out the differences between the Chinese and western mind:

> "The Chinese mind, as I see it at work in the I Ching, seems to be exclusively preoccupied with the chance aspect of events. What we call coincidence seems to be the chief concern of this peculiar mind, and what we worship as causality passes almost unnoticed.... Thus it happens that when one throws the three coins, or counts through the forty-nine yarrow-stalks, this chance details enter into the picture of the moment of observation and form a part of it - a part that is insignificant to us, yet most meaningful to the Chinese mind." (Jung 1965, p.591).

The meaning of many Western social concepts and theories introduced into Vietnam has changed, since the Vietnamese do not think of a theory as simply a theory. For the Vietnamese, a theory enters the mind and it is then adjusted in an ethical and emotional way until it is conceived as *the truth*.
When it is conceived as the truth, it is no longer a theory (in the strict Western meaning of the word). Marxism, for example, was conceived by many not as a theory or doctrine, but as *the truth*. In China and Vietnam, and possibly in other Asian countries, theory and practice go together, knowledge and action can be unified, and spirituality and ethics are all of one piece.

Researchers working on a postgraduate thesis in Vietnam (masters or Ph.D degree), are required to give solutions to practical problems. The author's observations suggest that giving solutions in a thesis is considered as one of the most, if not the most, important criterion. In an informal interview, one new Vietnamese PhD holder said: "Giving solutions counts for 30%-40% of the thesis." Causal relationships are not as important as 'sound' solutions. Theory and practice are all one. As a consequence, there are no 'theories' and often poor practice. The education system, however, does not focus on or encourage abstract thought. A research function of a 'Western' kind is totally absent in Vietnamese universities. There are, however, research projects that concentrate on 'solving' particular social or economic issues planned by the government. This kind of research project is called *nghien cuu khoa hoc* (scientific research), but it is not academic research in the Western meaning of the term. The focus, using Weber's terminology, is not on the 'mastery' of, but constant adjustment to the 'given' world. As a result, policies and laws keep changing or amending.

The perception of concreteness and low level of abstract thought are also caused in part by the 'high context' nature of the Vietnamese language. From his study of the Vietnamese language, Laycock (1994) found that the mode of self-reference in the Vietnamese language is unique. He gave the following example to demonstrate this:

> "Since self-reference via the English 'I' does not, in virtue of its very logic, involve belief in the existence of the person addressed, one is free in English (though not in Vietnamese) to entertain the possibility that solipsism might be true of the real world. The Vietnamese child, speaking to an imaginary playmate, certainly need not believe in this playmate's existence. But the same child, in addressing her parents, cannot escape belief in their existence." [p.10].

In Vietnam, people sometime have difficulties in introducing themselves and addressing others when they first meet. In a formal meeting, junior people sometimes do not know how to express themselves if they want to speak. They should address themselves as *toi* (I) in a formal meeting, but *toi* is not the right form when someone is addressing someone else older than they are, especially someone a generation older. The same problem arises when addressing someone else in a formal meeting as there is no one special word for 'you'. In a Communist Party meeting, one should address another member as *dong chi* (comrade). *Dong chi*, however, is still not really the 'right' way, especially for a junior to address a senior. In a normal situation, a junior addresses a senior as *chu* or *bac* (uncle). General words for 'I' and 'you' in a general situation (such as in a company meeting) are lacking.

From the above brief analysis of cognition together with the nature of the ethical emphasis of the Confucian culture we can draw some conclusions about several features of organisations and institutions in Vietnam. The forms of cognition of Vietnamese do not support the development of a system of laws that is (in Max Weber's terms) "rational", "formal", and "logical". We do not rule out the possibility of the development of a relatively rational legal system that can effectively facilitate exchanges, but our point is that the development of such system is unlikely to take place soon. Stable and long lasting legal codes that can effectively facilitate business transactions are not expected, at least in the near future. In the context of organisations, the form of cognition discussed above does not, as pointed out by Redding (1980), support functionally structured, formally planned and codified organisational and management practices.

4.2.6. Confucianism in Vietnam, China and Japan

The rise of Japan as a world economic power and the economic success of other East Asian economies (Hong Kong, Singapore, Korea and Taiwan) has attracted considerable attention from Western academics. They have explained these developments from many different perspectives including the economic, sociological and political. The cultural values associated with Confucianism have, however, frequently been seen implicitly or explicitly as a crucial variable. As Wilkinson (1996) pointed out:

> "The common culture roots lay in Confucianism, and during the past decade or so, many scholars, journalists, politicians and other pundits have implicitly accepted, or explicitly argued for, a Confucian explanation of economic growth in Japan and the ANICs." (p.422, original emphasis).

Theorists, however, have differed in their emphasis on the various aspects of Confucianism and their influence on different aspects of economic organisation. Hofstede and Bond (1988), for example, emphasised the entrepreneurial behaviour associated with Confucianism. Kim Byung Whan made a direct link between Confucian virtues and the ethical codes at the basis of industrial society: so loyalty to the rulers translates into organisation loyalty; parental benevolence translates into a benevolent management style; older-younger brother relationships translate into the acceptance of hierarchy; and trustworthiness between friends translates into co-operation between co-workers (Wilkinson, 1996, p. 424).

Naïve cultural theorists simply stated that "since conventional economic explanations for East Asia business success have failed, the explanation must lie in 'culture', and since the most advanced East Asian capitalist economies (Japan followed by Hong Kong, Singapore, Korea and Taiwan) were Confucianist, the explanation must lie in Confucianism." (p.423).

One of the problems of 'naïve' cultural explanations, as pointed out by Wilkinson (1996), is the absence of historical understanding. As noted earlier, Confucianism contains many interpretations within it. This section draws on similarities and differences between Confucianism in Vietnam, China and Japan. The two latter countries were chosen first because China and Vietnam share many cultural traits (summarised in this section) and because, given the fact that there has been little written about Vietnam, we can benefit from reference to the literature on China where appropriate; The second reason is that Japan, a neo-Confucianism country that has had extraordinary economic success, offers a model for comparison.

Vietnam and China

The five constant virtues of a gentlemanly ideal: *nhan, nghia, le, tri, tin* (benevolence, righteousness, propriety, intelligent and faith) and other Confucian order principles remained the same in Vietnam as in China. Law codes, the courts and the administration of the Confucianism examination system were, to a great extent, identical. Family concepts and practices were again almost the same. The distinction, as Woodside (1971) pointed out, is a difficult one. There are, however, some important differences such as (1) the relatively lower degrees of law codification and formal institutions in Vietnam compared to China; (2) the fact that the Vietnamese were less extreme or more 'tolerant' with regard to human relation issues; (3) the fact that the Vietnamese were more "static" or 'agricultural' than the Chinese; and (4) the fact that the Vietnamese were more 'traditional' and 'collectivist' than the Chinese. It is important to note that due to the lack of systematic comparative research on the topic, it is impossible to draw a neat comparison between the two cultures. The above list is certainly not exhaustive and the four points may overlap. A more comprehensive and detailed comparison of the two cultures remains to be carried out.

With regard to the codification of law, Woodside pointed out various differences between nineteenth century Vietnamese and Chinese formal institutions. One example was the examination systems:

"There were fewer bureaucratic control laws governing the Vietnamese examinations. There were also fewer achievement levels in the Vietnamese system between village and court, which in turn meant less standardisation in depth of the professional training of Vietnamese bureaucrats... Vietnamese examination sites were more informal and more highly improvised. There was less formal specialisation among Vietnamese examiners" (Woodside, 1971, p5).

In the civil administration, Vietnamese laws were less developed and effectively enforced than in China. The 'law of avoidance' (to avoid nepotism), for example, was poorly developed and practised in Vietnam. Woodside observed that:

"Particularistic proximities among provincial officials were tolerated, unless flagrant misgovernment occurred as a result. More "universalistic" than those of other South East Asian societies, perhaps, Vietnamese administration was less so in terms of promulgated rules than Chinese administration." (p.83).

With regard to notions of 'humanness' and 'tolerance', Nguyen Dinh Huy (1999) pointed out that compared to Chinese culture "Vietnamese culture is derived from agriculture and full of sentiment, and hence is more moderate and flexible in relationships" (p.10). The more tolerant and softer practices towards human relation issues were demonstrated by how crimes and the violation of family codes were punished. 'Crime punishment' in Vietnam was often less severe, compared with the dreadful stories told about how those who showed un-filial piety in China (*bu xiao* in Chinese, *bat hieu* in Vietnamese). So, for example, the story quoted by Hamilton (1984) describing the terrible punishment of a wife who had the insolence to beat her mother-in-law, could not be found in traditional Vietnam. It is difficult for Vietnamese to imagine the Vietnamese communist party acting as the Chinese communist government did in Tiananmen Square in 1989.

These more 'tolerant' and 'humane' features can also be found in the pre-modern Vietnamese law codes. The inheritance law that supported women is one example. Although, Vietnamese laws, especially, the one in effect in the 16th, 17th, and 18th centuries were influenced by Chinese law, they:

> "...treated women more generously than Chinese legal codes, in accordance with the traditions of a South East society whose women had on rare occasions been major politicians or writers. The Le court code allowed daughters to inherit family property almost equally with sons... No such legal principles could be found in China." (Steinberg,1987, p.73).

A third point of difference is that the Chinese were more dynamic and commercially-minded than the Vietnamese. Chinese merchants were very successful throughout history, the 'Silk Road' being a vivid example. Chinese merchants were and are very successful in Southeast Asia and in other parts of the world. In Vietnam, Chinese merchants out-performed their Vietnamese counterparts (Barton, 1983).

Another difference between the two cultures is that the Vietnamese tend to be more "traditional" and "collectivist" than the Chinese (Ralston, Nguyen and Napier, 1999). Using the Schwartz Value Survey, Ralston et al compared Vietnamese managers from both the north and the south with US managers and what they called "traditional" and "cosmopolitan" Chinese managers (managers from south west and south China, respectively). They found that both groups of Vietnamese managers "were significantly higher on collectivism than the other groups". They argue that "the Vietnamese, as a whole, may be more 'traditional' than even the traditional Chinese" and there is "a stronger adherence to eastern-culture collectivism in Vietnam than in China" (p. 11).

The two major explanations given for these variations between Vietnamese and Chinese culture and institutions are: (1) geographical and (2) the differences associated with borrowing culture and institutions. Although Vietnam and China have been always agrarian states, different patterns between the two countries can be discerned. Historically the majority of Vietnamese lived in a relatively small area located around the Red River. Their lives were bound by the wet rice fields and their villages. The climate of the Red River delta, with its monsoons and rainy seasons, is quite different from the North China plain (Woodside, 1971). The northern Chinese with their livestock farming were more nomadic than the southern Chinese and Vietnamese.

The nature of borrowed culture and institutions is frequently cited to explain differences. Since they are imported, it is easy to understand that bureaucratic institutions in Vietnam were less codified than in China. Although dominated by Chinese culture and institutions, Vietnamese society shares many unique features with other Southeast Asian societies. Jamieson (1984) argued that traditional Vietnamese social systems can be seen as the interaction between two conceptually distinct systems, which he termed "yang" and "yin". The "yang" system is, for example, predominantly male, legal in basis, orthodox, formal, autocratic and Sinistic in origin; whereas the "yin" system is more female, heterodox, informal, egalitarian and indigenous (p.324). Vietnamese society, according to this yin-yang theory is more 'yin' and less 'yang' than Chinese society.

68

In summary, from the analysis above we can draw a general conclusion that there are more similarities than differences between the two cultures. These similarities, especially those associated with Confucian values and practices, allow us to make use of the literature on Chinese management and institutions.

Japan

Japan is another a neo-Confucian country whose culture was also greatly influenced by Chinese culture. However, the influence of the Chinese on Japan was, to some extent more selective and indirect than in Vietnam. Unlike Vietnam, which borrowed the concept of family directly from China, Japan developed its own meaning of family which differs from those in Vietnam and China. In these two countries, family meant blood-link relationships or kinship and consanguinity is considered the most fundamental and reliable social relationship (Hall and Xu, 1990). Positions in the family's pedigree are very important. The distance of kinship is also important and precisely measured.

The tradition of equal division of inheritance encouraged a more horizontal culture and also competition from within. As Woodside (1971) pointed out, the merit behind the reward to family that in Vietnam and China could hold four or five generations in the same hall was designed to honour the discipline – dispensing family. The competition that arose among the sons' families with the appearance of their wives (non-blood members) was inevitable.

The Japanese culture is 'part ways' from the Chinese in that the Japanese emphasise the family as a community. They care more about the solid relationships of family members and less about the position in the pedigree. Property is not divided. An adopted son may be chosen over a son by blood as the family head (Hall and Xu, 1990). The Japanese notion of 'ie' (family or household) is the basic building block of what is often termed 'communitarian' or 'groupism' that characterises business organisations in Japan. Saito (2000) pointed out that the traditional Japanese family system differed markedly from that of traditional Chinese and other systems(*)(p.39). The family name was always desired and adoption could be used to create heirs (Saito, 1998). One Japanese scholar, Murakami, suggested that Japan should be differentiated from other 'Confucian' societies, arguing that the 'ie' social group, which is rarely found in other agricultural societies, had survived successive transformation until the present. It included "functional rather than kin membership, membership homogeneity rather than stratification, and a consequently functional hierarchy rather than one of class or status discrimination." (Clegg and Redding, 1990, p.42).

The traditional Korean household also differed from that of Vietnam and China. The typical traditional Korean household belongs to the authoritarian family (Todd, 1985). Unlike the exogamous community family, inheritance is not divided equally in the authoritarian family.

There were also critical differences in the Confucian emphases. The five Confucian virtues in China (and in Vietnam) were benevolence, righteousness, propriety, intelligence and faith. In Japan, loyalty was the key virtue along with propriety, courage, faith and honesty (Hall and Xu, 1990). Hall and Xu (1990) also pointed out that although loyalty was one of the Confucian codes, it was not as important in China as in Japan, where loyalty meant complete obedience to one's superior without exception.

> "The superior is considered to be the symbol of community and must be obeyed, even if it means self-sacrifice. Unconditional obedience is encouraged and even praised by the public. When filial piety to parents and loyalty to superiors are in conflict, the Chinese almost always choose the former, the Japanese the latter."
> (Hall & Xu, 1990, p.572).

Whereas, as Woodside observed, in Vietnam and China:

> "The three bonds (in Vietnam) were the bureaucrat's loyalty to his emperor, the son's obedience to his father, and wife's submission to her husband. As in China the family ethic was allowed to stand supreme over considerations of bureaucratic efficiency, as a result" (Woodside, 1971, p.38).

The political systems of traditional Vietnam and Japan both borrowed from China. The Vietnamese political system in general and the monarchy in particular, however, were borrowed more directly from a China in which Confucian ideas were dominant: "(they) searched for a perfectly ordered society, stipulated that men were born unequal in talent, argued that education was more important than economic luxury (or progress), and stressed the value of elitist example in politics" (Woodside, 1971, p.10). He also pointed out that the Sino-Japanese word for emperor had enough influence from Shinto teachings to mean "a representative of a divinely appointed unbroken imperial line" (p.13).

The above analysis is sufficient to allow us to conclude that there are significant differences within the Confucian culture, and that the validity of the so-called 'post-Confucian' hypothesis should be questioned.

Summary

This section has drawn out and discussed important cultural values that have a bearing on institutions, organisations and management in Vietnam. The most important point is that the Vietnamese share many cultural features with the Chinese. As in China, Confucianism is the dominant value system and several key cultural values associated with this value system have been discussed. These are: harmony, order and hierarchy, face and shame, conformity, oneness or holism, and reciprocity. We can also conclude that Vietnamese culture is characterised by large power distance and high collectivism, to use Hofstede's cultural dimensions.

In addition, the analysis of the Vietnamese family and village, indicates that, like the Chinese in Redding's (1993) study, the Vietnamese are equally characterised by limited and bounded trust, and limited co-operation. *The family is above everything else the most important thing in life*. This chapter will serve as a reference point for the analysis of the institutions and organisations described in later chapters.

Chapter 5: An overview of the Vietnamese economy in transition and the reform of state-owned enterprises

Unlike many developing countries, until recently Vietnam suffered severely from wars and struggles. As a consequence, the country faced many difficulties when it came to economic development. Vietnam is also different in terms of the development path it has followed. History matters. Human beings are not 'economic men' without a past and today's choices cannot be understood without referring to the development path a country has followed (North, 1990). A growing body of literature on 'path dependence' shows that what has happened to an economy or society in the past is important for understanding the present and for predicting the future (Arthur, 1989; David, 1985; and North, 1990,).

Paul David and Brian Arthur were among the first to introduce and clarify the issue of path dependence in economic and institutional studies. Paul David's "Clio and the Economics of QWERTY" (1985) was, perhaps, the first, and very influential, article on the issue of path dependence in economic studies. In it, David raised and attempted to explain the issue of how the peculiar organisation of letters on the typewriter keyboard became standardised and fixed, and why it persists despite the appearance of more efficient alternatives. There are many other examples of this type, such as the persistence of narrow-gauge rails and the survival of the gas engine over the stream engine in motor cars (North, 1990).

In general, one can find many examples of how a technology "once begun on a particular tract, may lead one technological solution to win out over another, even when, ultimately, this technological path may be less efficient than the abandoned alternative would have been" (North, 1990, p.93). It is possible that small historical events can lead one technology to win out over another. Arthur pointed out four major self-enforcing mechanisms that accounted for the path dependence phenomenon. They are: "(1) large set-up or fixed costs, which give the advantage of falling unit costs as out-put increases; (2) learning effects, which improve products or lower their costs as their prevalence increases; (3) co-ordination effects, which confer advantages to co-operation with other economic agents taking similar actions; and (4) adaptive expectations, where increased prevalence on the market enhances beliefs of further prevalence." (North 1990, p.94).

North extended the above ideas and explanations of path dependence in economics and technology to the context of economic and social institutions. He argued that if a country or a society has taken a particular development path, it is likely that the country or society would be greatly dependent on that path, and so the system adopted was likely to persist for some time.

Changes are incremental. Significant changes are unlikely to occur unless there are 'external shocks' such as wars and crises, or external pressures that trigger the process of change. This is because self-enforcing mechanisms are always present in a system once it has won over the others. Self-enforcing mechanisms in a social context result from the fact that human beings are not rational *per se*, their actions are shaped by ideas, theories, ideologies as well as their interests. Unproductive paths can, therefore, persist (North, 1990). It is likely that people who have power will shape the polity in their interests and resist change. History then, deserves a place in any analysis of the present.

The concept of 'path dependence' is very useful in an analysis of the transitional process taking place in Vietnam, China and other former socialist countries, since these countries have taken a development path that was, to a great extent, different from market capitalism. Seen from a path dependence perspective, a study of transition should and for certain purposes must, refer to the 'old' system and its bearing on the new one.

The issue of 'path dependence' and its influence will be examined in this and following chapters, especially those on SOEs. In Chapter 10, for example, we examine in some detail the issue of what is termed 'embedded materialism', a vivid example of path dependence, and its link to the problems of SOEs. This chapter provides background information and an analysis of the historical context in which the Vietnamese SOEs were established and transformed.

The story of the Vietnamese SOEs is really a phenomenon, since it is substantially different from that of Western business organisations and thus worth telling from the beginning. This chapter presents a history of the Vietnamese economy and the SOE sector in five parts. The first briefly summarises the Vietnamese economy during the time of French occupation. The second part describes the Vietnamese economy and SOEs under the Soviet-style development model whilst the third part describes the economic and SOE reform processes in Vietnam until the present. The fourth part presents the current situation of the Vietnamese economy and SOEs and the final part is a discussion of the reform process seen through the lens of culture.

5.1 The legacy of French colonialism

Before falling under French rule in the later half of nineteenth century, Vietnam was an almost purely peasant society living under subsistence conditions. The French invaders with their relatively modern weapons occupied Vietnam without much difficulty. It was said that in 1862 Phan Than Gian, a grand councillor (one of the most brilliant and dedicated mandarins in the country) who headed a diplomatic delegation to France in an attempt to regain the lost territory through direct negotiation with the French government, was so terrified when he saw machines and electric light bulbs that he decided to choose the ultimate withdrawal. He reported to the Vietnamese King at the time that "their (French) wealth and strength are beyond description" (Jamieson, 1993).

During the French colonial period, trade, industry and mining were introduced but at a peripheral level aimed directly at the short-term exploitation of Vietnamese human and raw natural resources. The French employed a humiliating discrimination policy against the Vietnamese people. One of its firmest principles was that the lowest ranked representative of France in Vietnam must receive a salary higher than that of the highest Vietnamese official employed by the colonial administration. Jamieson (1993) gave an illustrative example that "a brilliant and diligent Vietnamese who earned a doctorate at the University of Paris, and then returned to become a professor at the University of Hanoi, would earn less than the lackadaisical French janitor who maintained the classroom in which he taught" (p.97). Many Vietnamese had to work very hard in the mining industry, earning just enough to survive. The worst consequence of French rule was the death of more than one million Vietnamese in 1945 due to starvation. Table 5.1 provides a picture of the legacy of French colonialism in Vietnam.

Table 5.1. The legacy of French colonialism: Vietnam in 1930s

Population	18.8 million
Rice production (per capita)	300 kg
Modern industrial employment (% of population)	0.4-0.5
Hospital beds per 100,000 population	5.3
Doctors per 100,000 population	0.3
School children	0.5 million
Schoolteachers	9.300

Source: Fforde and de Vylder (1996, p.72)

The general conclusion that can be drawn from the above information is that the French colonial era left Vietnam, economically at least, a virtually primitive society.

Vietnam gained independence from the French in 1945. After 'independence', Vietnam continued to fight the French for another nine years, a period which consumed large amounts of human and other resources. There was no significant development in the economy during this period and the country only began reconstruction after the defeat of the French colonial forces in 1954.

5.2. The Soviet-style development model 1955-1980

5.2.1. The model

After the defeat of the French colonial forces in 1954 Vietnam was divided into two: North and South. In the North, the Democratic Republic of Vietnam (DRV), ruled by the Vietnamese Communist Party, began the task of economic construction and social development (Fforde and de Vylder, 1996). This development model followed the so-called neo-Stalinism or Soviet-style model, originally proposed by Stalin and applied in the former Soviet Union, Eastern European socialist countries, China and several other countries. The Soviet-style development model was characterised by the central planning of all economic and social activities, hence, it was known as the 'centrally-planned development model'. The term 'centrally planned', however, appears too technical. The development model pursued by the former Soviet block, China, Vietnam and other countries extended planning considerably beyond the economic sphere and was unique in history. The term 'Soviet-style model', thus, better captures the meaning of a historical period with its many unique characteristics not only affecting economics, but other aspects of society

The choice of the Soviet-style model by the North Vietnamese government at the time is easy to understand. First, North Vietnam was backed by socialist countries, especially, the former Soviet Union and China. The choice of the Soviet-style model at that time was, therefore, quite sensible both politically and economically. Second, the Soviet-style model appeared to be consistent with traditional Vietnamese society, being authoritarian and with a strong sense of egalitarianism. The Soviet-style model dominated the North from 1955 on, and applied to the whole country after national unification in 1975. The Soviet-style development model aimed at rapid industrialisation and modernisation by means of planning and direction by the state.

In Vietnam, much infrastructure and *nha may* (factories, later called SOEs) were built with capital and technical assistance from China and the former Soviet Union. The three SOEs investigated in the present research were established during this period.

Under the central-planning mechanism, factories were not business enterprises in any sense. Fforde and de Vylder (1996) summarised how a Vietnamese factory was run:

> "Capital resources were supplied by the state to SOEs in order to produce a certain product. These resources were essentially supplied free. Each unit was managed by a level of the state bureaucracy (a ministry, if centrally managed; a provincial or city department, if locally managed) that allocated labour to it. The unit was then given a regular production target, in quantity terms, and in order for it to meet this target it was provided with levels of current inputs calculated on the basic of simple arithmetic norms. These inputs were supplied directly to the unit by the state, and its output was also supplied directly to the state. The unit was there essentially to produce for the target, and with almost no freedom to choose either what it produced and who it produced for, the unit had little interest in either the value of what it produced or the

real costs involved in doing so. It was also not allowed to seek out better suppliers of its inputs. In this way the planners maintained central control over resources and could hope to ensure that they went to priority areas." (p.58).

These were no concepts of market, competition or customers at this time. The term 'state-owned enterprise' or SOE has only recently been used since the start of economic reform. During the period of the Soviet-style economy, SOEs were called *nha may* (factories). *Nha may* means literally a home (*nha*) which houses machines (*may*). The use of *nha may* is another example of the importance of *nha* (home or family) in Vietnamese society.

During the 1960s Vietnam War, the first priority of these factories was to manufacture products to serve the army. After national unification in 1975, the Soviet-style model was extended to the whole country. Many business enterprises in the South were nationalised and operated following the centrally-planned procedures outlined above.

Figure 5.1 illustrates the operating mechanism of a typical Vietnamese SOE (factory) under the Soviet-style economy.

Figure 5.1. The operating mechanism of a factory during the Soviet-style economy

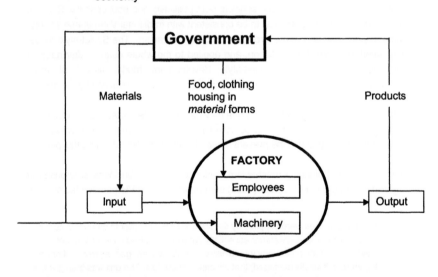

In the factory there were no departments or functions such as 'marketing', 'advertising' or 'sales'. Finance and accounting functions were essentially nominal because the market price mechanism was absent. Employees did not receive wages in money terms, as most of their income was 'materialised'. For example, each worker could receive 17kg of rice per month, five square metres of cloth per year (for

76

clothing), one kilogram of meat per month and so on. Housing, medical services and and schooling for children were all provided for free.

In the agricultural sector, farmers were organised into co-operatives. As with industry, all the inputs needed for farming were provided by the state. Farmers worked together in large farms, being given a certain amount of output depending on the number of days they worked for the cooperative.

The centrally planned principle was not only confined to economic aspects of life, but applied to all social spheres. In the universities, for example, the number of students enrolled each year was planned by the government and their jobs (after graduation) were fixed. Each student was entitled to a package of 17kg of rice, 350 grams of sugar, 400 grams of meat for a month and some other stationery. This package was not guaranteed during periods of economic shortage.

5.2.2. The failure of the Soviet-style model
The Soviet-style model was, at first, very successful by Vietnamese standards. During the Soviet-style development period, many Vietnamese factories, hospitals, universities and other basic social structure were built, and the economy enjoyed its peak during the first half of the 1960s. After that period, however, almost all human effort was directed towards the Vietnam War.

For a time, the Soviet-style development model in general was very successful in all the former socialist countries, where it was considered the ideal development model leading to full employment, no inflation and generous social welfare. The success of the model, however, did not last long: a verdict on it was provided by the collapse of the whole socialist system in the late 1980s.

In Vietnam, the weaknesses of the Soviet-style model became apparent earlier in time, when the war with the US ended and the country had to focus on the task of economic development. The Soviet-style economy fell into deep crisis in 1980 when Chinese aid was cut leaving the Vietnamese government unable to provide for the basic material needs of its people. There has been a strong consensus about the two major factors that accounted for the failure of the Soviet-style model: they are *information* and *incentives*.

Information
In a market mechanism, the price serves as a signal to allocate resources. The law of supply and demand ensures the efficient allocation of resources, albeit in relative terms. Each economic unit is itself an information processor. In a centrally-planned economy planners (various government bureaux) did the job of resource allocation. In order to allocate resources efficiently, planners need to gather and process a huge amount of information, which is beyond human capacity, especially at a time when information technology was limited. Even with the most advanced information technology, there are still many contingencies that are beyond human control.

Because of the nature of central planning, a small change in one sector of the economy may affect the whole system. The result can be a high degree of resource misallocation in the economy. In Vietnam, soon after the implementation of the Soviet-style model, the Vietnamese economy was increasingly characterised by sectional imbalances and micro inefficiencies (Fforde and de Vylder, 1996, p.12). The problems of resource misallocation and sectional imbalances became worse and worse in Vietnam, especially when aid from the Soviet Union, which used to help balance the economy, was reduced.

Incentives

The other major reason associated with the failure of the Soviet-style model was linked with incentives. One of the implicit assumptions behind the model was that human beings were like machines: they had no past, and would follow and carry out the orders of planning boards exactly. This assumption contradicted the fact that people do not normally try harder if they know that their extra work will not give them any greater rewards. In the Soviet-style economy, income was virtually fixed and, to a great extent, distributed equally.

There were no incentives for innovation, but a strong one for cheating and lying (Pejovich, 1990), a problem perhaps, more severe in Vietnam. The Vietnamese had no experience of managing relatively large economic organisations. Farmers, for example, as the author observed when he was in his village, did not work hard. They often took long breaks and productivity was not increased. The production of food staples in Vietnam between 1958 and 1975, increased by only 10.9% whereas the population increased 63.6% (Jamieson, 1993). In the factories, productivity and product quality decreased.

It is important to note that although factories in other Soviet-style countries suffered the same problem, this problem was worse in Vietnam. Almost all the machines and technology in Vietnamese factories came from China and the former Soviet Union. Any replacement parts therefore, also had to come from these countries. Indigenous technological development in Vietnam was insignificant.

The Vietnamese economy was in deep crisis in the late 1970s and early 1980s, when the problem of shortages was at its worst. Between 1976 and 1980, the annual growth rate for industrial production was only 0.6% and state industrial production actually decreased by 1.5% a year (see Table 5.2 p.118). The danger of starvation was real since productivity in agriculture was low and the SOEs were inefficient with outdated machines and equipment. Many enterprises had to stop or cut production because of material shortages. Chronic shortages in the economy as a whole, and the inefficiency of SOEs in particular, were the impetus for the reform of the economy and the management of SOEs (Fforde and de Vylder, 1996)

5.3. The reforms

This section reviews the economic reform process in Vietnam according to several important phases, each characterised by 'turning points'. It also pays special attention to the major *object* of the research, the reform of the SOEs.

The economic reform process in Vietnam in general, and SOE reform in particular, can be divided into the three stages shown in Figure 5.2 below.

Figure 5.2. Stages to capitalism

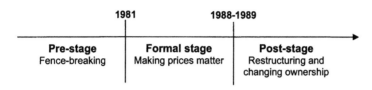

Summarised from Fforde and de Vylder, 1996

5.3.1. 'Fence breaking'

In the late 1970s and early 1980s Western and Chinese aid cuts in reaction to the Vietnamese invasion of Cambodia, combined with bad weather, put the Vietnamese economy under heavy pressure. As distortion and shortages emerged, an informal process of breaking out of the planning system began. Since the late 1970s, autonomous transactions (direct transactions between suppliers and producers and customers) had begun to take place informally. There were examples of direct deliveries of materials to producers (Fforde and de Vylder, 1996).

This incident was called *pha rao* in Vietnamese. *Pha rao* was translated into English by Fforde and de Vylder as 'fence-breaking'. *Pha* means 'break'. *Rao* means 'fence' – they type meant to protect a family's garden or to house animals. *Pha rao* is often used to describe situations in which animals are so hungry they break through a fence to find something to eat. 'Fence-breaking' was a rational response to the state of Vietnamese society. The 'fence-breaking' practice was informal and illegal, but it was either given the green-light or deliberately ignored by local authorities and line ministries (Fforde and de Vylder 1996). The 'fence-breaking' stage lasted until the formal reform programme began in 1981.

5.3.2. The formal stage – 'making prices matter'

As Fforde and de Vylder (1996) pointed out, unlike economic restructuring programmes in other developing countries which focused on 'making prices right', economic reform in Vietnam was more about 'making prices matter'. This process was formally begun in 1981. This year witnessed two important decisions made by the government: one (decree 25-CP) was about industry and concerned reform of the SOEs and the other (decree CT-100) was about the reform of agriculture.

Decree 25-CP introduced what was called the 'Three-Plan System'. Within this system, a state factory had *a single plan with three elements* that were called: Plan A, Plan B and Plan C.

Plan A: (also called Plan 1) was the most important of the three and was conditional on Plans B and C. Under Plan A, the factory had to produce outputs set by the state from inputs supplied by the state. Plan A was a must for the factory, and exactly the same as the plan system employed in the previous period. The difference in the new system lay in Plans B and C.

Plan B. Under Plan B, a factory was legally permitted to acquire input itself and could sell its products as it wished. This activity was limited to the utilisation of the factory's existing capacity – no factory was allowed to expand its activities freely. Plan B was an indication of the government's inability to provide adequate input for the factory. The factory was allowed to retain some profit from Plan B.

Plan C. Under Plan C, the outputs were 'minor' products. This type of production was free from control because the products were considered unimportant. Profits from Plan C were distributed to the employees to improve their living conditions. Employees were very enthusiastic about working for Plan C. For many employees at the time, Plan C (*ke hoach ba*) was more important than Plan A, and was often talked about at home and at work.

The three-plan system represented the introduction of the market concept to the SOEs. The system contributed to a reduction in the distortions in the economy, but was limited to 'minor' products. One of the positive outcomes of the three-plan policy was that many factory employees earned some extra income to survive. The early economic reform with the 'Three-Plan System' policy as a 'turning point', resulted in a sharp increase in industrial output, as shown in the Table 5.2 below.

Table 5.2. Industrial output growth: annual rate of growth (%)

	1976-1980	1980-1985	1985-1989	1989-1993
Total	0.6	10.0	6.6	10.6
State	-1.5	6.8	6.9	12.8
Of which = central	-3.5	4.7	7.6	16.9
Of which = local	2.9	11.1	5.8	3.9

Source: Fforde and de Vylder (1996, p.211)

Industrial output growth increased from 0.6% a year during the period 1976-1980 to an average of 10% a year during 1980-1985.

Parallel to the 'Three-Plan System' policy (25-CP) in industry, a decree named CT-

100 was issued in January 1981 to boost agriculture. Under this decree, farmers were allowed to contract out a certain amount of land from the cooperative, although they had to pay a certain amount of output for using that land. Farmers now worked both for the cooperatives and for their 'private' lots. As a result of this policy, agricultural output increased. Farmers took more care of their contracted lots and as a result, there was a sharp jump of around 20-25% in staple output (Fforde and de Vylder, 1996, p.141).

Reform was not, however, a smooth process. It was a trial-and-error, 'learning-and-doing' process in which economic rationale and ideological preservation interacted and confronted each other. The introduction of the three-plan system, for example, did not work out as intended. Factories spent much of their effort on Plan C, whose activities expanded. There were a number of efforts to 'tighten' market-oriented activities, for example, the issue of decrees 146-HDBT and 156-HDBT (see Box 5.1, page 119).

Although the earlier reforms of the three-plan system gained some successes, reform at this point was still limited to the improvement of incentive structures within SOEs. (ADB and MPI,1997). The reforms "were still basically managed by administrators, hence they (SOEs) had neither the autonomy nor responsibility for the results of their production and business" (Tran Tien Cuong, 1996, quoted in ADB and MPI, 1997, p.53). The two-price system still existed, one set arbitrarily by the State, the other determined by the open market. Opportunism was widespread. There were examples of products leaking onto the open market (Fforde and de Vylder, 1996). The economy enjoyed growth for a short while, but became stagnant again in 1983-1984. A new reform stage was required.

The Sixth Party Congress in 1986 marked the official abandonment of the Soviet-style model. A campaign of 'doi moi' (renovation) was launched. The term 'doi moi' has since became very popular both in Vietnamese society and in literature on Vietnam's economy.

The key messages from the Sixth Party Congress were support for a market mechanism for economic co-ordination and a move to 'open the door' to foreign investment. These ideas were put into practice via a number of new economic policies. In the area of SOEs, the promulgation of Decree 217-HDBT in 1987 was a turning point. Under Decision 217-HDBT and other subsequent regulations, SOEs were given a number of specific rights:

> SOEs were granted the autonomy to build and implement short-, medium- and long-term plans for business operations within the framework of the state plan as it existed at the time. SOEs were allowed to subcontract, to purchase, renew machinery and equipment and to handle unused assets through sale, lease, or transfer.

> The state no longer directly supplied inputs to SOEs. These had to be purchased directly from suppliers (except for a few products that had to be sold at Government mandated prices). SOEs could now sell their products on the open market.

> Profits were to be assessed on the basis of actual costs and revenues. This was significantly different from the period before. Before, profits were meant to be a percentage mark-up on approved input costs. Thus, higher costs meant higher profits (Fforde and Vylder, 1996, p.159).

> Enterprise directors were given greater flexibility in hiring and dismissing workers. Directors were accountable for the performance of their enterprise.

Box 5.1. Key documents of transition concerning SOEs

> CM, 21 January 1981, 25-CP: Introduced the 'Three-Plan System' thus legalising SOE market activities.

> CM, 25 August 1982, 146-HDBT: 'Supplementing and Correcting' 25-CP, tightened up in the interest of plan implementation. Stipulated superior levels as responsible for improving non-list output plans of enterprises.

> CM, 30 November 1984, 156-HDBT: On 'Problems of Management Reform in State Industry', again tighter, like 146-HDBT, Reducing profit retention on market-oriented output. But SOEs allowed to have foreign currency accounts and loans, and still permitted to keep back some output based on own-source materials and minor output. However, price-fixing almost entirely taken out of hands of SOEs. An un-implementable but revealed policy intent.

> CPV, 8 April 1986, 306 BBT: U-turn-encouraged SOE autonomy but failed to attack interference from higher levels.

> CM, 14 November 1987, 217-HDBT: Further encouraged SOE autonomy and outlined plans to reduce target indicators, etc.

Source: Fforde and de Vylder, 1996 (p.168)

Decree 217 and its subsequent regulations were an important step towards establishing commercially oriented state enterprises. SOEs now enjoyed increased autonomy. They had to operate on the principle of 'harder budget constraints'. Internal enterprise restructuring processes, including sharp reductions in SOE employment, were underway. Although, there was still much confusion, Decree 217 marked an era of the 'one price' system. Price now began to matter.

The post-stage of SOE reform in Vietnam – 'the governance structure and internal management'

At the end of the 1980s, the market price mechanism was applied to almost the whole economy except for some 'strategic' industries (e.g. electricity and steel). However, the price system alone was not enough to ensure efficient resource allocation and economic growth and in 1990, the government reviewed the SOE reform programme and highlighted the following problems:

> The large proportion of SOEs that continued to report losses.

> A growing concern about inadequate corporate governance and a lack of accountability over the use of state assets. Corruption (misuse of state assets for illegal activities) was not uncommon.
> Continued increases in the numbers of SOEs because of lack of effective controls.
> Administrative discretion resulting from the ambiguity and inconsistency of parts of Decree 217 and subsequent related regulations.
> Overlaps and conflicting responsibilities of different government bureaux in supervising and monitoring SOEs.

Source: ADB and MPI (1997, p.57).

The following measures were introduced with the aim of making the SOEs transparent and effective.

Re-registration, reorganisation and liquidation
In 1991, the government issued Decree 338-HDBT requiring all SOEs to be re-registered or liquidated. The Decree attempted to:
> Provide criteria for decisions on the establishment of state enterprises – commercial viability was a key concern for non-strategic enterprises. Also laid down was the minimum legal capital required for different categories of state enterprises;
> Clarify lines of authority in approving the establishment of state enterprises;
> Make clear what state enterprises were and what they were not.

As a result, the number of SOEs fell from about 12,297 to 6,254 by 1 April 1994 and employment dropped from four million to about three million (Watson Wyatt, 1998). Most liquidated and merged enterprises were small, locally managed enterprises with less than 100 employees and less than VND500 million (about USD 45,000) in capital.

In 1994, the Prime Minister issued a decision providing instructions on a second phase of re-registration. All re-registered state enterprises would continue to be monitored to ensure that they were operating in compliance with their certificate of registration. In addition, the new degree required that all umbrella entities, such as unions of enterprises and state corporations, should be registered as commercially viable business entities or dissolved. The second phase of re-registration helped to bring the number of state enterprises down to about 6,000 by the end of 1995.

Equitisation and divestiture
The Seventh Party Congress, held in late 1991, declared the need to change the ownership (which meant privatisation, called 'equitisation' in Vietnam) of state enterprises that had no need to be retained under state ownership. In 1992, the government issued a decision (Decision 202/CT, 8 June 1992) to implement a pilot equitisation programme. The equitisation process, however, was slow due to the cumbersome nature of the institutional implementation, lack of clear guidelines, and

resistance to change by those whose privileges were associated with the prevailing system. By September 1997, only 15 state enterprises had been equitised to become joint-stock companies. Reports show that those enterprises that equitised earlier subsequently improved their performance in term of turnover and profits (Le Dang Doanh, 1995). However, this evidence is insufficient to conclude that equitisation automatically improved performance, since such enterprises were carefully selected by the government for the pilot programme. All the equitised enterprises were good performers before equitisation (Dapice, 1999). Over the last five years, the government has issued many documents and guidance urging the speeding up of the equitisation process. The result has been much below the planned target. At the end of 1999, the number of equitised firms reached 224. Most of them are small and medium size, only a few were considered large (valued at about USD1 million) (World Bank, 1999).

State Enterprise Law

The National Assembly passed the so-called State Enterprise Law in 1995. The law established SOEs as separate legal entities, with liability limited to the total capital managed by them. State commercial enterprises were to operate on the same basis as private companies with profit as their key objective (MPI and ADB, 1997). The merit of the law was that commercial SOEs and private enterprises would operate on a level playing field with the same set of rules. The only difference was that SOEs were owned by the state, private enterprises by private investors. The law clarified the following issues:

- ➢ State enterprises as limited liability entities;
- ➢ State public service and commercial enterprises;
- ➢ Rights and responsibilities of state enterprises;
- ➢ Rights and responsibilities of chief executives and boards of management.

State public service and state commercial enterprises were to operate following different sets of guidelines and procedures. Only state public service enterprises in Vietnam belonged to the 'public sector', or 'public enterprises' in the body of public management literature. State commercial enterprises were designated profit-making entities. The three SOEs investigated in the present research are all commercial SOEs. They are limited liability entities and operate under virtually the same set of rules as other types of enterprises (e.g. privately owned) in the market.

Corporatisation

One of the most controversial decisions regarding SOE reform in Vietnam was the so-called corporatisation of SOEs. In March 1994 the government made two decisions, Decision-90 and Decision-91, concerning the groupings of SOEs into large corporations. The Decision-90 groupings, state corporations, were required to have at least five members (five SOEs) with a minimum capital of VND500 billion (about USD46 million at the 1994 exchange rate). Ministers and Chairpersons at the provincial or municipal level were allowed to decide on the establishment of

Decision-90 state corporations. The Decision-91 corporations were larger and more 'important' groupings that required at least seven members and a minimum amount of capital of VND1,000 billion. These corporations had to be approved by the Prime Minister. The person or administrative level that approved the establishment of a corporation also appointed the important personnel of the corporation. The garment and light bulb enterprises in the present research belong respectively to two corporations: the Vietnam Textile and Garment Corporation and the Vietnam Ceramic and Glass Corporation.

The government's rationale for the corporatisation decision was:

> ➢ Economies of scale (to enable large corporations to compete, especially with foreign firms). In addition, large corporations with their monopoly positions could control production, influence import policy and keep prices high for foreign customers (Dapice, 1999);
> ➢ The need to free state up administrative resources to focus on better managing a reduced number of businesses;
> ➢ Large state businesses were essential for the State to play a leading role in the industrialisation and modernisation of the economy.

(ADB and MIP, 1997).

It was said that the decision to establish large state corporations in Vietnam was greatly inspired by the success of the *chaebol* model in South Korea. This decision was, however, made before the *chaebol* crisis. Indeed, Daewoo used to be a reference for Vietnamese state corporations (Dapice, 1999).

State corporations were supposed to operate following the governance structure of the *chaebol* and Western corporations with a board of management and CEO. This was intended to remove the direct involvement of line ministries. However, the corporation model has not worked out as the policy makers intended. The administrative work arising from the state management of SOEs was not reduced but increased. Member SOEs of the corporation now have to report and be supervised not only by the line ministry, but also by the corporations.

There were also concerns about the problem of inefficiency as a consequence of strengthened monopoly positions resulting from the groupings and cross-subsidy amongst SOE members within a corporation. The organisation of the state corporations will be discussed in greater detail in Chapter 8.

5.4. The Vietnamese economy since the reform process and the position of SOEs in 2002

5.4.1. General

By 2002, the economic reform programme in Vietnam had gained notable successes in many socio-economic aspects. Between 1992 and 1997, GDP grew at an average annual rate of 8.6 percent (Vietnam Economic Times, 2002). Table 5.3 shows the growth and inflation rate of the Vietnamese economy in the period 1986-2000. The economy grew rapidly (over 8% a year during the period 1992-1997). The economy slowed, however, at the time of the Asian financial crisis in 1997-1998 but began to recover in the year 2000. The inflation rate was low throughout the period 1992-2000, though it was very high at the start of the reform (674.1% in 1986 and averaged 206.5% a year during the first six years of the reform: 1986-1991). From a condition of severe food shortages before the reform programme, by 2002 Vietnam had become the third largest rice exporter in the world and living standards had improved significantly.

However, to a great extent this success story has resulted from the fact that Vietnam began the reform from a low base economy in which human and natural resources were not utilised (Fforde and Vylder, 1996; Wolff, 2000). Vietnam today remains one of the poorest countries in the world, with an annual per-capita income of under USD400 (Shultz and Ardrey, 1997). Unemployment is high, with a rate of 28.2% in 1998 in the rural areas (World Bank, 1999). Export products are mainly raw materials (e.g. crude oil, coal, rice, coffee and rubber) and some labour intensive manufacturing products (garments and footwear). The reform programme still has many limitations, especially in those areas concerning SOEs. The problems of the SOEs will be examined in more detail later.

Table 5.3. Growth and inflation of the Vietnamese economy 1986-2000

Year	1986 - 91	1992	1993	1994	1995	1996	1997	1998	1999	2000
Growth (%)	4.70	8.70	8.08	8.83	9.54	9.34	8.15	5.76	4.77	6.75
Inflation (%)	206.5	17.5	5.2	14.4	12.7	4.5	3.6	9.2	0.1	-0.6

Source: Adapted from Vietnam Economic Times, 2002, issue 1 p.48

One of the essential components of reform in Vietnam was the acceptance of a multi-sectoral economic development strategy. That is, to formally recognise the permanent existence of a variety of forms of enterprise, and provide for their equal treatment under the law (Richards, Ha, Harvie & Nguyen, 2002, p.118). Since reform began, Vietnam has allowed and promoted the development of the private sector and encouraged foreign investment. The Vietnamese economy is now truly multi-sectoral. Besides the SOEs, there are also joint-ventures, foreign-owned enterprises, non-state businesses including private enterprises and household businesses. The rest of the section briefly presents some features of each sector and their role in the economy as a whole.

5.4.2. State-owned enterprises
The state sector in Vietnam has always played a key role in the economy. Although there are currently different types of business organisations operating in Vietnam, the

Vietnamese government has always strongly emphasised the 'leading role' of the state sector (*The People's Army*, 2001). As we can see from Table 5.4 (this page), although the government's reliance on the SOE contribution has decreased relatively, still nearly half of all government revenue comes from SOEs (40.2% in 1999). In terms of GDP, SOEs account for about 40% (Table 5.5, this page)

Table 5.4. Contribution of SOEs to the government's revenue

Year	1991	1992	1993	1994	1995	1996	1997
SOE contribution (% of government revenue)	59.8	56.7	9.9	48.8	41.1	41.5	40.2

Source: World Bank (1999)

Table 5.5. Share of GDP by sector ownership (%)

Year	1995	1996	1997	1998	1999
State	40.18	39.93	40.48	40.00	39.48
Non-state					
Collective	10.06	10.03	8.91	8.90	8.60
Private	3.12	3.35	3.38	3.41	3.39
Household	36.02	35.25	34.32	33.83	33.14
Mixed	4.32	4.05	3.84	3.83	3.64
Foreign investment sector	6.30	7.39	9.07	11.03	11.75

Source: Ministry of Commerce, 2000, p.49

The above statistical data, however, do not tell the true story of SOE performance. Although SOEs contribute nearly 50% of government revenue, the revenue comes from only about 300 or more large to medium sized SOEs of which many are, to a great extent, operating as a monopoly (Watson Wyatt, 1998). In Vietnam, all key industries such as electricity, petroleum, mining and post and telecommunications are run by the state. It has been estimated that only two-fifths of the total number of SOEs are profitable. In 1997, half the SOEs lost money (World Bank, 1999). Table 5.6 shows the current financial situation of the most poorly performing SOEs (about half the total number of SOEs in Vietnam).

The 'worst performing' group of SOEs have average debt *twice* (19.5:10) the value of state-capital. 'Poor performing' group of SOEs have average debt nearly equal (42.5:52) to the value of state-capital. The position of the SOEs is certainly not promising.

Table 5.6. Financial status of weak SOEs

SOE category	Worst SOEs	Poor SOEs
Number of SOEs	711	1,989
Number of workers (000)	183	583
Total debt (VND trillion)	19.5	42.5
Bank debt (VND trillion)	14	29
State capital (VND trillion)	10	52
Profit (VND trillion)	-0.25	5

Source: World Bank (1999), p.8

'Badly' performing enterprises are certainly a burden on the economy. As the World Bank has put it: "Vietnam's economic goals remain seriously threatened by a large number of inefficient and loss-making SOEs that absorb more than half of bank credit, without contributing to employment growth" (World Bank, 2001, p.6). Despite all this, SOEs are still enjoying considerable privileges and advantages over private businesses (Richards, Ha, Harvie and Nguyen, 2002).

5.4.3. The private sector
Before 1988 private businesses were not accepted by the government (Vu Quang Viet, 1998). However since reform the non-state sector, including private enterprises and household businesses, has begun to flourish. The number of non-state businesses is increasing rapidly year after year. The total number of private enterprises in Vietnam reached 66,071 at the end of 2001 (Vu Duy Thai, 2002). The non-state sector has played an increasingly important role in the economy. The sector has accounted for about 90% of employment (Dang Nhu Van, 2001). The non-state sector, however, consists mostly of household small businesses (i.e. teashops, restaurants). The contribution of the 'proper' private sector (limited liability private enterprises) is very limited. Table 5.5 shows that private enterprises contribute only about 3% of GDP and this share has not increased since 1996. Although the Vietnamese government has insisted on its development, the private sector remains more constrained in Vietnam than in other country in the region, including China (Richards, et al, 2002). The private sector still faces various unnecessary restrictions and problems including:

> License requirements
> Access to land

- ➤ Access to capital
- ➤ Access to export
- ➤ Red-tape and corruption

(Richards et al, 2002)

Given the high level of entrepreneurial zeal among the Vietnamese, the private sector in Vietnam has high potential. Change in government policy toward the sector is undoubtedly a necessary condition to ensure its success.

5.4.4. Foreign investment sector

An 'open door' to foreign investment is one of the key components of the economic reform in Vietnam. In 1987, the government promulgated a law on foreign investment which was considered one of the most liberal in the Asia-Pacific region (Price Waterhourse, 1996). Since then, foreign investment and trade have mushroomed. The flow of foreign direct investment (FDI) into Vietnam has increased rapidly since the reform, especially during the period 1992-1997 (FDI capital in 1997 alone is USD2.1 billion compared to USD186 million of the whole period of 1988-1992) (Nguyen Khai, 2001). At the end of 2000, the total number of foreign investment projects in Vietnam reached 3170, with a total registered capital of more than USD 39 billion (General Statistical Office, 2001).

Foreign direct investment has played an increasingly important role in the economy. Table 5.5 demonstrates that the share of foreign investment sector in the total GDP of the country is an increasing trend (6.3% in 1995 to 11.75% in 1999).

Table 5.7. GDP growth by sector ownership (%)

Year	1995	1996	1997	1998	1999
State sector	8.4	9.7	8.3	5.0	4.1
Non-state sector	8.7	7.2	5.7	4.3	3.5
Foreign sector	14.9	19.4	20.7	18.1	4.7

Source: Pham Do Chi & Tran Nam Binh (2001, p.146)

Foreign investment has grown faster than any other sector of the economy (see Table 5.7, above). Foreign investment into Vietnam has, however, slowed down during the last few years due to the Asian Financial Crisis and the slow pace of the reform in Vietnam (Nguyen Khai).

Despite all the positive developments in the sector, there are still many obstacles to foreign investors and foreign businesses operating in Vietnam. Those obstacles include:

> Poor infrastructure – roads, railways and electricity are still in very poor condition compared even to other developing countries;
> Bureaucracy and corruption;
> Lack of experience and knowledge of business, accounting and taxation concepts;
> Underdeveloped legal systems and weak law enforcement.

(Price Waterhouse 1996; Nguyen Khai, 2002)

Foreign investment in Vietnam would certainly be more effective if these weaknesses were remedied.

5.5. The reform process in Vietnam – 'adjustment to a given world'

From the above analysis, we can characterise economic reform in Vietnam in general, and SOE reform in particular, as a process of 'rational adjustment to the given world'. Figure 5.3 below shows a model of the reform process in Vietnam using a biological metaphor.

The reform was not a 'master-of-the-world' project. It was responsive rather than proactive. Fforde and Vylder (1996) pointed out that, in a strict sense, "the changes that took place in Vietnam during the 1980s and early 1990s should perhaps not be called reform at all." (p1).

The nature of the economic reform process during the last 20 years is consistent with Vietnamese culture and society. The widely used Vietnamese proverb *rach dau va day* (mend (clothes) only when and where it is torn) implied what Weber termed "adjustment to the world".

There is no development of abstract thought that can produce new and 'better' kind of clothes. The literati class today (government officials), as those of a thousand years ago, enjoy all the privileges of the existing system and do not want to change. The changes need to take place from the 'bottom' and, as Fforde and Vylder (1996) pointed out, recent reform in Vietnam has been a 'bottom-up' process.

Figure 5.3. Reform in Vietnam – 'adjustment to a given world'

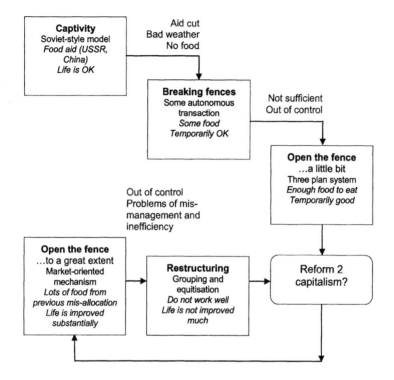

Chapter 6: The institutional matrix and the typical form of capitalism in Vietnam

One day, Deng Xiaoping decided to take his grandson to visit Mao. "Call me grand-uncle," Mao offered warmly. "Oh, I certainly couldn't do that, Chairman Mao," the awe-struck child replied. "Why don't you give him an apple?" suggested Deng. No sooner had Mao done so than the boy happily chirped, "Oh thank you, grand-uncle." "You see," said Deng, "what incentives can achieve." ('Capitalism', 1984, p.62, quoted in Eisenhardt, 1989, p.57).

6.1. The formal laws and institutions in Vietnam

The pursuit of the Soviet-style development model left Vietnam's institutions in a vacuum. Almost all the 'rules of the game' associated with a market mechanism and capitalism were absent, so the country needed to start from the beginning. Vietnam was also special in the sense that commercial trade had never developed to the same level as in other East Asian countries and China. In addition, Vietnam had not greatly benefited from the implementation of a western institutional structure during the French colonial period. The French employed a parallel legal system there in which a civil law system governed French and other European citizens, while the Nguyen code and customary practice governed the Vietnamese (Rose, 1998). Lee Kuan Yew made a perceptive comment on the different contributions of the British and the French to their colonies:

"Where they colonised, the French left a sense of civilisation--the language, culture and art. The British, by contrast, left behind the rule of law and institutions – a civil service, a judicial system and a police force ruled by criminal procedure codes ensuring the fairness of an investigation, about the presumption of innocence. This institutional setting was crucial to Singapore's success." (in Gardels, 1999, [p.2])

During the era of the Soviet-style economy trade was banned. Substantial private possessions were not allowed and the legal system was chiefly concerned with civil law, business law was excluded.

Since the introduction of 'doi moi' in 1986, Vietnam has begun to build an almost completely new legal system. A set of laws and regulations concerning businesses and market-related activities has been formulated step by step. Understandably, even today the legal system in general, and laws concerning businesses in particular, are still underdeveloped. The general feature of Vietnam's current legal framework, as Pham Van Thuyet (1996) pointed out, "remains largely informal and unstructured, as it had been for a long period prior to the transition to a market economy" (p.595). In addition, although Vietnam's legal system is expected to promote economic liberalisation it also, as Rose (1998) pointed out, has to preserve "a socialist, one-party state apparatus" [p.4]. This fact has impeded the development of what Max Weber would term a "rational" legal system.

This section examines some of the key feature of Vietnam's legal framework concerning transactions and private property following the three key characteristics of Vietnam's legal system (1) lack of codification; (2) incompleteness; and (3) weak enforcement.

6.1.1. Lack of codification

Since the late 1980s, a number of laws concerning businesses have been promulgated. These laws were developed in response to a particular situation rather than to achieve an absolute, stable and long lasting application. Laws and regulations continue to be modified and changed: almost every law and regulation in Vietnam has been changed or modified at least several times over the past ten years. Many laws and regulations are just temporary guidelines for business activities. As Mr. Le Dang Doanh, a key figure of the enterprise reform team in Vietnam, observed, many laws in Vietnam "are words, not really laws". (The Economist 1994, p.41). Many terms and concepts used in laws and regulations are not well-defined, and are open to different interpretations.

> "Individual interpretation of the law by authorities at different levels in the government can greatly affect the ways the law is put into practice. The law tends to be interpreted directly from what is written on paper and often its meaning varies depending on the authority who reads it. The concept of precedent is almost non-existent at present. Therefore, it is not uncommon to see the application of the same rule differ significantly in two cities within Vietnam. All of this means that one needs to be cautious and circumspect when dealing with legal matters in Vietnam." (Price Waterhouse, 1996, p16).

One example is the term 'force majeure', used in the Labour Law. Item 38.1d in the Labour Law states that employers may unilaterally terminate a labour contract in the case of "natural disasters, fire or other force majeures in which the employers tried all reasonable measures, but still had to reduce production and jobs". Owing to the Asian Financial Crisis, in 1999, many companies terminated many employment contracts and fired workers. Dong Yang, a South Korean company, for example, unilaterally terminated 88 employment contracts. They claimed that the Asian crisis was a 'force majeure' and the authorities had to accept that because the term was not clearly defined (Nguyen Van Binh, 1999).

In Vietnam, the concept of law itself is understood differently from the West. Ethics and laws are sometimes not separated as, for example, in the State-Owned Enterprise Law Item 32, concerning the criteria of a director or a deputy director of the enterprise, one criterion (sub-item 2) is that: "*they must be ethically good, honest and not self-seeking and they must have good attitudes toward obeying laws and orders*".

93

There are also communication problems amongst the different governmental bodies and organisations formulating and implementing laws and regulations. As *The Economist* pointed out:

> "Vietnam does not yet have a system to publicise even those laws and regulations it has passed. If, say, the National Assembly passes a trade bill, the trade ministry may not be told of some relevant regulations made by the finance ministry. So the linkages that give life to the law are weak. Sometimes a law does not apply to the government anyway. Vietnam recently announced that all domestic transactions must be in Dong (Vietnamese currency); but when this correspondent offered Dong as payment to a government agency, it was told that only dollars were accepted" (The Economist, 1994, p41).

6.1.2. Incomplete legal systems

Vietnam is now still in the process of formulating its legal system. Many business-related areas in Vietnam have not been covered by laws and many others have only been partially developed (Price Waterhouse, 1996). There have been many legal cases or incidents, but no legal framework available to settle them. The best way to illustrate this point is perhaps through case examples.

Box 6.1. Coca-Cola Chuong Duong joint-venture.

Coca-Cola Chuong Duong was one of the very first US-Vietnam joint-ventures. It was formed in 1995, just after the USA government's decision to lift the trade embargo to Vietnam. The joint-venture partners were Coca-Cola (Singapore) and the Vietnamese soft-drink company: Chuong Duong.

The original capital was USD48.7 million, Coca-Cola contributing 60% and the Vietnamese partner 40%. From 1995 to 1998, the joint-venture spent a lot of money on promotion and sold its products for almost nothing. A normal bottle of Coca-Cola was about only 5 to 10 pence. In 1998, the total losses of the joint-venture amounted to VND151 billion (about USD11 million).

Coca-Cola's strategy to get rid of its Vietnamese partner succeeded as the joint-venture became insolvent and Coca-Cola became a 100% foreign capital company, the first in the soft-drinks industry.

After this incident, the Vietnamese authority and local partner realised that they had paid a heavy price for the absence of **Antitrust Laws** and **price regulations**.

Summarised from the article titled: 'That's it, Chuong Duong!' Chu Thuong, August, 1998. http://www.fpt.vn/InfoStore/6B0B0001/1998/08/35E2A4E9.htm

---

With respect to businesses, there are still key areas that have not been covered by the legal system. Although the Vietnamese government is trying to promote private businesses, the private sector in Vietnam is still constrained in many areas: by the lack of an independent judiciary, the absence of private land ownership and other uncertainties in property law (Pham Van Thuyet, 1996). Land ownership and land use rights are still complicated and ambiguous (World Bank 1999).

6.1.3. Weak and lacking law enforcement

The above example indicates that the legal system in Vietnam is still underdeveloped. The government and society as a whole have had to pay a high price for the absence of laws and regulations. However, if the existence of laws is important, law enforcement is perhaps equally or even more so. North (1986), from his study of economic history, found that effective third party enforcement played an essential role in modern economies.

> "The gains from trade involved in the complex characteristics of modern economies cannot be realised without third party enforcement. It is no accident that no high income country in the world has achieved this result without effective third party enforcement. Government must play an essential role in enforcing contracts in such economies" (North, 1986, p233).

Weak law enforcement is an obvious feature of the legal system in Vietnam. Vietnamese people do not, and perhaps never have, trusted the legal system, a fact reflected in the widely used proverb *con kien kien cu khoai* (an ant sues a tuber of sweet potato). The proverb is meant to show that since an ant is tiny compared to a tuber of sweet potato, power is extremely unbalanced between them. The ant (ordinary people) is always in a state of hopelessness and unlikely to win in any legal case.

In today's business context, legal areas which are important to businesses such as contracts and dispute resolution are vague, 'the law exists but the system of enforcement has not been implemented' (Price Waterhouse, 1996, p16). The violation of contracts, especially overdue payments, is ubiquitous in Vietnam but such disputes have not been resolved by laws. In an interview, a director of a private company (VB Steel) summarised how businesses in Vietnam solved the problem of contract violation.

> "As you already knew Vietnamese people are afraid of *hau toa* (going to court), but if you try your best and still cannot settle the disputes yourself or are too angry with your business partners - in the case of overdue payment, for example, you have to take the issue to court. It takes some time for officials from the different departments to investigate. In the case of overdue debt, it is rather simple. The court will follow the signed contract and decide, for example that party A must pay party B an amount of x dong before date y. But one year after date y, party B may still not have received any payment. Party A has to constantly ask and press party B, and may raise the issue in the newspapers. In order to reduce the tension, party B may sometimes pay a small part of the debt. So it is both time consuming and makes you angry" (interview December, 1999).

The findings of a study of trading relationships in Vietnam carried out by McMillan and Woodruff (1999a) give further evidence on this issue. In their interviews, McMillan and Woodruff found that Vietnamese managers did not believe in using the courts. One of the managers said: "they [the court] normally just create more problems" (p.640). From a survey of 259 Vietnamese firms about their contracts with customers and suppliers, McMillan and Woodruff (1999b) found that 91% of the managers sampled said that the courts could not enforce a contract with a customer. This figure is much higher than those found in two other transitional countries, Ukraine (55%) and Russia (58%). They also found that only 2% of Vietnamese managers said they would take disputes to court or appeal to local authorities.

The Bankruptcy Law is another example of weak law enforcement. The Bankruptcy Law was promulgated and officially came into effect in 1994. But the law was not actually activated! Nguyen Van Huy, a senior official of the Vietnam Enterprise Reform Committee estimates that currently, Vietnam has in total over 40,000 business enterprises, of which about 6,000 are SOEs. About 25% of these make a loss, with 11% of SOEs having repeatedly made a loss unable to settle payments. The number of private enterprises in this position is much greater yet despite this, at the end of 1999, only 64 companies were declared bankrupt (VASC, 2000).

Intellectual property rights are another obvious example of weak law enforcement in Vietnam. Legislation exists to protect most forms of intellectual property in Vietnam but in practice, infringements are widespread (Price Waterhouse, 1996). One can easily find many examples of the violation of intellectual property rights in Vietnam, such as the case of the mineral water, brand name: 'La Vie'. La Vie is popular (possibly the most popular mineral water brand name in Vietnam) and a product of the Long An Mineral Water Joint-Venture Company, a joint venture established in 1992 between Perrier-Vittel SA (Nestle' Group), France and Long An, Vietnam. Because of its success in the market, a number of companies launched almost identical products on the market. One can easily find several kinds of mineral water bottles with the same size, the same design, and with a little modification of the name such that La Vile or La Vila. It is said that the joint-venture has made several appeals to the relevant authorities, but the situation has not changed.

Chu Thuong (2000) told a story about a musician, Le Vinh who, according to the author, is "the first ant"[*] ever who won an intellectual property court case. His song 'Hanoi va toi' was modified and printed without permission but it took three years before the case was finally settled. Le Vinh appealed to the court on May 6, 1997. A year later, on July 27, 1998, the court in Hanoi Court investigated the case and declared Le Vinh the winner, a verdict accepted by the other party. But ironically, Le Vinh had to pay the court fee of over VND2 million yet received only about VND400,000 in royalties and so was financially worse off. He decided to appeal and on May 19, 2000, the Vietnam Supreme Court decided that Le Vinh had won and should receive over VND34 million. This example demonstrates how the courts work in Vietnam.

6.1.4. Banking and the stock market
Apart from laws, any analysis of the formal 'rules of the game' should include the formal institutions (e.g. banking system and stock market) which have a profound

---

[*] Chu Thuong uses the metaphor 'ant' as in the proverb 'con kien kien cu khoai' mentioned earlier in this section.

effect on how businesses are developed and run. Capitalism cannot work effectively without efficient capital markets, and the level of interest rates in capital markets is perhaps the obvious quantitative evidence of the efficiency of the institutional framework (North, 1990). This section briefly analyses the banking sector and stock market in Vietnam.

Banking system

The concept of banking as normally understood in the West was totally absent during the era of the Soviet-style economy. There were banks, but their functions were completely different from those in a market economy. Since 1989, in parallel with other economic reforms, Vietnam has undertaken a reform programme on monetary and fiscal issues (Wolff, 1999) and as a result, the banking system has started playing a role in the economy. However, Vietnam's banking system remains fairly underdeveloped. Banking systems are highly inefficient and dominated by undercapitalised state-owned commercial banks (Wolff, 1999), and burdened with the debts of inefficient state-owned enterprises (Wolff, 1999; World Bank, 1998 and 1999). A World Bank (1998) report shows that:

> "Currently (1998), for all banks (state-owned-commercial and joint-stock), over-dues are around fourteen percent of all loans, though for two state-owned commercial banks, the level exceeds twenty percent and for several joint-stock banks, it is higher still. This level of over-dues is worrying, particularly because weaknesses in the loan classification system may understate the actual extent of the problem." (p22).

The banking system still favours the state sector, so it is difficult for private businesses to get bank loans (Richards, Ha & Nguyen, 2001). Private firms face the problem of bureaucratic procedures, especially in fulfilling collateral requirements (World Bank, 1999). A survey of 95 private small and medium enterprises showed that 53% of the surveyed sample were "unable to get investment capital" (World Bank, 1999, p.15).

In Vietnam today, most transactions are still settled in cash. Only businesses and a small number of people use the banking system. Trust in banks amongst the population is very limited (Price Waterhouse, 1996).

Stock market

The stock market is a totally new concept in Vietnam. The Vietnamese government is aware that a stock market is a must in a market economy and since 1995, has issued a number of degrees and regulations concerning the establishment of a stock market. In 1996, the government decided to establish a special committee to prepare and manage the coming stock market (Decree 75-CP). The first-ever stock market officially opened in July, 2000 but only two companies have registered so far. There are still concerns about criteria, regulations and how the stock market will work.

6.2. Informal norms in economic transactions

Vietnamese (left) and Western scales

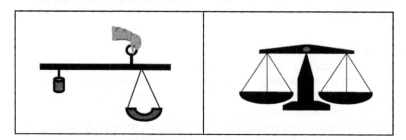

The last section described the current state of development of the formal rules governing business transactions in Vietnam. Formal rules are important, especially so during the transitional period in Vietnam and other former socialist countries, when they are needed to direct economic activities. When formal rules have already been laid out, the question then is whether people follow them. The same set of formal rules does not work out in the same way in different countries with different cultural backgrounds. North (1990) gave an illustrative example:

> "The US Constitution was adopted (with modifications) by many Latin American
> countries in the nineteenth century, and many of the property rights laws of
> successful Western countries have been adopted by Third World countries. The
> results, however, are not similar to those in either the United States or other
> successful countries. Although the rules are the same, the enforcement
> mechanisms, the way enforcement occurs, the norms of behaviour, and the
> subjective models of the actors are not. Hence both the real incentive structures and
> the perceived consequences of policies will differ as well" (p.101).

Following Max Weber's *'The Protestant Ethic and the Spirit of Capitalism'* and his work on the sociology of religion, an increasing amount of literature has been written about the role that culture plays in the economic sphere. Granovetter (1985) argued that transactions, even in a modern western society where the legal system is highly developed, cannot rely solely on laws. A certain level of trust is always needed in any exchange. In any economic transaction, an exchange party's deepest concern is perhaps whether the other party 'lives up to the agreement'. This 'lives up to the agreement' issue has been elaborated in the literature with different terms such as trust, distrust, honesty, goodwill, opportunism, fraud and malfeasance. All these terms are inherently interrelated. The most frequently used term was perhaps 'trust'. Trust appeared to be the central concept in social exchange literature, as next briefly discussed.

A lot has been written about trust from a range of perspectives in the fields of economics, sociology and organisation studies. Examples are Arrow (1974) and Williamson (1993) in the field of economics; Luhmann (1979), Granovetter (1985), Zucker (1986), Coleman (1990) and Giddens (1990) in the field of sociology; and

Whitley (1992), Orru, Biggart & Hamilton (1997) and Dore (1983) in the field of organisation and business studies in the Far East. Trust has been defined and treated differently by different authors in different fields.

Barney and Hansen (1995), for example, defined trust and trustworthiness so:

> "An exchange partner is trustworthy when it is worthy of the trust of others. An exchange party worthy of the trust is one which will not exploit others' exchange vulnerabilities...Trust is an attribute of a relationship between exchange partners, trustworthiness is an attribute of individual exchange partners" (quoted in Korczynski, 2000, p.4).

Although there are variations in the definition and treatment of the concept of trust, there is a common acceptance that trust is intimately tied in with vulnerability, risk or uncertainty about outcomes. It is widely agreed that trust plays an important role in facilitating exchanges and fostering co-operation. North (1990), for example, pointed out that "trust, honesty and integrity simply lower the cost of transacting and make possible complex, productive exchange." (p138).

Trust is arguably one of the pre-conditions in the development of modern or advanced societies. Giddens (1990) pointed out that trust is crucial in *disembedding* space and time. Disembedding is fundamental to "advanced" societies or "high modernity" in Giddens' term. This statement could equally mean that trust is fundamental to the nature of advanced contemporary societies (Korczynski, 2000, p.8). Weber (1958) argues that capitalism in fact relies upon pre-modern, social habits and values (e.g. trust and honesty) to function effectively (Korczynski, 2000). Dore (1983) argued that trust is one of the keys to the success of Japanese organisations and Japanese economy as a whole.

Trust is fundamental if business transactions are to be possible in a context where legal systems are underdeveloped, and third party enforcement is absent or weak. Trust has been widely treated as a cultural trait. Trust is one of the 'informal' aspects in our analysis of institutions, and influential writers on economic organisations and management in East Asia: Redding and Whitley (1990), Redding (1993), Whitley (1992), Orru, Biggart & Hamilton (1997) and Dore (1983) all implicitly or explicitly treat trust as a cultural trait which has a strong bearing on management and organisations.

The remaining part of this section examines some important Vietnamese cultural traits (e.g. trust and honesty) in the context of transactions.

6.2.1. Trade and the city

The city is important in any analysis of capitalism. Cities gave birth to capitalism in Western countries and Confucianism, as Max Weber pointed out, with its patrimonial nature, impeded the development of trade and cities. He pointed out that, compared to Western cities, Chinese cities lacked political and military autonomy and the unity to act as a corporate body. There was also a lack of legal guarantee for guild privileges that compelled the guilds to function self-sufficiently (Weber, 1951). If trade and cities were not developed in China by Western standards, in Vietnam they were not even developed by Chinese standards.

Vietnamese cities, as Tran Ngoc Them (1997) pointed out, were often established in an arbitrary fashion by the government. The city's location, for example, was often chosen by geomancers. Cities did not have autonomous status but were strictly controlled by the central government. Cities in Vietnam shared many characteristics with the village. The city administrative system more or less followed that of rural areas (Tran Ngoc Them, 1997) and the lifestyle of its inhabitants was not distinctly different from that of those living in villages. From a historical study of the nineteenth century Vietnam, Woodside (1971) pointed out:

> "Nineteenth century Hanoi was divided into blocks or wards, each of whose inhabitants followed the same trade-hemp stores, tin shops, sail shops, bamboo basket shops, sugar retailers - and often came originally from the same native place or village. But from the standpoint of comparative social history, the wards suggested a super-aggregation of rural economic units rather than more significant urbanisation (p.32).

In fact, instead of urbanisation there was a process of 'ruralisation' in Vietnam. Only a few years ago, city people still grew vegetables and raised pigs and chicken in their home areas (Tran Ngoc Them, 1997). Mai Ngu, a Vietnamese writer, described Vietnamese cities in the 1970s and 1980s:

> "Many streets, in the afternoon, look like villages. People take showers, wash clothes, wash vegetable and rice, and wash and slice fish and meat around a water tank or a water fountain on the pavement. Children play at tipcat and flying kites. Noon is sounded by inviting words from pig castrating specialists. Midnight is sounded raucously by dogs baking." (in Tran Ngoc Them, p.257, the author's translation).

The merchant class was held in contempt in Confucian society: the merchant was ranked least important in the Confucian hierarchical class structure: literati – peasant – artisan – merchant. Vietnam was no exception to this. Woodside (1971) pointed out that in comparison with nineteenth century Japan and China, the merchant class in Vietnam was underdeveloped.

> "Chinese court ideology scorned merchants (overtly but not covertly) because it considered them parasitic and unproductive, compared to scholars and farmers. Vietnamese rulers and bureaucrats tended to discriminate against merchants more because successful merchants commanded immoderately large resource in a poor society. Their acquisitiveness seemed grotesque and immoral. In Nguyen Vietnam, it was as much the visible results as the functions of entrepreneurship that were invidious." (p34).

Merchants were considered as 'animals' in Vietnam, and often called *con buon*. *Buon* means trade (buying and selling), *con* is, in this context, associated with animals. In Vietnamese, *con* is a generic particle denoting a unit of animal or animal-like thing, for example, *con ga* (chicken), *con kien* (ant), *con trau* (buffalo) and so on. *Con buon* is used to denote derogatorily merchants as animals. *'Do con buon!'* (you are a merchant!) is amongst the worst Vietnamese swearing phases (Tran Ngoc Them, 1997).

The popular negative attitude toward merchants and the rural lifestyle of the city people in Vietnam were perhaps the major reasons for the insignificant development of trade and the slow pace of industrialisation in Vietnam. Woodside (1971) threw some light on this point by comparing Japan and Vietnam in the early nineteenth century:

> "In Tokugawa Japan in the early 1800s, for example, the distribution of goods seemed to follow a pattern of producers-wholesalers-small merchants-customers, whereas in Nguyen Vietnam the pattern was producers-periodic markets-customers...There were no Vietnamese equivalents of those large, specialising dry-goods stores of pre-modern Tokyo like Matsuzakaya (from 1707) and Daimaru (1726), for instance, which accumulated capital, developed large-scale operations, and then evolved into modern department stores in the twentieth century." (p.32).

Fforde and de Vylder (1996) pointed out that a negative attitude towards the merchant class was consistent with, and believed by many to be the cultural root of, the adoption of the Stalinist development model. During the Soviet-style economy, business and merchants were considered as a root of capitalism, to be banned at all costs.

Until recently, trade in Vietnam was limited to basic products like food and simple farming tools in irregular markets. Large volumes and impersonal exchanges were never developed in Vietnamese history where the basic symbolic token of modernity, scales, was not used. In the 1980s and early 1990s, farmers did not even use scales when they bought and sold agricultural products such as rice, fish, and small pigs. For fish and small pigs they relied on rough estimations.

6.2.2. Limited trust and honesty in economic transactions

Max Weber pointed out that distrust and dishonesty were amongst the chief cultural traits associated with Confucianism. He noted that "the Confucian gentleman, striving simply for dignified bearing, distrusted others as generally as he believed others distrusted him" (Weber, 1951, p.244). A number of studies on East Asian business and management, for example, Redding (1993), Redding and Whitley (1990) and Whitley (1992) confirmed many of Weber's observations and theories about Chinese traits and their bearing on the characters and forms of Chinese businesses. Redding (1993), for example, pointed out that one of the characteristics of the Chinese is *bounded and limited trust*. He elaborated the point:

> "The key feature would appear to be that you trust your family absolutely, your friends and acquaintances to the degree that mutual dependence has been established and face invested in them. With everyone else you make no

assumptions about their goodwill. You have the right to expect their politeness and their following of the social proprieties, but beyond that you must anticipate that, just as you are, they are looking primarily to their own, i.e. their family's, best interests. To know your own motives well is, for the Chinese more than most, a warning about everybody else's" (p.66).

All the theories and evidence about the distrust and dishonesty of the Chinese are also true for the Vietnamese. It was no accident that the Vietnamese regarded merchants as animals. Tran Ngoc Them (1997) pointed out that one of the key attributes of the Vietnamese merchant class was their practice of cheating, lying and forcing their customers. The Vietnamese saying *buon gian ban lan* was and is still widely used today. *Buon gian ban lan* means literally as 'trade is deceitful, selling is cheating'. Cheating was not an exception, but considered a necessary attribute in any merchant business ranging from small scale (e.g. buying and selling fish and rice in the market or between markets in a local area) to larger scale (buying and supplying various products to cities). 'Small' merchants may, for example, buy rice, chickens and fish from one corner of the market and sell them in another corner, or buy from one market and sell in others. They could make a little 'profit' that could be enough to feed their families. These 'part-time' merchants needed to be 'good' at bargaining and cheating. 'Cheating' skills include the practice of using the box (a unit to measure products such as rice used instead of scales) in buying and selling. The price per box in both transactions could be the same, but merchants still made a little 'profit' from their 'skilful' use of the box. Merchants sometimes colluded with others in their gang to cheat farmers in the market.

'Bigger' merchants, who bought products from farmers and sold them in cities, and city wholesalers and retailers, also practised cheating tactics. It was not uncommon for merchants to force and threaten their customers to buy or sell their products. The Vietnamese called merchants *dan cho bua* (market people) to mean an immoral class, characterised by lying, cheating and violence.

Bargaining is a fact of life in Vietnam today. Weber wrote about the Chinese retail trade nearly 100 years ago that it, "to be sure, seems to know little of such honesty; the fixed prices appear to be fictitious even among native Chinese." (p.232). This is still true today, as almost everything needs to be bargained for. It is very often the case that sellers of fashionable products, for example, clothes, set the initial price much higher, even as high as three times more than the lowest price at which they would be willing to sell. It is quite normal for academic people (university students or lecturers, who are not very good at bargaining) are 'cheated' when they buy, for example, clothes or shoes from the market. People can also be easily cheated when buying basic goods such as meat and fish. To avoid this, many people take their own scales with them to the market to compare that with the seller's scale. Farmers, who are so poor in Vietnam, are even poorer because they are vulnerable to being cheated, and may spend all their savings on fake products.

Vietnamese parents sometimes use the expression *khon nha dai cho* (just clever at

102

home, but foolish or naïve in the market) to their children to mean that they should be clever in the market. *Dai cho* (foolish or naïve in the market) could mean too honest to be cheated or not good at bargaining. They should be 'alert' enough to not be cheated and are even encouraged to tell lies in order to cope with the situation. Lying and cheating were necessary in life. Hickey (1964), from his intensive ethnographic study of a Vietnamese village in the 1950s gave an example that "one devout Buddhist villager gave up rice merchandising because one had to be 'a teller of lies' to be a merchant" (p.173). This fact was partly reflected in the saying *that tha an chao, bo lao an com*. The phase means that if you are honest, you eat soup (*chao*), if you are dishonest or cheating you eat proper rice (*com*)'. *Chao* is rice cooked with a lot of water to get enough quantity (in Vietnam, people were so poor that they did not have enough rice, they had to cook rice with a lot of water in order to share it easily).

The 'price of trust'

Distrust and dishonesty undoubtedly "handicapped all credit and business operations" (Weber, 1951, p.244). Weber made this point clear by making the comparison "... what is repeatedly maintained as the incompatible dishonesty of the Chinese, even toward their own defence attorneys, could scarcely be reconciled with the obviously remarkable reliability of merchants in big business – compared to countries with a feudal past such as Japan, for example." (p.232). It was evident that distrust and dishonesty prevented the Vietnamese from forming and sustaining any reasonable size of business operations. Hickey (1964) gave evidence for this in his study of the village, showing that villagers did not trust each other enough to co-operate in economic or trade activities. The rice merchants, for example, did not "trust one another sufficiently to form workable partnerships and business arrangements" (p. 173). Another example described the failure of *hui* (Chinese style informal rotating credit association) in the Vietnamese village. The *hui* was formed once, but did not work. The reason, as Hiskey pointed out, was the lack of trust.

> "The trust and co-operation needed to make a success of the organisation clearly was lacking. In their last meeting before it disbanded, some members openly admitted reluctance to entrust money to the group, and there was a great deal of dissension." (p280).

Barton (1983), from his study of Overseas Chinese businesses in the precommunist South Vietnam of 1960s, pointed out that one of reasons that Chinese merchants were successful in Vietnam was their practice of *sun yung* (*tin dung* in Vietnamese). *Sun yung* literally means 'the use of trust' and is often translated into English as credit or credit ratings. In economic aspects, *sun yung* is expressed in business co-operation and credit ratings. Vietnamese merchants failed to achieve the level of success attained by the Chinese because, as Barton pointed out, they were generally lacking in *sun yung*. One Vietnamese merchant claimed that "it would be impossible for him to form a partnership even with his best friend for as soon as they had pooled their money, he could be sure that the next day his friend would be off with the funds to Paris" (Barton, 1983, p.53). One clear indication of the lack of *sun yung* or trust amongst Vietnamese merchants was the high interest rates they had to pay. Barton (1983) found that "on average Chinese merchants paid interest charges of 2-3% per month, while interest charges paid by Vietnamese traders averaged 4-6% per month" (p.61). If trust is treated as a commodity, this commodity was obviously expensive in Vietnam. Trust was expensive because it was rare (to use the language of the law of demand and supply).

In a survey of 127 managers working in joint-ventures in Vietnam about their perceptions of excellence in leadership, Truong Quang, Swierczek and Dang Thi Kim Chi (1998) found that "dependable and trustworthy" and "honest" were rated as the two most important leadership characteristics. One implication of this finding is that trust and honesty are lacking in Vietnam. The findings of their research "demonstrate that joint venture leadership in Vietnam *should* be open and fair in its management style" (p.365, the author's emphasis).

Lying, cheating and distrust in business dealings are still common in Vietnam. The 'price of trust' is high. Interest rates paid by private firms in informal credit markets are as high as 4-7% per month (McMillan and Woodruff, 1999a, p.641). Disputes with trading partners are common. From their research, McMillan and Woodruff (1999a) found that 25% of 259 surveyed firms had experienced a customer failing to pay for a product after it had been delivered, and 6% said a supplier had failed to deliver products without returning advance payment. Getting money back in Vietnam "is an art which is very difficult to explain", as a manager said (McMillan and Woodruff, 1999a, p.642). There have been cases in which criminals were used to collect debt. Limited trust and honesty obviously limit the scale and scope of trade. Business parties have to spend time, resources and use particular tactics (e.g. sending staff to talk with the customer's neighbours and visiting customers or suppliers frequently) to scrutinise trading partners (ibid.). Long distance trade is limited. In their sample, McMillan and Woodruff found that 60% of sales were made to firms located in the city. The reason, as one manager said, was that "it is difficult to have accurate information about them (customers at a distance)" (McMillan and Woodruff, 1999a, p.645).

6.2.3. Opportunism and corruption in current business practice

Corruption is not unusual in developing countries, especially in Southeast Asia, but "Vietnam has a reputation for being one of the worst offenders" (Brooks and Brooks, 1995, p.3). One can find corruption almost everywhere, in every activity and every administrative level from low ranked to even top officials. According to a BBC report, a senior member of the Vietnam's ruling Communist Party, Pham The Duyet, has admitted that "there is evidence of corruption among the relatives of figures in the Politburo" (BBC news, 2000). Another Vietnamese top official, vice-chairman of the National Assembly, Mai Thuc Lan, in an interview, compared the current situation in Vietnam with *ghe ruoi* (fly-like scabies). It (the scabies) spreads out over the whole body and causes itching everywhere on the body. (*Thanh nien*, 2000 in VASC). It is common to find that one needs to know 'someone' or bribe somebody to get work

104

done. Parents 'bribe' their children's teachers, students 'bribe' lecturers and university officials, patient's relatives 'bribe' doctors and hospital administrators. The most respected class in Vietnam – medical doctors and teachers, sometimes take bribes and treat their customers and students unfairly. Many people are scared to go to the hospital because they do not have money to 'bribe' the hospital's staff.

Vietnamese describe the current corruption situation as *van hoa phong bi* (envelope culture). People put money into envelopes to bribe others and the popularity of the phenomenon is reflected in the use of the word *van hoa* (culture) in the context. In business, corruption (bribery of officials) is the rule.

Every manager from the three SOEs interviewed said that they had to bribe the customs office almost every time they fulfilled an export or import or export contract. A senior manager of the garment enterprise said:

> "Giving money to the customs office is a must in Vietnam, if you do not give them money, they will cause problems and you will have difficulties in fulfilling orders. I believe every company involved in import or export activities has to do that."

He also stressed the importance of giving money to the customs office: "In this company, every expense has had to be approved and signed by the director or sometime deputy directors. Only bribery expenses, like the one to the customs office, can be decided by managers and staff and reported later." (Mr. Than, head of the administration and personnel department at the garment enterprise).

In the case of the garment industry, Vietnam still needs a quota to export to the European market. Enterprises must bid for their quota and the government body responsible for administering and organising the bid is the Ministry of Commerce. Behind the scenes, problems are the norm and the selling and buying quotas is common practice. A manager from the garment enterprise told me in an interview that:

> "It is very frustrating, last year we had to buy quotas from the "market" with a high price to keep the workforce going. Some companies or people do not have the ability or capacity to meet production targets, but they still got the quota and resold it with a profit".

Corruption can be attributed to poor living standards, and Vietnam is amongst the poorest countries in the world. It could reasonably be argued that when people are so poor, they may do things they would not normally do under better living conditions. However, a purely economic explanation cannot account for the different degrees of corruption in countries with a similar economic standard. Through their comparative study, Blunt, Richards and Wilson (1989) argued that bribery, for example, is linked to particularism and not to low economic resources. They supported their argument by giving evidence that bribery is not uncommon in a very wealthy Asian country, Brunei. Moreover, economic explanations cannot account for the corrupt activities of many officials whose living standard is very high compared to working class people. In Vietnam, as National Assembly vice-chairman, Mai Thuc Lan, pointed out: "There are opinions attributing corruption to low salary, this is only partly true. Some people are already very rich, but still continue to be corrupt." (*Thanh nien*, 2000, the author's translation). This argument is also true in the case of the customs office. Some high ranking customs officials justified the decision to increase customs fees (decree 45/2000/TTLT/BTC-TCHQ) as a measure to reduce the phenomenon of 'giving money' to customs office staff (currently in Vietnam the customs office take 35% of total fees as a source of its earnings). The *Thanh nien* pointed out that the explanation was unrealistic or naïve, and that 'giving money' to the custom office staff had not declined since the decision to increase fees was put into effect.

Many people in Vietnam attribute the spread of corruption to the market economy and capitalism. This is true in the sense that capitalism creates more jobs and more wealth giving officials have more opportunities to be corrupt. Corruption, however, is deeply rooted in Vietnamese history and a part of Vietnamese culture.

In traditional Vietnam, the officeholders (*quan*) enjoyed many privileges. Tran Ngoc Them (1997) pointed out that *quan* received *bong* and *loc* (any form of valuable materials: gifts and money). They got *bong* from people below and *loc* from people above them. *Bong* and *loc* were unofficial incomes. The official income (*luong*-salary) in the book was often smaller than the informal income: *bong* and *loc*. The expression *nhe luong nang bong* (light *luong* or salary, heavy *bong* or unofficial income) told the story (Tran Ngoc Them, 1997). *Quan* were highly corrupt. This fact was reflected in the following popular Vietnamese folk-song that parents sang as a lullaby to their children:

'Con oi nho lay cau nay
Cuop dem la giac cuop ngay la quan'

The song literally translates as: 'baby please remember this sentence: robbers at night time are thugs, robbers in the daytime are *quan*'. *Quan* were considered much more dangerous than thugs, and everyone could see them exploiting people. The saying *mieng quan tron tre* '*quan's* mouth, baby's anus' means that words from quan are unreliable and uncontrolled like a baby's anus.

During the Soviet-style economy, it was difficult for officials to obtain bribes since people were so poor. At the same time, communist ideology and materialist economy made it difficult for officials to get a significant amount of wealth in material terms. Corruption, however, was not unknown. To find products leaking from the state distribution channel onto the open market was not uncommon, and there were cases in which products were distributed 'at leisure', for example, bicycles intended for sale to farming families in Bac Thai Province were sold on the free market instead (Fforde and de Vylder, 1996, p.25). In the materialist economy, stock keepers and managers who were at the junction of distribution benefited most. A widely familiar saying: *giau thu kho, no nha bep* 'warehouse or stock managers are rich, cooks are

106

full' reflected this situation: stock managers and keepers were in 'good' position to 'steal' products. There were also many other examples of corruption, for example the distribution of rice. I myself witnessed people who had to start queuing from as early as three or four o'clock in the morning in order to get rice. The rice was often terrible and full of grit so many people (elders and children) spent hours everyday to taking the grit out of the rice before they could cook it. 'Important people' or people who 'knew' the rice distribution staff, however, did not have to queue and got the best quality rice chosen from the store.

The privileges enjoyed by government officials today are, in essence, not very different from those of the Confucian officeholders Max Weber described nearly 100 years ago. 'Educated' men, who inherited a Confucian way of life, are living according to the concept of unbroken faith. They look primarily to their own, that is, their family's best interests, collude with each other and form networks to exploit the powerless in society. The network is strong and self-enforced because it serves the interests and the ultimate purpose of life (the family) of its members. It is organic in its nature.

6.3. Guerilla capitalism

The last two sections completed our discussion of both the formal and informal aspects of the 'rules of the game' in Vietnam. The formal rules and informal norms form the institutional matrix, as summarised below (Figure 6.1). The formal rules in Vietnam are still incomplete. The formal rules will, step by step, be completed as the 'game' goes on. The informal aspects are cultural norms and are unlikely to change in the near future. The next section examines the type of capitalism associated with the type of 'rules of the game' or institutional framework analysed above to support the argument that the institutional framework in Vietnam, as outlined above, is likely to produce a type of capitalism: 'guerilla capitalism'.

Figure 6.1 The characteristics of the Vietnamese institutional matrix

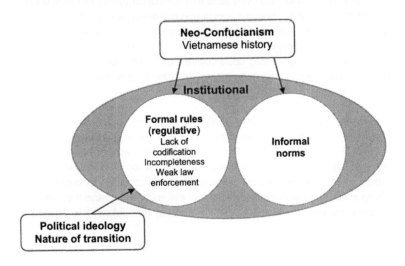

6.3.1. Pattern of firms

One obvious conclusion that can be drawn from the above analysis is that the Vietnamese institutional matrix or the prevailing 'rules of the game' in Vietnam is characterised by high transaction costs and insecure property rights. The consequences of these are not difficult to infer, following the simple logic that "a person who can secure his property, and can keep the fruits of his labours, will try harder" (Redding, 1993, p.232). The above examples show that it is still far from certain that one can keep 'the fruits of one's labours' in Vietnam. The Vietnamese institutional matrix does not create incentives for entrepreneurs. Below are illustrative examples:

Land is an obvious example: no-one will invest his or her money in building a modern, expensive factory if they are uncertain about (or distrusts) government policy regarding the land on which the factory is to be built. In Vietnam, all the land belongs to the state. Entrepreneurs can, however, buy the *right to use the land* for a certain period of time. Currently, private businesses can rent the land directly from the government for up to 50 years. They can also rent from state organisations or enterprises for up to 10 years. Businesses can also re-rent the land from other private businesses or organisations. In an interview, the director of a private firm (Mr. Vinh) gave several clues about the advantages and disadvantages of renting land from different type of owners:

> "Renting land directly from the government is less risky. In addition, you can use the land use right certificate as collateral. Renting from state organisations or private businesses is risky. If, in the future, the state wants the land to do something, you will be in difficult position. They can compensate you but as you know, in Vietnam, the

amount compensated is never compatible to what you've lost. In addition, if you re-rent from a private business, when it goes bankrupt (which is not uncommon), a new boss will take over, and you have to deal with a new person who you do not know, and then you might be in trouble. But why did I not rent land directly from the government? It's not difficult to understand, a lot of paperwork. And, you have to pay a bribe of about 40% of the total fee!".

In making his decision, Mr. Vinh considered both 'formal rules' (e.g. the state might want the land to do something and it will not compensate adequately) and 'informal norms' (he might have to deal with a new boss whom he does not know so he cannot trust him). It is, therefore, easy to understand why Mr. Vinh would not invest a large sum to build a long-term, stable infrastructure on the land.

Another example is a complaint about unstable laws and regulations from a Vietnamese businessman, published in an official Vietnamese newspaper:

"In the last few years, many times we were told (forced unexpectedly without being informed beforehand) to stop exporting or importing (by the authorities) while we were carrying out the contracts. Taxes were increased when the contracts had not been completed. The government authorities calmly give orders without considering the loss to investors. Frequent change of policies is the biggest risk that investors have to bear. These leave investors in a constant state of worry and they dare not put all their money into a business because they have to keep some in reserve for unexpected (sudden) risks."

Source: (Tuoi tre (Youth) Newspaper, 19-2-1995, cited in Tran Ngoc Them, 1997, p.622-623)

It is easy to understand why private firms will not invest heavily in R&D projects if they are uncertain about the future and if they know that when a new product is launched, other firms will immediately copy, manufacture and sell the same kind of product.

Inefficient transaction costs limit transactions, and the absence of effective law enforcement means that firms have to spend significant resources on scrutinising business partners and building trust. Firms also have to pay 'corruption' fees to make transactions go smoothly. Efficient transactions are limited to networks of family members and close friends.

In an environment of insecure property rights and inefficient transaction costs, business firms, as North (1990) pointed out, "will tend to have *short time horizons* and *little fixed capital*, and will tend to be *small scale*. The most profitable businesses may be in trade, redistribution activities or the black market." (p.67, the author's emphasis). This is exactly the current situation in Vietnam. According to Tran Ngoc Hiep, a Vietnamese economic analyst, "companies put no priority on expanding their net worth, fixed assets and equity" but "were chasing immediate profit." (quoted in Le Anh Tu, 1997, p.4). A number of private firms in Vietnam had lifetimes as short as 'zero' years. In 1999 when the government issued new regulations about VAT, a number of 'firms' were established just to obtain VAT sheets, and resell them for a profit. Those firms disappeared after a just few day! (see for example, *Vietnam Economic Times*, 1999 and *Nguoi Lao Dong*, 1999).

6.3.2. The internal structure of the firm

The above analysis demonstrates that the institutional matrix in Vietnam (the rules of the game) is likely to develop a pattern of firms characterised by *short time horizons, little fixed capital,* and *small scale.* Extending this analysis of institutions to the internal structure of the firm, we know that the institutional environment in Vietnam is characterised by insecure property rights and high transaction costs. Transaction cost economic theorists like Williamson and Ouchi would argue that in a high transaction cost environment (inefficient market) there will be vertical integration. Firms will choose the 'make' instead of the 'buy' decision and as a result, large corporations (hierarchy) will be formed to avoid 'unnecessary' transactions. This section briefly describes Williamson's market/ hierarchy reasoning and the 'embeddedness' perspective.

Granovetter (1985) argued that it is the nature of personal relations embedded in economic transactions that matter. He criticised Williamson's market/ hierarchy dichotomy by pointing out that the conception held unrealistic assumptions of social actors. Granovetter argued that Williamson's analysis, with its strong Hobbesian flavour, suffered from the problem of under – and over – socialised assumption of social actors. In a market/ hierarchy concept the firm (or hierarchy in Williamson's term) resembles Hobbes's over-socialised sovereign state while the 'market' resembles Hobbes's *state of nature* (Granovetter, 1985, p.494-495). The efficacy of the hierarchical power within the firm is overplayed and this underlined an over-socialised assumption of social actors (Granovetter, 1985). The 'market' is implicitly assumed to be atomised and anonymous – an under-socialised conception that "neglects the role of social relations amongst individuals in different firms in bringing order to economic life." (ibid p.495). He also claimed that "both order *and* disorder, honesty *and* malfeasance have more to do with structures of such relations than they do with organisational form." (p.502-503). He, accordingly proposed that researchers should "pay careful and systemic attention to the actual patterns of personal relations by which economic transitions are carried out." (p504).

Empirical evidence does not always support Williamson's thesis and the Vietnamese case is one example. Given the high transaction cost nature of the business environment in Vietnam, transaction cost theorists would predict that there would be vertical integration amongst firms. McMillan and Woodruff (1999a) took the transaction cost approach to study business transactions in Vietnam and found that Vietnamese firms remained small, despite transaction costs being high. Since the absence of vertical integration in a market characterised by high transaction costs in Vietnam does not follow Williamson's standard model, McMillan and Woodruff (1999a) explained this phenomenon by reference to capital and capital market-related factors. They argued that "to buy out a customer or supplier in order to solve a specific-assets problem would mean expanding in a discrete jump, for which financing would typically be unavailable (in the Vietnamese context)" (p.644). They implicitly predicted that Vietnamese firms would eventually vertically integrate (e.g. buy-out and merge) into large organisations to avoid high transaction costs when financial conditions allowed them to do so! Their argument may not yet be empirically challenged since the private Vietnamese firms are still under-capitalised.

The evidence from Chinese-style businesses in Hong Kong and Taiwan, however, rejects the transaction cost argument. The Taiwanese case, for example, clearly does not support Williamson's vertical integration thesis (Hamilton and Biggart, 1988). Despite the fact that the Taiwanese economy in general and Taiwanese firms in particular has been successful for years, firms are still limited in size:

> "Although there are exceptions, the small to medium-sized single unit firm is so much the rule in Taiwan that when a family business becomes successful the pattern of investment is not to attempt vertical integration in order to control the marketplace, but rather to diversify by starting a series of unrelated firms that share neither account books or management." (Orru, Hamilton and Biggart, 1997, p.125).

Limited and bounded trust (trust is not extended beyond the family and the closest friends) is widely accepted as the major source of explanation for this small and family – controlled type of business (see, Redding, 1993; Whitley, 1992; and Orru, Biggart and Hamilton, 1997).

With regard to the internal structure of the Vietnamese firm, we agree with Granovetter (1985) that if opportunism, distrust and malfeasance are rife in economic life, "there are not necessarily more transactions between firms than within" (p.495). Therefore, if a business environment is characterised by high transaction costs between firms (caused by opportunism), it is also characterised by high 'co-operation' costs within the firm. Given the fact that in Vietnam trust is not extended beyond the family and close friends, and the relatively low degree of co-operation, Vietnamese private businesses are unlikely to leave important business decisions to 'outsiders'. The firm may grow larger, but it is likely that it will continue, for a long time to come, to be controlled and run by the family or close friends as is the case with the Overseas Chinese in Southeast and East Asia (Redding, 1993). The evidence about the management problems of the Vietnamese SOEs presented in Chapter 9 supports the argument on the *family structure* of the Vietnamese firms and Granovetter's embeddedness.

In summary, the institutional matrix in Vietnam is more likely to produce, or be most 'suitable' or *ideal* for, a special form of capitalism, *guerilla* capitalism characterised by firms with *short time horizons, little fixed capital, small scale, and family-controlled*.

Part 3: The Vietnamese state-owned enterprises during the reform period

The previous section established and verified the proposition about the form of capitalism and the *ideal type* of business – the small-scale, little fixed capital, short time horizon and family-controlled firm – found in Vietnam.

This third section provides empirical evidence about the behaviour of SOEs. These were established in Vietnam and other former socialist countries on the Soviet-style development model and were, by and large, the products of a social event rather than a market-based rationality. Vietnamese SOEs, to a great extent, diverge from the ideal type. Many of them are large in size with significant amount of fixed capitals and more importantly, are not owned and run by the family but by officials. This section presents our findings about the behaviour of Vietnamese SOEs with a reference to the ideal type, and the peculiar features of the economic reform process in Vietnam.

Chapters 7 and 8 are concerned with the structure of SOEs. Chapter 7 focuses on the authority relations within SOEs while Chapter 8 is concerned with industrial governance, the relationship between government bureaux and SOEs. Chapter 9 focuses on research findings and discusses 'management problems' whilst Chapter 10 analyses what is called 'embedded materialism'. The argument runs that Marx's labour theory of value, with its emphasis on materialism, was the building block of the old system and still exercises a great influence in Vietnam. The current 'rules of the game' (i.e. payment policy and incentive systems) applied to SOEs are still heavily material-orientated. We argue that this embedded materialism either accounts for or makes worse some of the problems presented in Chapter 9. Based upon these research findings and the analysis contained in the rest of the monograph, Chapter 11 provides several suggestions about how to overcome some of the problems associated with SOEs and improve their performance.

Chapter 7: Authority relations within Vietnamese SOEs

This chapter, which presents the findings of research into authority relations is in three parts. The first part presents the data collection methods and assessments used in the present research, the second our findings about authority relations in the three enterprises studied. The chapter concludes with a discussion that places the authority relations found in the SOEs studied in a broad societal context.

7.1. Research process and assessment methods

The research process and assessment method was partially guided by a study of six Chinese SOEs carried out by John Child and his MBA students (Child and Lu, 1990). Child and Lu (1990) investigated the authority relations within and between Chinese SOEs and the related government bureaux. They examined the extent of decentralisation in the six Chinese SOEs by investigating 48 key decisions concerning the establishment of the hierarchical management levels authorised to make these decisions. Child and Lu (1990)'s research on decision making in the six Chinese SOEs followed the assessment method from the well-known research programme, the 'Aston Studies'. The original Aston Studies on the 'centralisation' dimension of organisation structure covered 37 major decisions in organisations. Given the complexity of industrial governance in China, Child and Lu (1990) increased the number of decisions investigated in the original Aston Studies to make a total of forty-eight decisions.

The Aston Studies have been highly influential in organisation studies, and have been replicated many times. Starbuck (1981), for example, referred to them as "one of the most important clusters of organisational research during the last 20 years-possibly the most important cluster" (quoted in Greenwood & Devine, 1997, [1]). There have also been many critiques of this research programme for its employment of a mechanical and functional approach to organisation studies. Although different views about the central thesis underlying the research exist, the Aston Studies have provided a well-defined set of language to describe and compare organisations. The present research, bearing the interpretative approach in mind, was not intended to replicate the Aston Studies, but use the instrument as part of the data collection process. This enabled the easy comparison of authority relations in Vietnamese enterprises with others elsewhere available in the literature. Given the similarity between the industrial governance policies pursued by Vietnam and China, the use of Child and Lu (1990)'s instrument allowed a comparison of authority relations in Vietnamese and Chinese SOEs and in other transitional countries.

This research examined only 38 of the 48 decisions investigated by Child and Lu (1990). This was because some decisions investigated by Child and Lu were not relevant to the present research (Child and Lu carried out their research in the late 1980s when the SOE reform programme in China had not gone as far as reform in Vietnam in 2000). Some decisions included in Child and Lu's investigations are irrelevant in Vietnam, for example decision number 47 in Child and Lu (1990, p.41) which aims to establish the lowest hierarchical position "able to represent management in discussions with trade union leaders". This question was based on a Western concept of trade unionism whereas the concept and the role of trade unions in Vietnamese state organisations (probably as in China) are significantly different. The 38 decisions investigated in the present study covered all key decision areas of an enterprise and can be compared with Child and Lu (1990)'s studies and other Aston-related studies. The complete list of the decision areas investigated is given in Appendix 1.

The Aston data was generated by interviews with different management levels in the enterprises and by an analysis of documents from both the enterprises and the government concerning the management of SOEs. In order to make such a comparison, we have tried to follow the procedures set by the Aston Studies and Child and Lu (1990) exactly. The aim of the data collection was to establish "the lowest hierarchical role in which the incumbent could authorise action to be taken without this requiring further ratification" (Child and Lu, 1990, p.24).

In addition to the Aston data on the centralisation of decision-making, data from interviews, observations and government documents are also used to establish and verify various propositions about structures and authority relations in the Vietnamese SOEs. We also examine the role of the Communist Party Committee and trade union within SOEs.

7.2. The Aston data of centralisation of decision making

This section presents our findings on the *Aston* 'centralisation' dimension of the three investigated enterprises. The overall conclusion was that these enterprises are highly centralised compared not only to Western organisations but also to their Chinese counterparts. The data coding procedure followed exactly the Aston Studies and Child and Lu (1990). Hierarchical levels of the enterprise are numbered as 5, 4, 3, 2, 1, 0 and the same coding has been used in the tables and figures associated with this line of analysis. The keys to hierarchical levels are given below.

Key to hierarchical levels:
5 = Above enterprise director (i.e. bureau or board with non-executive majority)
4 = Enterprise director or enterprise management committee
3 = Head of several departments (e.g. deputy director)
2 = Head of department, workshop or functional area
1 = Work group leader or supervisor
0 = Operative or functional specialist (e.g. buyer)

114

7.2.1. The shoe enterprise

Figure 7.1 shows the distribution of decisions by hierarchical level of the shoe enterprise. Some 28 decisions were made by the director herself. Only eight decisions were left to deputy directors and one decision to department levels. The decisions 'delegated' by the director to her subordinates (deputies and at departmental level) mainly concerned technical related activities. The majority of decisions delegated to deputy directors and department heads were in the area of production. All the decisions involving personnel and transactions were made by the director herself. The only decision that head of departments could make was to allocate work to be done amongst available workers or staff.

Figure 7.1. Distribution of decisions by hierarchical level – shoe enterprise

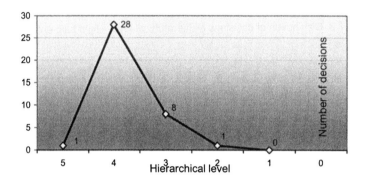

7.2.2. The garment enterprise

Figure 7.2. Distribution of decisions by hierarchical level – garment enterprise

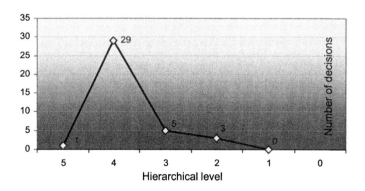

115

Figure 7.2 shows the distribution of decisions by hierarchical level in the garment enterprise. As in the shoe enterprise, the director himself made 29 out of a total of 38 decisions investigated. Three decisions were delegated to deputy directors and three down to department level. Like the shoe enterprise, decisions delegated to deputy directors and department level involved production issues.

7.2.3. The light bulb enterprise

The light bulb enterprise was even more centralised than the other two enterprises (Figure 7.3). Thirty-four decisions were made by the director and only three decisions delegated. The three decisions delegated were:

> The allocation of work among workers in a department or production unit;
> The maintenance schedule and procedure;
> The deputy's right to make decisions in the absence of the director.

Figure 7.3. Distribution of decisions by hierarchical level – light bulb enterprise

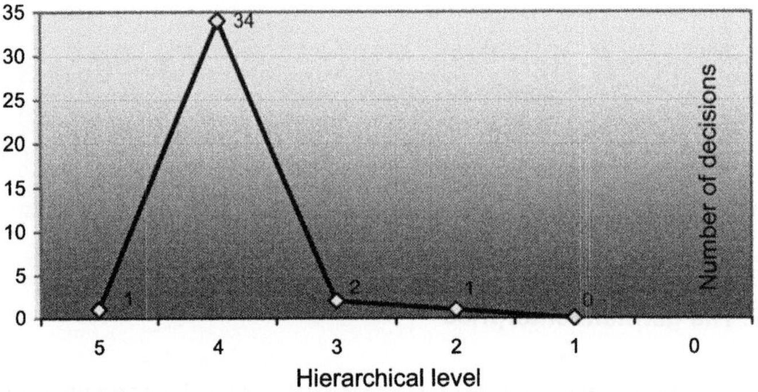

7.2.4. Overall

Table 7.1 summarises the distribution of decisions by hierarchical level and the average figure over the three enterprises. On average, 30 out of 38 decisions were made by the enterprise's director, and only two delegated to department level.

Table 7.1. Distribution of decisions by hierarchical levels.

Number of decisions from a total of 38 delegated to each of five hierarchical levels

Enterprise	No. of decisions made by different hierarchical levels				
	(5)*	(4)	(3)	(2)	(1)
The shoe enterprise	1	28	8	1	0
The garment enterprise	1	29	5	3	0
The light bulb enterprise	1	34	2	1	0
Average (approximately)	1	30	5	2	0

7.2.5. Comparison with China

Given the fact that Vietnam is a developing country with collectivist cultural traits, it should be no surprise to discover that Vietnamese enterprises are more centralised than their Western counterparts. What is interesting is that Vietnamese SOEs are much more centralised than their Chinese counterparts, as emerged from Child and Lu's research (Child and Lu, 1990). It is important to note that the size (number of employees) of each of the enterprises in the present research was comparable to that in the Chinese cases studied by Child and Lu. In fact, the Vietnamese SOEs investigated were relatively larger in size than the Chinese SOEs. In our three enterprises most of the decisions (an average of 30 out of the total of 38) were made by the director, a far greater number than in the Chinese cases (about 17 decisions on average) in Child and Lu's research. In addition, on average only two decisions (compared to around 17 in the Chinese case) were delegated to the departmental or functional level. Figure 7.4 shows a clear difference in the distribution pattern of decisions by hierarchical levels between the Vietnamese and Chinese SOEs.

Figure 7.4. Distribution of decisions by hierarchical level in Chinese and Vietnamese SOEs

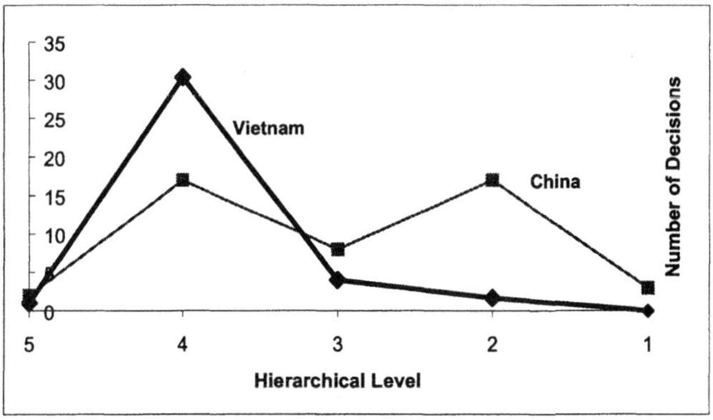

Note: The line denoting the distribution of decisions in the Chinese case in this figure is adapted and redrawn from Child and Lu (1990).

7.3. The Central Domain

7.3.1. Limitations of the Aston Studies' assessment method

Although the data from our study shows a clear and comparable picture of the centralisation dimension in the three SOEs, it tells only part of the story of authority relations in Vietnam. The Aston Studies, although replicated in different countries and different kind of organisations, underlined a Western (or at least Anglo-Saxon) concept of organisations, that is that individuals, depending on their positions on the organisation, can act freely and are encouraged to do so within a relatively well codified boundary. Thus, it is relatively clear what one can and cannot do. This feature of Western society can be observed in all aspects of social organisation from the family to political systems. The Aston research programme was designed in this spirit.

Because of the 'Western nature' of the Aston Studies, some difficulties were encountered in generating Aston data during the data collection process. Decisions were attached to lower hierarchical levels in the enterprises based not on absolute criteria, but on reasonableness. In the enterprises studied, no clear boundaries were set for the lower hierarchical levels in which juniors could act freely. For example, the head of the planning and production management department of the shoe enterprise said in an interview:

> "In principle or on paper, the director allows me to organise my own staff in the department. But if the director wants to change, she can do it, of course... Because she is the boss, she has the right to do it. In my department, I can assign and organise people to do the work, but mostly the 'normal' work. The people who have direct contact with the suppliers (buyers) were actually decided by the boss. I am the one who 'assigned' them, but the boss gave the green-light before that."

A deputy director (responsible for production and marketing) said:

> "In Vietnam, deputy directors are only assistants (*nguoi giup viec*) to the director. If the director really trusts a deputy director, he can delegate and allow them to make some decisions. In this enterprise, I and the Director worked together for a long time when we were still workers in this factory. She trusts me and delegated some decisions to me. But speaking of delegations, I can make some buying decisions (e.g. to buy from different suppliers). It is O.K if the price is the same or lower. If the price increase I have to ask her. In general, if there is a change in suppliers or prices, you need to ask or should ask her. Also, the director sometimes tells you to buy from that suppler rather than from this supplier for some reason, for example, because she has personal relationships with that supplier."

> "Last month when she went to Canada three weeks for a Trade Fair, do you know that the enterprise had to spend a lot of money on faxes? Although, I can sign some decisions on her behalf, many things still have to be decided by her."

As the above quotations indicate, it was not always clear when those in lower hierarchical levels could or couldn't make certain decisions *without this requiring further ratification*. The research findings point to the limitations of the Aston Studies both in terms of its conception and its empirical operability. Our findings also suggest that the big difference between the distribution of decisions by hierarchical levels in the Child and Lu Chinese SOEs study and the Vietnamese SOEs in this study could have partly resulted from the bias in Child and Lu's research design, in which Western pre-conceptions predominated.

7.3.2. The Central Domain
In order to supplement the decision making data and gain further insights and offer a more comprehensive interpretation of authority relations in Vietnamese enterprises,

this section discusses the nature of authority relations in Vietnam in general. This method allows us to make some generalisations about management in Vietnam as a whole.

As mentioned in the chapter on Vietnamese culture, Hamilton's (1984) distinction between *patria potestas* and *xiao* (*hieu* in Vietnamese) provides insights into the logic of patriarchal domination in Confucian societies. *Xiao* represents a domination principle resting on duties prescribed to positions, the essence of *xiao* being to be dutiful. *Patria potestas* allowed the institutionalisation of power in Western societies and organisations that rest on an acceptance of boundary constraints and stress order. The acceptance of boundary constraints supports an atomic bureaucratic structuring principle. *Xiao* stresses roles, the superiors act out the role of a superior, subordinates act out the role of a subordinate.

In a family, parents have a duty to take care and educate their children. Children in turn have a duty to obey and respect their parents. Both parents and children expect to live up to the responsibilities of their roles in life in the absence of commands, or even in the absence of someone to command (Hamilton, 1984). Children and parents are not *'independent'* individuals. There is no clear boundary within which children can act freely without paying attention to their role as a son or daughter. Parents decide or at least play an active part in almost all important decisions concerning their children, ranging from which clothes to buy, which friends they play with to which university they might enter.

The concept of *xiao* applied not only to the family but to other social contexts (Hamilton, 1984). In any organisation, whether political or economic, the same principle is applied to the superior-subordinate relationship. *There are no clearly defined boundaries within which a subordinate may act freely without paying attention to his or her role as a subordinate.* Power does not pass down to the lower levels of the organisation in the Western meaning of it. The head of the organisation, like the father in a family, is legitimised to make any decisions concerning the function of the organisation. Subordinates can make their business decisions in certain circumstance depending on the nature of the superior-subordinate relationship (e.g. level of trust), but this does not mean that subordinates *have the right* to make those decisions. This structure of domination pervades every type of organisation from the family to political to business organisations.

From the study of polity in three Confucian societies: China, Korea and Vietnam, Woodside (1998) observed that there is a shared feature amongst these countries: the very strong sense of a political 'centre'. There has always been a 'Central Domain' that has the right to make decisions that in a Western country would have been left to regional authorities. The 'Central Domain' has its roots in the Confucian classics and is thus more or less peculiar to these societies. Woodside correctly criticised work on traditional political systems in those countries that failed to acknowledge the 'Central Domain'.

"There is a Western temptation to associate "traditional" kingdoms with decentralised medieval polities consisting of dispersed dominions and relatively autonomous local lordships, and "modern" states with more centred political systems that have absorbed the formally autonomous lordships; the "Central Domain" myth makes this work very poorly in Confucian Asia outside of Japan" (p.198).

Woodside also pointed out that "the administrative term in nineteenth-century China and Vietnam that Western scholars so freely translate as 'province' (*sheng* in Chinese, *tinh* in Vietnamese) really means a branch "department" or a branch 'secretariat' of the central government" (p.215).

This feature of the administrative system has not changed in today's Vietnam. The provincial administration is actually a branch department of the central government. All important decisions, especially those concerning personnel matters, are decided by the 'centre'.

The 'Central Domain' is institutionalised in the administrative system in Vietnam. Documents concerning external transactions are invalid without the signature of the head, or deputy head at least, of the organisation. This administrative procedure is applied to almost every type of organisation in the country. In the universities, for example, the signature of the head of department or faculty is not considered valid in any external transactions (e.g. appointing students or introducing students to a company for a placement).

In the context of SOEs, the 'Central Domain' is explicitly stated in the State Enterprise Law, issued in 1995, which explicitly considered the director as the 'Central Domain'. His role and responsibility is similar to that of a family head. The director has the right to make any decision regarding the business activities (within those areas left to the enterprise level, of course).

Deputy directors have the right to "help the director manage (*dieu hanh*)[*] the enterprise with respect to the allocation and delegation of the director, and are responsible to the director for tasks that the director has allocated and delegated" (Item 39.4). Deputy directors can make decisions that are delegated to them, but these are only routine decisions concerning logistics, as the term *dieu hanh* indicates.

The Law clearly considered functional departments as secretariat units as specified in Item 39.6: "the function of administrative departments and functional departments is to suggest and carry out secretarial work for the director in order to manage and *dieu hanh* work" (Law of State Enterprise). According to this Item, functional departments are not delegated to make any management decisions.

Institutionalised patriarchy can also be found in the Law of Private Enterprise. According to the Vietnamese Law of Private Enterprise (issued in 1990 with amendments in 1994), the owner of a private enterprise (not hired executive or

120

director) is the person responsible for *every* business activity of the enterprise. The owner (not hired director or any other staff) is the person who represents the enterprise in court or in any business dispute (Item 19, Law of Private Enterprise, 1997).

The enterprise is considered as a family, the family's head is responsible for making every decision and, on behalf of the family, for any external transaction or dispute.

7.3.3. Formalisation and centralisation

Written documents, such as detailed job descriptions or detailed contract terms, are hardly ever found in Vietnamese enterprises. However in the three case studies two enterprises (the shoe and garment enterprises) had written documents about job descriptions and report procedures. The main reason was that they were required to do so by ISO-9002 (a quality assurance certification). The shoe company was awarded ISO-9002 in 1999 and the garment enterprise, at the time of this research, was preparing for the certificate. Having the ISO certificate is fashionable in Vietnam. Before the appearance of ISO-9002, there were no written job descriptions or detailed areas of responsibility.

To qualify for the ISO-9002 certificate, these two enterprises were "formalised", but the degree of formalisation is still limited. As one manager said in an interview:

> "In order to get the certificate, we had to write out job descriptions of each department, each work group and in some case each individual. But the written documents are based on what we have been doing and are very general".

As a requirement of the ISO 9002 (or so the author was told), the author was not allowed to access the shoe enterprise documents. However, the author was given a copy of job descriptions in the garment enterprise. Mr. Tung, deputy head of the department, who was responsible for compiling the documents said:

> "The documents are written based on what we have been doing. They are very general...It is possible to define the areas of departments and managers, but it is very difficult to assess the performance of a department or a manager. They (departments and managers) cannot decide important decisions in their areas of responsibility. They depend on each other and of course on the boss. It is difficult to set out the performance criteria of a department manager, for example. His work depends much on other departments; also he is not free to make decisions."

Box 7.1 (below) provides an example of a job description from the garment enterprise as a requirement for the ISO 9002 certificate. In addition, from observations in the shoe enterprise, the author found that managers there did not believe that ISO 9002 made any difference in terms of the management and organisation culture within the enterprise. The light bulb enterprise was not preparing for ISO certification. A key person of the enterprise said in an interview: "We do not need ISO-9002 at the moment, as you see you can 'buy' it for about VND300 million. Our products are well known in Vietnam, we do not need such a thing, at the present, at least." Our findings on employee attitudes towards quality certification in Vietnam is in the same spirit as Kirkbride and Westwood's (1998) findings about the purpose of building a corporate culture in Hong Kong companies. The intention behind cultural change or ISO certification is to cultivate an image for *external* audiences. ISO 9002 appeared to have had little effect on the *internal* management (e.g. formalisation) of the shoe enterprise.

Box 7.1. Responsibilities and rights of the head of the administrative & personnel department

➢ Is the person who as an assistant to the director is responsible for implementing tasks in the units as well as managing (dieu hanh) the activities of the enterprise according to functions and tasks assigned. Sum up the (current) situations of the enterprise.

➢ To compile (construct) and submit to the director (for approval) working rules, procedures of the department and detailed tasks of each individual, to assure a lean and effective machine (the unit); compile and submit to the director legal documents, in order to carry out the tasks of the units and other activities of the enterprise well.

➢ To lead and manage the unit to obey (or follow) the aims, policies and laws of the government; to take care and protect the rights of the members (of the unit); responsible for working protection, work safety, fire safety of the area of the unit.

➢ To be directly responsible for tasks of personnel organisation and administration policies (about personnel matters). Tasks of external and internal relationships and responsible to the director when a unit member makes mistakes, or does not fulfil his/her tasks.

➢ Has the right to allocate general activities among the unit, comment and rate, propose rewards or punishments, training, propose pay rises, involve (take part) in the recruitment committee and disciplinary committee of the enterprise.

Source: from the garment enterprise documents

When asked about the codification of the manager's job (e.g. duty, responsibility and performance criteria) a manager of the trade department (at the garment enterprise) who has a Western MBA degree said:

> "We do not have the right to make decisions, you see, some people in my department are very incompetent. They (higher levels and the Personnel Department) ep xuong (put or press down) people who do not know how to do the jobs. In Vietnam, management is very complicated, you have to be keep a balance between many different relationships."

When asked about his responsibility as a department head, the head of the planning and material department of the shoe enterprise said:

> "How can I take responsibility for the performance of the department since I am not allowed to make decisions on supply matters. In order to fulfil time requirement of several orders, we did try to buy a certain amount of materials from a private firm. The quality is the same or even better, the price is lower than the usual one. But after

that she (the director) asked me to come to her office and I was talked to (di).... Also how can I take the responsibility if I am not free to allocate work within the department." (interview December 1999).

The above quotations demonstrate how culture, and in particular social and authority relations, exclude formalisation or codification.

7.3.4. Party, trade union and management – all in one piece

Further insights into the structures, and especially authority relations within Vietnamese SOEs, may be gained by examining the role played by the Communist Party Committee and trade union in the enterprise.

One of the particular features of management in socialist countries is the powerful position of the Communist Party organisation in the enterprise. During the Soviet-style economy, the Communist Party Committee operating within the organisation took care of almost everything from shop floor to housing and schooling for employees and their families. Since the collapse of communism, The Communist Party (CP) has played no role in the business enterprises in the former socialist countries in Eastern Europe. However, the picture is different in Vietnam and China, which are still ruled by the Communist Party. In these countries, CP Committees are still in place in almost every state organisation, including SOEs, although the role of the CP Committee in Vietnam's state enterprises (also in China see various studies carried out by Boisot, Child and their students), has been significantly reduced by the reform process. In principle, the role of the Party has shifted from direct involvement in the economic sphere to being confined to guarding ideological and political correctness.

Scholars with a Western way of thinking have often seen Eastern institutional arrangements, from governmental level to economic organisations, as ambiguous or 'hidden' structures. A Western concept of an institutional arrangement with its assumption of atomic, separate and independent parts is quite unlike the relationship between management, party and trade union within Vietnamese SOEs.

The author's observation and interviews in the three enterprises gave an interesting picture of institutional arrangements between management, party and trade union, one that was quite consistent with the Vietnamese traditional concept of governance: a strong sense of 'Central Domain', harmony and oneness. Western scholars such as Child and Boisot saw the existence of party organisations within the Chinese enterprises a source of potential conflict with the management, and indeed conflict could occur between party, management and trade union at a particular case or particular time (e.g. the early period of transition). In the present research, based on observation of three Vietnamese SOEs, party, management and trade union are absorbed into one, both in conceptual terms and also in personnel. The enterprise configures towards the traditional form of organisation which, to some extent, resembles the Vietnamese family in which there is a 'Central Domain' (the family head) who leads and controls both economic and ethical aspects.

There may be conflicts within an enterprise, but they are resolved within the enterprise: it is an internal or 'family' matter. During interviews, three senior party members from all three enterprises showed their pride in their enterprises and in the fact that party, management and trade union had worked well together to 'prevent' employees from taking complaints to external authorities.

The 'Central Domain' and oneness are clearly indicated by the fact that: in all three cases, the director was also party secretary (head of the party committee in the enterprise).

> All deputy directors were also in the Party Central Committee.
> All the people with management positions at all level were party members.
> Most of the people holding key management positions at the top or department level simultaneously held key positions in the party organisation.
> The trade union leader was a member of the Party Central Committee.

It is an unstated law that management positions from deputy department head upwards must be occupied by a party member. The convergence of party and management, according to the people inside, is easy to understand. A member of the Standing Party Central Committee observed that:

"In principle, party members are those who are the most ethical and competent. Management requires those ethical and competent people and therefore, it is logical if someone who is the head of a department should also be the head of the Party Committee of that department. In Vietnam, the party leads, if someone is competent, but is not a party member, he should not be given a management position. The question is why he is not a party member? There are two possibilities, first, he does not meet the criteria to become a party member (if he is competent, there must be some ethical problem), so that he does not meet the criteria of a manager. Second, if he is competent but does not want to be a party member that means he does not believe in the direction and the lead of the party and as you know, Vietnam is led by the Communist Party, so he should not be given a management position."

Thus, it is not surprising that the same people show up to management and party meetings. The management team and the Party Committee are not, to a great extent, different parties or institutions. Normally, the party is not involved in management decisions, but this does not mean that the party is not powerful. It is powerful when it matters. In any Vietnamese state organisation, from government departments to economic units like SOEs, important personnel decisions are made by Communist Party organisations. The directors of SOEs are appointed by party organisations so, for example, although the shoe enterprise is under the direct supervision of the Hanoi Industrial Department, the director is appointed by the Hanoi Communist Party Committee. The director could also be obliged to move to other positions if required by the higher levels of the party organisation. At the time of the data collection process, the now former director of the garment enterprise left the enterprise and was appointed to a government position to fulfil a new duty assigned by the party.

124

Within the enterprise power resides in one person, the boss of the enterprise. This power comes from two sources, the party and management so it could be said that a boss has two kinds of tools, and can use them as and when necessary.

The example below illustrates the power of the boss as a party secretary:

> Mr. T was a deputy head of the import-export department. According to a deputy-director, he was very competent but saw no prospect of promotion because the head of department was still young. He decided to move to another enterprise where one of his relatives was the director. It was difficult for the shoe enterprise to keep him, since employment contracts in Vietnam are not *codified*. In an interview, he told me that he really wanted to move and did not care about economic losses as a consequence of the transfer. But the problem was that the director did not want him to go. One of the reasons was that she was aware of the potential problem of trade secrets leaking to Mr. T's new enterprise, since Mr. T had been working in the shoe enterprise for a number of years. She decided to make the move difficult on party grounds (according to Mr. T). He could move, but if the director insisted he would lose his party membership on ethical grounds (e.g. not being loyal to the enterprise). If he lost his party membership, he would not be appointed and promoted to a management position in his new enterprise. After several months, the director finally decided to let him go. A deputy director told me that the director wanted to make the move difficult to set an example to others, to show that people could not move without any conditions.

The concept, as well as the practice, of trade unions in Vietnamese SOEs is very different from in Western societies. In conceptual terms as defined in Trade Union Law, the trade union is a representative organisation of labourers led by the Communist Party (Trade Union Law, Item 1.1). In practice trade unions, as observed during the course of this research, are responsible mainly for *ritual* and charity activities such as visiting staff who are ill, helping staff arrange funerals for their relatives and organising staff holiday trips. The operating fund is partly funded by member fees but most of the funding comes from the enterprise, with the director, of course, deciding the amount to be contributed.

Trade unions, management and party are complementary rather than opposing or interlocking forces. If an employee is not happy about a particular issue, he or she can talk to a trade union manager. The trade union manager will then explain things to the employee or report to the director. Trade unions, therefore, serve a function in helping the director take care of employees. Almost all trade union managers are full-time employees of the enterprise. They get some extra pay for taking on extra work in the trade union, depending on the policy of the particular enterprise. There are full-time posts, the number depending on the size of the enterprise. In principle, full-time posts are officially paid for by trade union organisations, but they are entitled to receive a bonus, rewards and other benefits as if they are employees of the enterprise (Trade Union Law, Item 19).

The following quotation from the trade union chief of the shoe enterprise sums up the role of trade unions within Vietnamese SOEs:

"The trade union in our enterprise is working well, we have organised many activities: collected funds for employees with financial hardship, organised holiday trips for employees and so on. The director gives strong support to the trade union. The enterprise pays me the same salary level as the deputy director... In general, trade unions are nominal in Vietnam. Trade unions do not work well if they are not supported by the enterprise director."

The above findings and picture of relationships between management, party and trade unions are consistent with the authority pattern of a Confucian society. The strong sense of oneness and 'Central Domain' is as fresh as ever. To some extent, this structure of the Vietnamese SOEs resembles the *ideal* monarch described by Hobbes in his *Leviathan*. The director of the enterprise resembles a Christian king able to unite both civil and ecclesiastical powers in his own person and become both 'civil sovereign' of his people (the director as a chief executive) and 'supreme pastor' (the party secretary). This comparison is, of course, crude. The director of an SOE is powerful within the enterprise, but he or she is also subject to external control from two sources: the party and the state.

Chapter 8: The industrial governance of SOEs

As Chapter 5 revealed, one of the key elements of the SOE reform programme in Vietnam was to make prices matter, an objective that has to a great extent been achieved. Commercial SOEs now, in principal, operate on a profit-maximisation basis and compete with other types of enterprises (e.g. joint-ventures, foreign owned and private enterprises) in the market place. The enterprise reform programme in Vietnam is now focusing on how to run the SOEs to ensure that they are profitable.

In the last chapter, we explained how many important management decisions have been delegated to the enterprise level, so that the enterprise director has the right to make important decisions regarding the management of the enterprise. There are, however, big differences between the 'right to do' and having the 'resources to do it'. Findings from this research indicate that the relationship between Vietnamese SOEs and the various government departments is much more complicated than the picture that emerged from the Aston Studies' instrument.

The governance structure of the current Vietnamese private enterprise is very simple. Almost all, if not all, private businesses in Vietnam are small and managed directly by their owners. Private businesses are, therefore, free from the problems arising from the separation of ownership and management. In a large private corporation in capitalist countries the situation is different, so that ownership and management are kept separate. The governance structure of large Western corporations can be examined through the principal/agent theory of Western management literature (briefly described earlier) but this is not the case with Vietnamese SOEs, whose governance structure differs both from large Western organisations and from Vietnamese private owner-managed businesses. This is because state ownership in Vietnam is very complicated. Everyone (director, managers, employees and various government bodies) could be said to be the owner of the enterprise indeed, there may be no 'real' owner at all. The following section presents evidence about the nature of the relationship between the government and the enterprise in Vietnam.

Different types of SOEs have different governance structures. Administratively, most SOEs belong to two broad categories: central and local. Central SOEs are under the direct supervision of the central government through, for example, different ministries. Local SOEs are under the direct supervision of local governments through different provincial bureaux. SOEs are also classified as both those with boards of directors (e.g. state corporations established following Decisions 90 and 91) and those without board of directors (non-board enterprises). Thus the shoe enterprise in the present research is a local (Hanoi) and non-board enterprise. The garment and light bulb enterprises, on the other hand, belong to two centrally-owned state corporations established according to Decision-91. The next section presents the formal governance structure of the various types of Vietnamese SOEs followed by our findings on the nature of governance structure.

8.1. The governance structure – a formal framework

The administrative framework in the Vietnamese state enterprises is, in general, very similar to that of the Chinese SOEs presented in Child and Lu (1990). SOEs are directly or indirectly under the control of various government bodies, although the framework is slightly different for different types of SOEs. Below are brief descriptions of the different frameworks applied to different types of SOEs.

8.1.1. Central SOEs

Figure 8.1 shows the administrative framework governing a typical central industrial SOE. The Central Industrial Ministry is the direct supervisory body of the SOEs. It is called *bo chu quan* in Vietnamese, which literally means 'owner-managed ministry'. The Central Industrial Ministry is the body that 'takes care of' the enterprise, being entrusted by the government to act as if it were the owner of the enterprise. The ministry is delegated to make important decisions regarding its management including the appointment of the director and deputy directors, approval of its annual plans, and investments. It is also responsible for regular monitoring of the enterprise.

Figure 8.1. The administrative framework in Vietnamese central SOEs

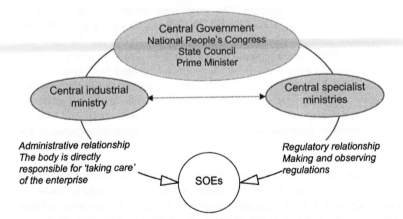

Important central specialist ministries are the Ministry of Finance, Ministry of Trade, Ministry of Labour, Invalids and Social Affairs and the Ministry of Planning and Investment. These ministries are responsible for making regulations and ensuring enterprises follow those regulations. The Ministry of Finance, for example, is responsible for ensuring that regulations concerning taxation and other financial and accounting matters are observed. The Ministry of Labour, Invalids and Social Affairs is responsible for regulations on labour issues: salary policy, employment policy and other labour related matters and the Ministry of Trade is responsible for making regulations and controlling issues regarding trade matters, especially, import-export areas. The Ministry of Trade has the power to grant export quotas for a number of export products, including various garment products. Depending on the type of businesses in which it is operating, the enterprise may also be under the purview of other specialist ministries such as the Ministry of Technology and Environment.

8.1.2. Local SOEs

The administrative framework applied to local or provincial SOEs is very similar to that of the central SOEs, except for the issue of control which is local rather than central.

Figure 8.2. The administrative framework in Vietnamese local SOEs

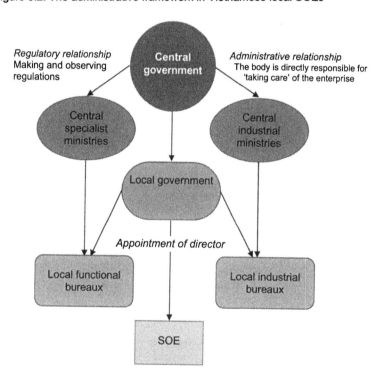

Figure 8.2 shows the administrative framework applied to local SOEs. In principle, the same administrative procedures are applied to both central and local SOEs, the difference being one of degree. Local governments and local bureaux in Vietnam, as mentioned in the last chapter, are branches of the central government and do not have the autonomy typical of local governments in many Western countries. The

shoe enterprise in the present study is a local SOE (Hanoi), and follows the administrative framework outlined in Figure 8.2.

8.1.3. State corporations

The garment and light bulb enterprises belong to the Garment and Textile Corporation and the Glass and Ceramic Corporation, respectively. Both are Decision-91 corporations and the governance structures of the two enterprises are similar. Before joining the corporation, these enterprises operated under the administrative procedures applied to other central SOEs. They now operate following the framework for Decision-91 corporations (see Figure 8.3).

Figure 8.3. The administrative framework in the Vietnamese Decision-91 state industrial corporations

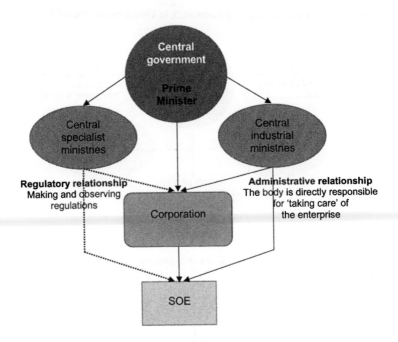

The garment enterprise and light bulb enterprise are now under the control of not only the ministries, but also of a government corporation. One of the objectives of the establishment of corporations, as we saw, was to replace the direct control or active involvement of various ministries in the enterprise. This objective has so far underachieved and the enterprise still has to deal directly with the ministries. As the ADB and MPI (1997) report noted:

130

"One of the main stated objectives of abolishing the business management function of line ministries-is not being realised under the measures implemented to date. Ministry officials continue to be actively involved in a full range of management decisions involving State Corporations." (p.77)

The garment enterprise, for example, has to deal directly with the Ministry of Trade on export quota issues. In interviews, managers from both the garment and light bulb enterprises complained that they have had to deal with *more* administrative procedures and paper work since the enterprise joined the corporation. The corporation can, however, be powerful in the sense that it is delegated to appoint directors and deputy directors from the SOE members and can make certain important investment decisions.

Governance structure of a corporation

At the top level, each corporation has a board of directors which is supposed to follow the model taken from large corporations in the West. Board members are appointed directly by the Prime Minister. Below the board is a management team headed by a general director (similar to a Western CEO). The general director is a board member, but not the chairperson of the board. He is appointed by the Prime Minister as are his deputies, unless someone else is delegated to do so by the Prime Minister. The board of directors forms a control committee, responsible for checking the general director, the management team and the SOE members over management and financial issues to ensure that they follow the regulations, corporation decisions and government laws in general (Item 16, Decision 39/CP, 27/6/1995).

Figure 8.4. Formal structure of a Decision-91 corporation

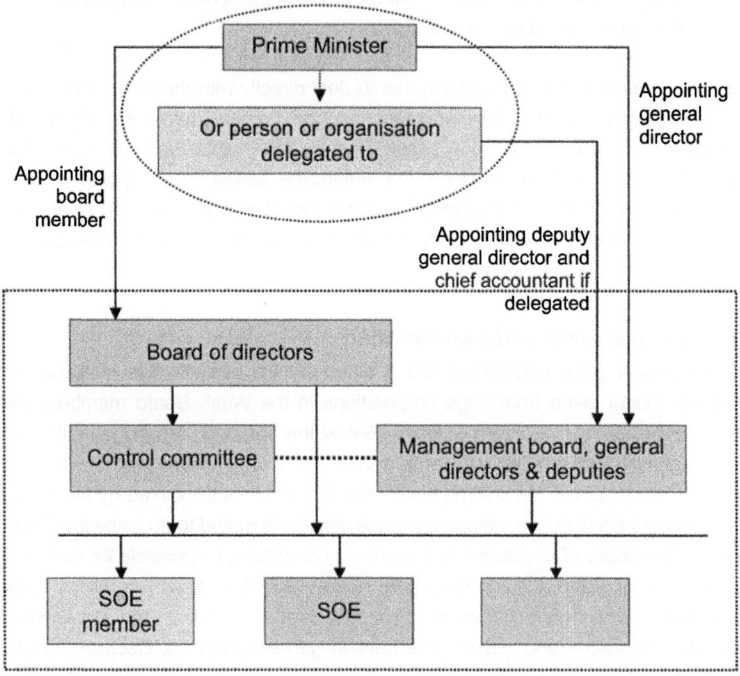

8.2. The nature of the relationship between the enterprise and the higher hierarchical levels

8.2.1. Formal administrative relationships

The administrative procedures can be summarised as follows:

At the end of each year, the enterprise is required to produce a one-year plan for the following year. This plan must be presented and approved by the employee's congress (*dai hoi cong nhan vien chuc*) and follow a certain format in which a number of indicators are specified. The most important indicators are profit, revenue and the total production value (TPV)[*]. The salary budget is calculated based upon these figures and follows the salary regulations issued by the Ministry of Labour, Invalids and Social Affairs. The plan is then submitted to the supervisory body (Central Industrial Ministry if the enterprise is a central SOE, Local Industrial Bureau if the enterprise is a local SOE). The government body then considers the plan, approves it and then sends it back to the enterprise as an order. The plan must be set following the principle that the financial indicators (e.g. revenue, profit and PTV) of the current year must be higher than those of the previous year, and this increase is often based on the government's growth rate target. So, for example, the government sets an overall growth rate target of 10% for the next year which it then

132

divides among different sectors and industries. The ministry, then, divides the percentage given among member enterprises.

The plan does not, therefore, always reflect the true capacity of the enterprise. As a deputy director of the shoe enterprise humorously observed in an interview about the way the government imposed a plan on the enterprise.

> "They [the Industrial Bureau] do not know anything about the business, they simply set the plan, let's say, 10% higher than the previous year." If every enterprise grows 10% every year, Vietnam will soon become the USA".

The enterprise sometimes responds to the arbitrarily imposed plans by hiding the true data about the enterprise's performance in certain years, as occurred in both the shoe and light bulb enterprises.

Monthly, the enterprise has to report on, and review with the relevant government department, the actual implementation of the plan. The enterprise is also required to submit quarterly reports to different government departments. It is also subject to investigation by delegations from the relevant government bodies (e.g. tax, finance and environment). Despite this seemingly tightly control and monitoring mechanism, a 'loss of control' by the government over the actual financial situation of SOEs is not uncommon. As Nguyen Minh Tu, a researcher and government official pointed out: "The government cannot inspect the financial affairs of state businesses, it does not know whether enterprises are gaining interest or suffering losses in order to have a clear settlement with them" (Nguyen Minh Tu, 1997, p.6). A manager (head of the production planning and materials department) of the shoe enterprise said in an interview that "in a state enterprise, you can report that it's making a loss or alternatively, you can also report that it's making a profit". He supported his point by showing how one way to do that was to value the stock differently.

8.2.2. Centralisation and patrimony
As the last chapter revealed, within SOEs the director of the enterprise resembles the family head in that he or she makes almost all important decisions concerning the management of the enterprise. SOE directors are, however, only powerful within limits as their freedom is restricted by administrative procedures and regulations.

The director can, for example, decide on employee pay but in doing so has to follow the regulations set by the Ministry of Labour, Invalids and Social Affairs. These regulations are very detailed and specify the payment levels for different jobs and management positions that the enterprise must follow. The enterprise can in theory decide to launch new products onto the market, but this requires capital investment that must be approved by government bureaux. Many important business decisions involve spending money or investment yet directors of SOEs in Vietnam are not given a budget that they are relatively free to decide how to spend. Except for routine operational decisions, the enterprise has to get approval on a case-by-case basis from higher hierarchical levels for every decision involving capital investment or that involve spending a relatively large sum of money. Various government regulations place SOE directors in the position where they can only disburse funds on what 'must-be' spent items (e.g. production costs: materials, electricity and labour costs). Other spending associated with market mechanisms (e.g. advertisement) is tightly controlled. For example, the total expenses for marketing, advertisement, sales promotion, conferences and external affairs altogether, as regulated by the government, must be less than 5% of the total cost (Circular 99/1998/TT-BTC).

If one has the 'right to decide' but no resources to implement the decision, then the right becomes nominal. This is similar to a situation in which one is free to buy whatever one wants, but one does not have any money.

This fact makes the enterprise, to a great extent, dependent on the various government departments. Again, the authority pattern between the government bodies and the enterprise director and those above him is very similar to that between him/her and their subordinates. There is no 'boundary' within which they can freely act without asking for approval. The 'boundary' in this case, can be understood as the budget in which a director can decide to invest or spend on what he/she thinks is best for the enterprise. The director of a non-board SOE, or the board of directors of an SOE with a board can, however, decide to spend on investment projects within the capital budget from retained profit (the capital actually created by the enterprise itself) but:

> "The persons (e.g. the director or board members) who approved the re-investment plans (with capital from the profit), that if wrong, lead to investment projects (e.g. renewing machines and equipment) that are inefficient, do not meet the pay-back time, or are lost, not only face administrative discipline, but also have to pay back the investment. The amount of compensation is defined by regulations or laws" (Item 2.2, Circular 24/1998/TT-BTC, the author's translation).

This regulation means that 'you can act, but you have to be careful!' This unbalanced relationship provides room for opportunism. Personal relationships between the enterprise and government officials are important, and the degree of importance is manifested in money and other favours.

One of the favours is to give jobs to people 'introduced' by government officials. We found this in all three enterprises: the head of the personnel department in the garment enterprise did not hesitate to tell me in an interview that they have to recruit people who are introduced by *important* people (e.g. from government bureaux or boards). He used the term *diplomatic posts* to describe those positions. A deputy director of the shoe enterprise said:

> "In a state-owned enterprise, how can you improve productivity? You have two or three cleaners, in fact you need only one cleaner, but what can you do if they are relatives of people in the city! When recruiting new management staff, he or she should have degrees from the National Economics University or Trade University; these are most acceptable but here, some of them graduated from the Agriculture University."

134

Giving money to various government officials and government departments is a fact of life. We found that, in all three cases, the enterprises gave money to government officials and departments on the following occasions:

On the occasion of big holidays (e.g. Tet holiday, National Day);

When delegations from, for example, the tax department, visited the enterprise to 'check' whether it was following regulations;

To the customs office to 'smooth' import or export orders.

Source: interviews with enterprise managers

The garment enterprise also gave money to the trade department of the Ministry of Trade which grants export quotas. Giving money to government departments is not considered to be 'corruption' in Vietnam. In fact, some departments actually asked the enterprises for money.

For example, when the light bulb enterprise performed well and made a substantial profit, one Tet holiday the Industrial Ministry asked the enterprise for money in order to make an extra payment to its employees (the information is from an interview with one of the enterprise's managers, Mr. Quan).

The enterprise can benefit significantly from the 'return' it gets from government officials and departments. The light bulb enterprise, for example, is the only enterprise that manufactures vacuum flasks, an import protected item. During the research period, the enterprise was preparing to submit a proposal that extended the protection period and was actively 'lobbying' for that to happen. Maintaining good relationships with government officials is therefore important to any enterprise. Those with special relationships with government officials (relatives of the enterprise's director or managers holding important positions in the government) often have many advantages over others (UNIDO and DSI, 1999, p.158).

Chapter 9: The management problems of the Vietnamese SOEs

The last two chapters presented our findings and discussion on authority patterns within state enterprises and between the enterprises and the government bureaux. The authority pattern in Vietnamese society is what Max Weber termed "patrimonial", where power is not institutionalised. There is no clear boundary within which subordinates can act freely without asking for permission or approval from their superior. The authority pattern in the SOEs and Vietnamese society as a whole is very similar to that found in the Overseas Chinese businesses, as studied by a number of authorities in the field including Westwood (1997); Westwood, Tang and Kirkbride (1992); and Redding (1990). Drawing on his study of the Overseas Chinese businesses, Westwood (1997) heuristically derived the concept of 'paternalistic headship' to characterise leadership in the Chinese context. 'Paternalistic headship' refers to an authority structure similar to that in a traditional Chinese family, where the family head has absolute power and expects and receives respect and obedience from the rest of the family. Such a power form, as Westwood pointed out, "cannot really exist unless it is connected to ownership; it is the non-separation of ownership and control in the Chinese case that facilitates the flourishing of patrimony in Chinese enterprises" (p.455).

Since the Vietnamese share many cultural traits with the Chinese (i.e. Confucian values), it is possible to extend Westwood's concept of 'paternalist headship' to the Vietnamese business context. However, given the fact that SOEs are not family, owner-managed businesses, the *full* meaning of the concept 'headship' in the context of the Overseas Chinese family businesses may not be extended to the context of the Vietnamese SOEs. It is, therefore, necessary to clarify the use of the metaphor 'headship' or 'family head' in the context of the Vietnamese SOEs.

Every metaphor can only reveal certain aspects of reality, and thus may at the same time be misleading about other aspects. It is, therefore, important to explain what we mean by using this particular metaphor. In other words, the 'metaphor of metaphor', or what Alvesson (1993) called the second level of metaphor, is important and requires explanation. In this case it is necessary to explain what we really mean by the metaphor 'family head'. The 'family head' has so far been used to characterise only the authority and power pattern. It is common when talking about a family head to mean that he is the one who takes care of all family members and tries to make the family prosper. This meaning of 'family head' may not be extended to the context of the state enterprise, since the state enterprise is not his family, far from it. The property is not his property: it belongs to the state and most of the enterprise employees are not his relatives. In this chapter, we present our findings on how

136

people react to the situation in which they (the SOE director, managers, and officials) have a 'father's authority' in the work context, but their 'grace and dignity' is to prosper their own family.

This chapter introduces evidence about the problem of opportunism in the Vietnamese SOEs in *general*, and will also focus on the 'bonus' problem in economic transactions. It then presents a *specific* in-depth case study, the shoe enterprise, which was the main focus of the fieldwork. The case shows how a director used her power to gain her own ends, and provides insights into how people use their power to get what they want. The chapter then presents evidence about opportunistic behaviour in the other two enterprises, and concludes with discussion of the problems of management in Vietnamese SOEs in *general*.

As the title suggests, the chapter is about the 'problems' of managing Vietnamese SOEs. It is important to explain the use of such normative terms as 'problems' and 'opportunism' in the present research. 'Problems' and 'opportunism' are considered by a number of social theorists as too subjective to describe social phenomena in *scientific* research. We agree in principle that the social sciences should be objective however, objectivity and subjectivity are relative. We believe that the use of 'problems' and 'opportunism' is appropriate in the context of this study since throughout his research, the author found that 'problems' and 'opportunism' were the actual words employed by the subjects of the study. The government, Vietnamese newspapers and research publications, managers and employees from SOEs, and people at large, all talk about 'opportunism' and 'problems' of the SOEs. The use of these terms is in fact, a reference to what Schutz would call "subjective reality". They express contemporary consciousness in Vietnamese society. Secondly, as mentioned previously, this study takes a critical theory perspective, which holds that in trying to understand and explain social phenomena we cannot avoid evaluating and criticising them.

It is important to clarify the concept of 'opportunism' that will be used in the following sections. Williamson (1975) defined 'opportunism' as "self-interest seeking with guile" (p.255). What he really meant by 'opportunism' was "the rational pursuit by economic actors of their own advantage, with all means at their command, including guile and deceit" (Granovetter, 1985, p.494). Williamson treated 'opportunism' as a human behaviour variable in his transaction cost conception. This assumption of human behaviour has been severely criticised (Perrow, 1986; Pfeffer, 1982 and 1997; Donaldson, 1985; Ghoshal and Moran, 1996). While agreeing that 'opportunism' is not a *universal* human trait, we would ague that 'opportunism' is useful as a working hypothesis in the study of social exchanges in certain settings. In '*The bureaucratic phenomenon*', Michel Crozier, for example, found situations in which the "active tendency of the human agent (was) to take advantage, in any circumstances, of all available means to further his own privileges" (1964, p.194).

In addition, like other social concepts, 'opportunism' is not context-free. People from different cultures would, for example, perceive 'bribery' differently. In the context of the present research we found the term 'opportunism' appropriate to describe the behaviour in which people use their power or position to get money and other material gains illegally. That is the behaviour of individuals who cheat their companies by receiving money or valuable gifts personally through economic exchanges. The context in which the term 'opportunism' was used in Williamson (1975) and in the present research is, however, different. Williamson used 'opportunism' to describe behaviour in the market (between firms). In this research we use the term to refer to behaviour within the context of the firm ("hierarchy" in Williamson's term).

9.1. Other people's money – the 'bonus' problem

An analysis of the cases presented later in this chapter, especially the shoe enterprise study, will provide insights into *how the opportunistic process works* in a particular way. This section presents our findings about opportunistic behaviour in Vietnamese SOEs in *general*, and addresses the question of the *popularity* of opportunistic behaviour (the opportunism problem) in the Vietnamese state sector as a whole, rather than how people use their power to get their own ends. The first section discusses the nature of economic transactions in Vietnam with particular attention to the transactions involving SOEs, and then examines this issue in the context of SOEs.

The research ideas and questions arose from the author's own observations. A number of interviews were carried out to confirm initial observations and then a questionnaire designed to obtain quantitative data and information about opportunistic behaviour in state enterprises through the study of economic transactions. Since the official income of employees of SOEs (including management) is clear, the opportunistic behaviour (if any) must deductively be found in economic transactions.

9.1.1. Qualitative evidence

Being Vietnamese and 'grounded' in the environment was certainly a great advantage in carrying out this research, as the author was able to observe and gain an insight into the nature of the patterns of personal relations in business transactions. It is not difficult for anyone to discover the fact that in Vietnam, it is not uncommon for a seller to be willing to make the price on a receipt higher than the actual price, or to give the buyer a sum of money if required. Vietnamese people, especially businessmen, call this phenomenon *luat* (law). It is the *law* that buyers who buy products for their companies will get a certain amount of money for themselves. The use of the term *luat* in this case indicates that the phenomenon is a fact of life. Everyone knows it, and would accept it as commonly held knowledge.

Examples abound of people who, through transactions, took money from their organisations. During fieldwork, the author several times accompanied a friend to buy office supplies for his department. The author witnessed the sellers asking quite naturally: "How much do you want me to write on your receipt?" By accident, when the author was reading in a library he witnessed a saleswoman from a book company entering and telling the librarian that "if you buy books and journals from my company, you will get about 5% discount for yourself." Since the author is a close friend of the librarian, he had the opportunity to join in the conversation. The saleswoman told me: "To increase sales, my company motivates sellers by giving them a 10% discount on total sales. For example, if I sold an amount of books and journals or magazines worth USD1,000, I would get USD100 for myself. But in order to encourage or persuade the buyers, I normally 'offer' them a 5% discount. Of course, in the contract or receipt, we still write down the original price."

In order to get more information about this phenomenon the author interviewed a number of managers. During one interview Mr. Ngoc, a manager in a private company specialising in computer equipment and software business, said:

> "When people buy something for their companies, ink for their printers, for example, they ask us to give them some money. We often give them VND50,000 (nearly USD4) for a roll of ink. If we do not give them that, they would buy from other companies. It is normal that when we sign a contract for the sale of an accounting software package to a company, especially an SOE, we need to give them (the people who deal with us) a certain amount of money. For example, on the contract, the price may be USD1,000, but what we actually receive is about USD900, maybe USD700 or USD800, of course it all depends. During the Y2K period, we signed several contracts and were paid, but what is interesting is that we did not have to do anything. This was because every company that uses computers had to fix the Y2K problem, which was much discussed. But technically, it was very simple to fix - people from the IT departments could fix it themselves. We signed several contracts with the companies to fix the Y2K problem for them but then the IT people from companies did the work themselves. They got the money and gave us about 20% of the amount written on the contract because they used our name, and also because we had to pay tax on that 'revenue'. That is the Vietnamese way of doing businesses, and it has become the unwritten law."

Another example came out of the author's interview with Ms. Hong, an employee from an auditing company:

> "We have often given an envelope containing about USD100 or USD200 or more to our customers (people who gave us the jobs to do the audit for their companies or people who introduce us so that we got the jobs)."

9.1.2. Quantitative evidence

The evidence from the author's observations and interviews gave rise to an initial idea about the general pattern of transactions in Vietnam. In order to examine the popularity of the phenomenon and try to reduce potential bias the author designed a survey instrument, a questionnaire designed after spending a considerable time on observations and interviews. The content of the questionnaire was unique in the sense that it was concerned with issues and problems that have rarely been dealt with empirically. Granovetter (1985) pointed out that the difficulty of getting information partly accounted for the fact that little attention has been paid to studying actual patterns of relations in transactions. Personal relations in transactions are sensitive issues, so the questionnaire needed to be designed in a way so that on the one hand, it covered the issue under investigation, and on the other, was not so 'sensitive' that respondents were unwilling to answer. Details of the questionnaire are given in Appendix 3. The questionnaire was designed to get information on the problem of personal opportunistic behaviour in transactions.

A total number of 47 questionnaires were distributed to 47 enterprises in Hanoi of which 32 questionnaires were completed and used for the analysis. Respondents had to be members of the companies with jobs that involved transactions. The 'must' criterion was that regardless of the position held in their companies, they must understand the nature of business transactions in those companies. They had to be directors, deputy directors, sales or marketing managers, accounting managers or employees of the marketing or accounting departments. The questionnaires were filled in by director/deputy directors (six in total) and managers and staff of the marketing, sales, accounting and planning or the materials department (24 respondents). Two respondents did not reveal their job positions in the companies. In any study of relations in transactions, it is an ideal to get information from both parties on a transaction: i.e. from seller and buyer. In the present study, since the questionnaire was designed to get information about 'sensitive' issues, it was designed for respondents on the seller or supplier side of transactions only. In fact, it is difficult if not impossible to get reliable information from buyers about whether they cheat their company (by obtaining money personally from the seller) in a transaction. It is, however, quite normal in Vietnam to ask a seller whether or not they would be prepared to give money to an anonymous buyer. In the questionnaire, 'opportunism' was clearly defined. It referred to the situation when the buyer asked a seller to record a price higher than the actual price paid to the seller, or asked the seller to give him or her a certain sum of money. The difference between the actual sum paid to the seller and the amount written on the receipt (which goes into the buyer's pocket) is often called *thuong* or 'bonus' in Vietnam. We also used the term 'bonus' in the questionnaire.

The sample was not chosen randomly from the business population in Vietnam. This was partly because of time limitations but more importantly, because the purpose of the questionnaire was to obtain evidence on transactions in Vietnam in order to construct rather than quantitatively test theories. The general information about the sample (e.g. ownership type and size) is given in Appendix 4.

Although the sample is small (32 replies), it covers a variety of enterprises with different types of ownership operating in various industries ranging from medicines, footwear and garment to steel production and computer equipment and software. The questionnaires were handed directly to the respondents either by the author (17 questionnaires) or by contacts of the respondents (intermediaries). When he handed out the 17 questionnaires, he took the opportunity to interview five of them to get more information. Below are the findings from the questionnaires and interviews.

Popularity

In the first question we asked respondents about the frequency with which their buyers or customers asked for a 'bonus'. 18 out of 32 respondents (56.3%) replied that for their buyers (customers) to ask for a 'bonus' was *generally popular*. Twelve out 32 (37.5%) respondents replied that their buyers sometimes or occasionally asked for a 'bonus'. *None* of the respondents replied that their customers never asked for a 'bonus'.

When a buyer or customer asked for a 'bonus', in general the seller accepted their request. In the sample, 31 out of 32 respondents (96.9%) replied that their companies accepted the 'bonus' requests of their customers and gave them an acceptable amount. Only one respondent, from a software company, replied that the company "in general, did not accept" the 'bonus' requests.

Unwritten law

In the questionnaire (question nine) we asked respondents about their general perception of the "bonus" phenomenon in Vietnam. Not surprisingly, 12 out of 32 respondents (37.5%) *definitely* agreed with the statement that the 'bonus' incident "was popular in Vietnam and further, was an 'unwritten law' that it was pointless to discuss." 43.8% of the respondents *generally agreed* with the statement. Only one respondent did not generally agree with the statement.

The 'bonus' amount

In question five, we asked respondents to give information about the average 'bonus' they normally gave their customers. We found that the 'bonus' was a proportion of the sale ranging from 1% to 30% depending on sales, the customers and the kind of products being sold. The 'bonus' amount of the equivalent to GBP100 (1% of a modest sale amount of GBP10,000) was equal to about two months' income for a worker in the shoe or garment enterprise. The 'bonus' amount is, therefore, economically significant in the context of Vietnamese living conditions.

9.1.3. Private vs. public

Two separate questions in the questionnaire asked respondents about the frequency with which their private (enterprise) buyers, and buyers for SOEs requested 'bonuses'. Again not surprisingly, the difference was significant. 65.6% of the respondents answered that their SOE customers frequently requested a 'bonus', compared to only 6.3% of private (enterprise) buyers. The mean score was also significantly different between the two customer groups (3.53 compared to 2.28).

Table 9.1. The frequency with which private buyers and SOE
buyers requested a bonus

	Frequently	Sometimes	Rarely	Non	Mean
Private buyers	6.3%	25%	59.3%	9.4%	2.28
SOE buyers	65.6%	21.9%	12.5%	0%	3.53

Frequently = 4; sometimes = 3; rare = 2; non = 1. Sample size: N=32

The mean score of 2.28 indicates that private buyers rarely asked for a 'bonus', which is understandable since the private sector in Vietnam is newly developed. Most private firms are small in size and managed by family members. Almost all business transactions are decided and carried out by family members or close friends. One respondent (the director of a steel tube producer) said in an interview:

> "Private firms buy for themselves. I mean the owner or his wife or sons or relatives or very close friends make all important decisions and buy important things themselves, so there is no point in asking for a bonus".

In addition, we found that 59.4% of respondents generally agreed that their SOE customers would not buy from their companies if they do not get any money for themselves one way or another. Also, 81.3% of respondents generally agreed that keeping personal relationships (giving gifts and money on important occasions) with the buyers (the individuals who make the purchasing decisions) was very important.

The 'bonus' phenomenon is somewhat *institutionalised*. Circular 01/1998/TT-BTC concerning the payment to 'agents' is an example of this. The term 'agent' here means any individual or organisation playing an agent role for the company, especially those helping it sell its products. According to this regulation, an agent could receive up to 30% of the amount gained by the enterprise or 3% of the total sales that they generated. The regulation paved the way for any enterprise to give a 'bonus' in order to 'smooth transactions'. It is interesting that the circular required the 'agent' to sign the receipt when they received the money from the enterprise. To sign receipts is a matter of fact in every legal transaction; so the reminder to sign the circular indicated the government's lack of trust of in the enterprises' conduct. More interestingly, the circular also gave a green light to the enterprise: "In the case that (the enterprise) cannot get the signature of the agent (who received money), (the enterprise) has to write down their names." (01/1998/TT-BTC,1998). The use of agents in businesses is not uncommon. The interesting thing is that an agent in Vietnam could be any individual, even someone without a business licence. A person who bought equipment for his/her company could also be considered an agent.

9.2. The shoe enterprise

This section provides empirical evidence of how people in the shoe enterprise used their power to achieve their ends. There is a particular focus on the firm's sales activity, through which power was exercised by Mr. Thong, an employee of the sales department (and a son of the director). He, together with his mother (the director), used their power to obtain their own ends. His position at the transaction junction between the enterprise and the market enabled Mr. Thong to take advantage of his knowledge of the market to get what he wanted.

9.2.1. Research strategy

Pfeffer (1992) lists a number of symbols of power in organisations including payment structure (the degree of difference in pay among different levels and positions in the organisation) and office conditions (e.g. size and location). These symbols are important in helping the observer establish working hypotheses about the power pattern of the organisation. It is often the case that power is associated with material gains in some form (salary, housing, car or job security). From their study of a university budget, for example, Pfeffer and Salancik (1974) found that departmental power was significantly related to the proportion of the budget received. They accordingly argued that "it is possible to obtain unobtrusive measures of organisational political systems without direct interviewing" (p.135). These symbols and measures of power are, however, not in evidence in the Vietnamese SOEs, at least in the official sources. SOE employees including management (director, deputy directors and other management positions) are officially paid according to the overall performance of the enterprise. The payment policy is regulated and guided by the Ministry of Labour, Invalids and Social Affairs. The salary budget must also be approved by the relevant government bodies following various regulations, and is tied to the performance of the enterprise as a whole. The enterprise can decide, as noted earlier, on its own payment policy but only within limits. Although SOEs operate following market principles, their regulated payment structures still, to a great extent, reflect the socialist ideology that dominated the country in the recent past and still does today, albeit to a lesser degree.

The salary budget is still based on the principle of the theory of labour value. For example, a shoe enterprise can only pay a maximum of x Dong for the labour (labour cost) needed to produce a sold pair of, say, canvas shoes. Various government regulations are in place to ensure roughly equal payment systems within and amongst SOEs. On paper, the payment structure of a Vietnamese SOE does not indicate a distinct class or 'political' structure (the payment policy applied to SOEs is presented and analysed in detail in Chapter 10). Pfeffer and Salancik's (1974) proposition that one may not need direct interviewing or observation to obtain measures of organisational political systems might only be relevant in the case of a university budget, as in their study, or to organisations in US and Western developed countries. The information on official resource allocation, salary and other benefits suggested by Pfeffer (1992) and Pfeffer and Salancik (1974) as a source of power must be set aside in the context of the present research.

Pettigrew (1972) used the document analysis method to examine a case in which a manager named Kenny used his power to exert biases in favour of his own demands in a large-scale, capital investment decision. In that study, Pettigrew was able to look at various documents, including written correspondence from Kenny to the customers (computer manufacturers). It would be a work of fiction to apply the same document analysis procedures in the Vietnamese context. Business communications in Vietnam, especially those similar to the ones in Pettigrew's study, are rarely in written form. We cannot, therefore, rely on 'tangible' or 'hard' evidence such as official payment structures and written business correspondence to establish the power and the use of power in the Vietnamese context.

The best, perhaps the only way, to gain an insight into the power structure of the Vietnamese enterprise is to observe and interview the people involved. Since the issue under study was sensitive, it was impossible to get information directly from Mr. Thong. Neither was it always easy to get information on such sensitive issues from other people in the enterprise. During his fieldwork, the author gradually built up a relationship with some managers and employees from the enterprise who came to trust him enough to give him the information he sought. Since it is a sensitive issue, their real names are not used here although the story is, of course, real. The people he was able to interview included the head and his deputy of the production planning and materials department, the head of the accounting and finance department, the head of the sub-contracting and statistics department, and the head, deputy head and several employees in the sales department.

Being aware of the problems of bias and validity in interviews, the author also tried to get evidence from other sources. He observed and interviewed two of the enterprise's agents: one from Hanoi and one from Haiphong. However, there could be no better source of information than those interviewed, people whose work involved them directly in sales activity. They also worked with Thong day to day, especially the head and deputy head of the sales department who were officially Thong's direct bosses.

9.2.2. The formal structure of the enterprise
In order to understand why and how people obtain and use their power, we must know where they stand in the structure of the enterprise. This section presents the formal structure of the enterprise, with particular reference to the context of its sales activity.

Figure 9.1 (see below) shows the formal structure. The diagram has been redrawn and translated from the enterprise's own chart[*] though the positions of the boxes and arrows remain the same. The names inside the boxes have been translated from Vietnamese by the author. Given the fact that Western business practice is still new in Vietnam, there are many problems in translating terms from Vietnamese into English. The best way is perhaps to use terms that are familiar to Western readers and explain them where necessary. To avoid confusion and since our major focus is on sales activity, not all the boxes in Figure 9.1 have been filled in with names.

Figure 9.2 and Figure 9.3 further illustrate the sales department.

Figure 9.1 shows the overall structure of the enterprise. The director sits at the top with the trade union, youth union and party office placed below. The arrows indicate that these offices are under the control of, or subordinate to, the director. Within the director box, the title 'party secretary' is placed above the title "director" indicating that the party is the highest and leading force. 'Party secretary' and 'director' are, however, in the same box denoting the same person. This structure shows that the director has absolute power within the enterprise. Even the trade union is under the direct control or subordinate to the director.

Below the director are four deputy directors responsible for different areas of business activity. Each deputy director is in charge of several departments.

➤ The deputy director of technology and production technique is in charge of two functional departments responsible for technology and product designs and pilot production.

➤ The deputy director of production and quality is in charge of four functional departments covering important business areas that include material supply, production, and domestic sales. Interviewed managers believed him to be the second man in the enterprise. He is also the enterprise's deputy party secretary.

➤ The deputy director of equipment and safety is in charge of two functional departments, one for machinery and equipment (e.g. maintenance) and the other dealing with security issues.

➤ The deputy director of social insurance and environment is in charge of two functional units, one for industrial hygiene and environment while the other is a medical centre.

Besides having overall responsibility for the enterprise, the director herself is directly in charge of three departments: import-export, accounting & finance and administration and personnel (see Figure 9.2). These three areas are the most 'important' areas in the enterprise. Since the lion's share of the enterprise's revenue comes from export, the import-export-related activities are important to its success. The other two areas, personnel and accounting, are important not only in the Shoe Enterprise but in almost all Vietnamese SOEs in general. Since accounting is a very sensitive issue in Vietnam, the enterprise director is not allowed to appoint the enterprise's chief accountant. For the shoe enterprise, the chief accountant was appointed by the Hanoi Industrial Bureau.

Personnel matters are also very important and sensitive issues. In Vietnamese state organisations and SOEs, the Communist Party often has a decisive influence on personnel decisions. All important personnel decisions in government state organisations are made by the Communist Party. Figure 9.2 shows the location of the sales department within the enterprise's hierarchy. Hierarchically, the department reports directly to the deputy director of production and quality.

Figure 9.1. The formal structure of the shoe enterprise

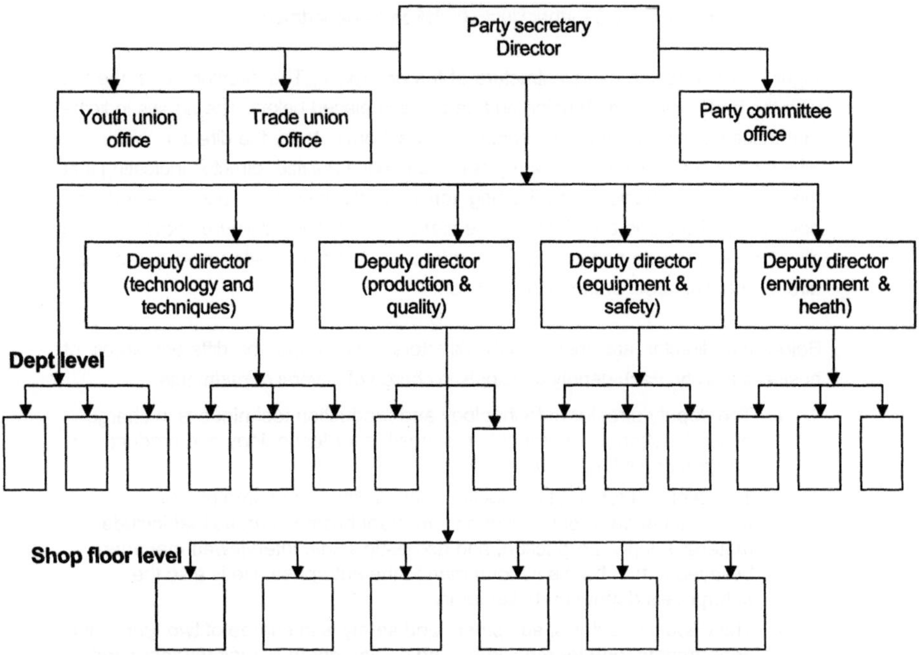

```
                          ┌─────────────────┐
                          │ Party secretary │
                          │    Director     │
                          └─────────────────┘
   ┌──────────┬──────────┐         │         ┌──────────────────┐
┌────────┐ ┌────────┐              │         │ Party committee  │
│ Youth  │ │ Trade  │              │         │     office       │
│ union  │ │ union  │              │         └──────────────────┘
│ office │ │ office │              │
└────────┘ └────────┘
  ┌──────────┬──────────────┬──────────────┬──────────────┐
┌────────────┐ ┌────────────┐ ┌────────────┐ ┌────────────┐
│Deputy      │ │Deputy      │ │Deputy      │ │Deputy      │
│director    │ │director    │ │director    │ │director    │
│(technology │ │(production │ │(equipment &│ │(environment│
│and         │ │& quality)  │ │safety)     │ │& heath)    │
│techniques) │ │            │ │            │ │            │
└────────────┘ └────────────┘ └────────────┘ └────────────┘
```

Dept level

Shop floor level

Source: internal company document

9.2.3. The organisation of sales

Pfeffer (1981) pointed out that standard operating procedures (e.g. how a certain activity or area of business is normally carried out) "have in themselves implications for the distribution of power and authority in organisations and for how contested decisions should be resolved" (p.32). It is, therefore, important to discuss how sales are carried out (the standard operating procedures of the sales activity) and, in the present case, the power structure underlying the 'standard operating procedures'.

146

Figure 9. 2. The enterprise structure – 'important areas'

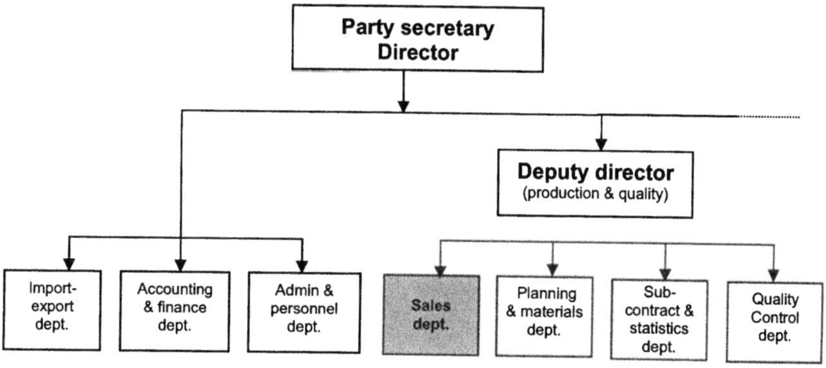

At the time of writing, two departments were responsible for sales activities: The import-export department and the sales department. The import-export department was in charge of export sales and the sales department for domestic sales. The next section looks at sales policy.

Sales policy

The enterprise sold its products though sales agents or wholesalers, called *dai ly* in Vietnamese. *Dai ly* is often translated into English as 'agent' and for convenience, the term 'agent' will be used in the rest of this work. At the time of the research, there was one agent in each key province or geographical area. These agents bought shoes from the enterprise and resold them directly to final customers or retailers or smaller wholesalers located within their geographical area. The enterprise did not control the price at which the agents sold the goods to their customers. The contract terms between the enterprise and its agents were simple:

➢ All agents had to pay a small sum (over USD100) as a deposit;
➢ Agents were not exclusive but were required, at least on paper, to display the enterprise's products in a certain area of space in their shop;
➢ They also had to follow the payment policy (e.g. the proportion they had to pay immediately the products were delivered and the amount they could pay later).

In general, the agents were actually independent wholesalers and so not 'liable' for the sales of the enterprise. The first requirement (to pay a deposit) was not significant since the amount was too small. The second requirement could be of some significance because the rent for apartments and shops in shopping areas in big cities was often much higher than in other areas. This requirement was not often followed strictly by the agents, especially those from provinces outside Hanoi.

"During his fieldwork, the author observed the agent in Haiphong City (the second largest city in the northern part of Vietnam). It was a shop located in the city centre of Haiphong. He was surprised to see that there were no signs showing that the shop was an agent of the shoe enterprise. The shop was relatively small (about 25 square metres). It sold many kinds of products (different brands of shoes and sportswear). It looked as normal as other retail shops. It had, however, sold a large number of the enterprise's products every year. Its main customers were retailers from the city and nearby districts" (from observation, October, 1999)

The third requirement was merely a payment procedure.

In summary, agents had the privilege of being the sole wholesaler for the enterprise's products in their local area whilst at the same time not being liable for the overall sales or sales promotion of the enterprise. However, the amount they gained from that advantage depended on the difference between the price paid to the enterprise, and the price at which they could resell the products to their customers.

Figure 9.3. A formal hierarchical structure – the sales context

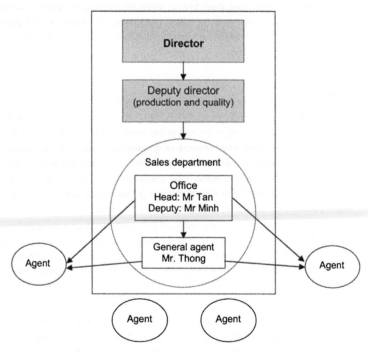

The sales department was responsible for organising sales procedures, checking on the agents and providing market information for the enterprise. The department had a total of 30 employees with two management positions, the head of the department, Mr. Tan and a deputy head, Mr. Minh. The department *had* a few display shops (which displayed and sold the enterprise's products) located at the entrance to the enterprise. It also took care of the so-called 'general agent' (GA) located in Hanoi,

148

through which a large number of products were distributed to the enterprise's agents. The GA was officially part of and under the control of the sales department. Employees (sellers) who worked at the GA belonged to the department. Mr. Thong, as noted before, was in charge of the GA. He was an employee of the sales department and his direct bosses were Mr. Tan and Mr. Minh.

Figure 9.3 shows the hierarchical context and organisation of the sales activity. Products were distributed to the agents through the sales department but there were also two 'places' at which agents could buy goods: the sales department office and the GA. An interesting point was that certain product models could only be bought through the GA.

Pricing

Pricing is one of the most important business decisions in any for-profit enterprise. In the present case, the director had the final say on any price decision, as was the case in the other two enterprises studied. In fact, the State Enterprise Law states that the enterprise director is the person who should make pricing decisions.

In the shoe enterprise three departments – sales, production planning & materials and the accounting & finance – were involved in the pricing process. Their influence on the final decision was, however, limited to the calculation of costs. The production planning & materials department provided information on materials and labour. The accounting & finance department provided total and unit costs associated with different quantities produced. The director would then decide on the selling price. According to the head of the accounting & finance department, the pricing process for the domestic market was very simple. The director employed a cost-pricing method in which the price was often set "a little bit higher than the cost regardless of the demand of the market" (according to the head of this department).

The director's major justification for this pricing method, according to the head of the sale department, was that the most important purpose of the enterprise was not profit but to protect jobs. According to the deputy director of production and planning, the enterprise often made only a little or no profit from the domestic market.

9.2.4. The general agent (GA) and the exercise of power

The role of the GA was not clear. It was, in some ways, an independent trading unit, since it also sold products from other shoe brands to make a profit of its own. Officially, however, it was a unit of the enterprise and, together with the sales department office, was in charge of delivering orders to agents and customers following the enterprise's policy. With regard to the enterprise product models that customers and agents could only buy through GA, it emerged that in this case the GA, particularly Thong, 'booked' or 'ordered' high demand or fashionable product models from the enterprise and charged agents and customers at high price to earn his own 'profit'. In an interview, Mr. Tan, the head of the sales department complained that:

"Although I am the head of the sales department, and am supposedly in charge of the enterprise's sales Mr. Thong, the son of the director, controlled a large proportion of sales. If there was a good load of products (product models that sold well, high demand), he 'took' the load and sold the goods at a higher price than that set by the enterprise to put into his own pocket. You teach business and economics, you know about demand and supply."

The enterprise did not have its own marketing department and the major source of market information was not market research or marketing experts but Thong and the director herself! Ms. Tuan, the head of production planning & materials, said:

"You know, 'her family' (the director and her son, Thong) sells shoes. Market information and new product models come from her and her son. If, for example, she sees some shoe brand in a trade fair or market (e.g. overseas market), which she thinks could sell in Vietnam, she brings a pair as a sample and orders the enterprise to make shoes resembling to the brand and her son or 'the GA' will sell them."

Given this control of market information, Thong was able to 'order' from the enterprise certain product models in limited quantities so that he could 'sell' them at a higher price. In an interview, Mr. Tan, head of the sales department, said:

"The enterprise could have sold much more, I would say more than a million pairs of shoes a year. Thong controlled production, you know that the demand of shoes is very seasonal. There were periods when demand was very high, especially, of fashionable models, but we did not have enough shoes to sell. Thong was, therefore, able to charge the customers a high price."

The above findings clearly support Pfeffer's (1981) argument that norms and standard operating procedures underlie the distribution of power. In the present case, all the standard operating procedures: the pricing method, the market information source, the terms of contract with the agents and the unclear role of the GA was 'designed' so that Thong was able to take advantage of the system. The cost-pricing method enabled Thong to take advantage of the difference between the price set by the enterprise and the market price determined by supply and demand. The director's claim that the cost-pricing method increased sales and therefore helped the enterprise secure jobs was not justified, since the enterprise's official price of many product models was not the one paid by the customers. The absence of a marketing unit or any specialised or professional marketing job placed Thong in a unique position that enabled him to control and take advantage of his knowledge of the market. The unclear role of the GA could only give Thong further advantages. Although GA 'ordered' or 'booked' certain product models from the enterprise (that sale agents could only buy through them), if the GA, for some reason, could not sell all the products it had booked, it was not responsible financially for the unsold products because it was not an independent trading unit. According to Mr. Minh: "There is a fair amount of 'its' (GA) unsold product in the enterprise's stock. We will finally have to sell them at a low price." In addition, the nature of the contractual relationship between the enterprise and its agents clearly favoured the latter. This partly explained why the sale agents covered up for the GA and Thong. On paper,

150

the GA and Thong appeared to be doing nothing wrong. Mr. Minh had an insight into this point:

> "There are a lot of rumours about Thong charging the agents a price higher than that set by the enterprise and by doing so, limiting the sales and production of the enterprise. Thong is very clever. He reacted to the rumours by asking the agents to pay the enterprise directly through the accounting & finance department. But we all know his trick. In fact, some agents told us informally what Thong had asked them to do. You see, sales agents have nothing to lose, they followed exactly what Thong told them to do."

9.2.5. Sources of power

Clearly, many people in the enterprise, especially those involved in sales and production activities, knew that the director and her son, Thong, had used their power for their own purposes, both in sales activity and material supply decisions, where Thong was also involved. In an interview, both the head and deputy head of the production planning & materials department (Mr. Tuan and Mr. Hung, respectively) said that the enterprise's current supplier of rubber (material) was 'introduced' by Thong. This supplier was from the south of the country, and Thong acted as the 'middleman' between the enterprise and the supplier. Both Tuan and Hung were unhappy about the price of rubber charged by the supplier, but they "could not, should not do anything about it," said Tuan. Hung gave the following evidence:

> "You know, in November (1999) due to the floods in the central region (of Vietnam), rubber supply from the south could not get through. We had to buy rubber here in Hanoi. Do you know that the price of rubber we bought from here was nearly 10% cheaper than we normally pay for Thong's rubber?"

It is interesting that everybody knew what was going on around them and seemed very unhappy about it, but at the same time they all accepted it. In an interview, Tuan observed that:

> "In order to appear democratic, she (the director) often 'asked' us in the meetings about how the enterprise should improve sales. Nobody said anything about the GA and Thong. We just said something very general like: we might consider producing more models to meet the market demand. She also praised the GA for its contribution to the enterprise's sales in front of all the enterprise's employees. Everybody appeared to agree with her."

French and Raven (1959) pointed out there were five types of power, which they termed: reward, coercive, legitimate, referent and expert power. In this case, the major source of power was French and Raven's *legitimate* power. The director had power and was able to exercise it because she was the director. People in the upper social ranks have 'legitimate authority' which enables them to exercise their power if they wish to do so. In the shoe enterprise, the director held the highest position within the organisation and no counter-force existed. Subordinates were highly dependent on her. When asked why everybody accepted the situation, the head of the production planning & materials department (Tuan) gave a brief but insightful summary:

> "First, people who know the truth are managers. She appoints most of the managers. Therefore, in the personal relationship (tinh cam), they owed her something, so they could not betray her. Second, all the managers also have "some benefit" in one way or another. She cannot 'eat' alone. Frankly, I myself, for example, earn some income by subcontracting to the enterprise(*). If she does not like me, she may give the contract to other people. You know that everybody cares about himself. Nobody is stupid enough to speak out. If the director does not like you, she can use a very simple trick to remove you from your position, or you may be still in the position (e.g. department head), but may not be able to 'earn' anything. Thirdly, there is no written evidence, so if you speak out about something, you need to prove it: how do you prove it, who will support you?"

The deputy head of the sales department, Mr. Minh, shared this views:

> "If, for example, I complained about the GA, the director might agree and allow me to take full charge of the sales activity. She could set a high sales target and could easily remove me if we did not meet that target. In Vietnam it would be a disaster if someone from a lower position criticised his or her boss."

What we can infer from the above quotation is that it is difficult, if not impossible, to assess performance in quantitative terms. The director can set a high or a low target if she wishes to do so. This fact is consistent with the nature of Vietnamese society in general and the form of cognition of the Vietnamese people in particular. Everything connects to everything else. Things are not functionally organised and quantitatively measured. It is the social relationships that exclude the "mechanical and quantitative, the forced and the externally imposed" (Needham, 1956).

What enabled the director to act as she did was, as Tuan and Minh pointed out, the fact that she was the director, so able to reward particular persons in the organisation (e.g. give someone favours). This evidence does not support the claim made by some organisation theorists that middle managers in organisations in developing countries possess "inadequate management and administrative skills" and are "risk-averse, unwilling to take independent action or initiative" (see Hickson and Pugh, 1995, p.232). Middle managers in this case, including Tuan, Hung, Tan and Minh, were not in fact allowed to take responsibility. In interviews, they appeared knowledgeable and competent. Most middle managers in the company had acquired knowledge about business and management in a market economy from universities whereas the older generation, the generation of the director and deputy directors, had no such opportunity.

It is also important to note that in his interviews and from his observations, the author did not see something many Western academics have romanticised about the Chinese, Vietnamese or Confucian culture in general: that subordinates respect their boss unconditionally. Loyalty and mutual respect are perhaps present in other contexts where the interests are in line, but not in the SOE under investigation. In

Vietnam and China, loyalty and respect are not unconditional. Subordinates respect their boss only if the boss is charismatic and ethical. Lao Tse's "high stands on low" says it all. In the present case, subordinates listen to and follow their boss because bosses are powerful. This does not necessarily mean that they respected their boss. There were people from the enterprise who were not very happy with what the director did, but were afraid to speak out. It is quite understandable, they cannot cause the director to lose 'face' since 'face' is very important in Vietnamese and Chinese culture. Instead, they wrote letters (anonymously[*]) laying out what the director did and sent them to the relevant the government bodies. In an interview, Mr. Tuan revealed:

> "Last year, there ware rumours that someone from the enterprise had written a letter pointing out the director's 10 wrongdoings and sent it to various bureaux. There were 'investigations' into that, but nothing happened because when asked face to face, nobody here gave any evidence."

The only counter-force that could challenge the director's power was that represented by the people 'above' her – government officials. The nature of the relationship between the director and relevant government officials was not, as we have mentioned, 'rational' like those between management and board in large Western organisations. They do not even know the true capacity of the enterprise and do not have a direct stake in the enterprise's profit as do shareholders in the context of private businesses. The enterprise's director has, in fact, been awarded a best director prize by the Hanoi Industrial Bureau. It seemed ridiculous, but quite understandable given the Vietnamese context. The following explanation from Tuan shows why:

> "I think she deserved the award despite her all wrongdoing, because our enterprise performed better than many others from the same industry did. I believe that in Vietnam, almost all directors and managers in SOEs will try, one way or another, to take money from the enterprise. In this enterprise, although the director took a lot of money from the enterprise, she 'an' (ate) from the output (through sales). This means that the amount her family earned was proportional to sales, and they cannot 'earn' much this way if the enterprise's products are not saleable. In many other enterprises, directors and managers 'an' (eat) input. That's why many of them are making a loss."

9.3. Additional evidence from the shoe enterprise and from the garment and the light bulb enterprises

9.3.1. Additional qualitative evidence from the shoe enterprise.
One impression from the author's fieldwork at the shoe enterprise was that there was a lack of co-operation amongst different functional departments. People from one department negatively perceived those from others (e.g. thought that they were stealing money from the enterprise). Managers from the sales department including Tan and Minh, the import-export department (Mr. Cuong), and the administration & personnel department (Mr. Nguyet) whom the author had the opportunity to interview all said, for example, that they believed some people from the production planning &

materials department took money from the enterprise. The import-export department was also one of the major targets of criticism. Several managers interviewed believed that the head of the import-export department, Mr. Mai colluded with customers to 'take' money from the enterprise. Before giving proof of this, it is necessary to summarise the 'standard operating procedures' of the export sales.

The import-export department was responsible for helping the director in managing overseas contacts, negotiating export orders and carrying out procedures to make sure that orders were fulfilled. Most Vietnamese enterprises are not able to sell their products directly into foreign markets under their own names, including the footwear industry. The shoe enterprise was one of the best performers in the footwear industry, but its knowledge of international markets was very limited. At that time, the enterprise sold its products to foreign markets through 'agents', so for example several dealers acted as the 'middleman' between Vietnamese enterprises and their enterprises in Taiwan or Korea. The final destination of the products could be Australia, America or Europe. The enterprise's involvement in the market was limited to the contact with the 'agents'. The process was as follows.

The agents gave the enterprise sample products. The enterprise then produced 'counter' samples and if these were close enough to the sample and the 'agents' accepted them, the order would be signed. In some cases, the enterprise designed its own samples which the agents might accept. The agent would also be responsible for arranging import materials so the enterprise was largely dependent on him. As the head of the import-export department said:

> "After the products have left the port, we have no idea where they will go. Our products may be sold at a price tenfold higher than the price we sell to the agent. But we cannot do anything about it."

Lacking any information about the market the enterprise was, to a great extent, dependent on the agent. A manager whose job involved direct contact with the agents noted that it was common for agents to ask the enterprise to write a price on the contacts higher than the price actually paid. By this practice, the agents would 'get' some extra money paid for by their company in Korea or Taiwan. The enterprise then balanced its books by asking the suppliers of import materials (also arranged by the agents) to write the import price higher than it actually paid.

It was believed that this was not a transparent transaction, and that the head of the import-export department 'took' money and put it into his own pocket. Mr. Hung, deputy head of the production planning & materials department said in an interview about the head of the import-export department:

> "It is very obvious that he 'earned' a lot of money. A few years ago when he first joined the enterprise, he was still very poor, now he's got a big house with many expensive things, so where did the money came from? His official income from the enterprise is just about USD100 per month. Did you know, several months ago for some reason, the import materials did not arrive on time so we had to buy them from

another supplier here. They were the same kind of materials, but we paid 20% less! So you can imagine how much he earned."

Not only people from other departments believed that Mai 'took' a lot of money, his deputy, Mr. Cuong who moved to another enterprise, also believed it. In an interview, Cuong said:

"Of course, he 'earned' a lot of money. It is often the case that in contract negotiation meetings (e.g. about price) between the enterprise and the agents, only he and the director were present. The director cannot talk directly to the agents because she cannot speak the foreign language. There must be things 'behind the scene' between him and the agents."

This information could be regarded as highly objective given the fact that the interview with Cuong took place after he had moved to another shoe enterprise. More importantly, at the time of the interview he was in charge of the import-export department of his new enterprise, where the director was his uncle. He had been given the opportunity to deal directly with the agents (the same people who deal with the shoe enterprise).

9.3.2. Qualitative evidence from the other two cases

Due to time limitations, the author was not able to study the other two enterprises in the same depth as he did the shoe enterprise. However, from the author's interviews and observations he again found evidence of disguised structure and opportunistic behaviour in these cases.

9.3.2.1. The light bulb enterprise

Information about this case came from interviews with managers from the accounting & finance department, the personnel & production organisation management department and from the marketing department.

Disguised structure

From the author's own observations he discovered that Mr. Quan, the deputy head of the accounting & finance department was, in fact, the 'second man' in the enterprise who helped the director with almost everything. He wrote investment proposals, dealt with various government officials and produced almost every important report. Within his department, although he was only a deputy head, he was actually the man in charge of almost every important area. In an interview he revealed:

"The head of my department knows almost nothing. Did you know, her education is only class-four (het lop bon)(*) ! I had to decide and do almost everything."

From observations, it appeared that other managers and staff were 'afraid' of him. The author tried to interview other managers and employees about the management of the enterprise, several of them told him to ask Quan. A deputy head of the personnel & production management department said: "If you need any information about this enterprise, just ask Quan; he knows everything."

The reason why Quan, who officially held a relatively low management position in the enterprise, was trusted by the director to take care of almost everything in the enterprise was that he was the director's younger bother. The fact that Quan did not hold a higher management position was probably because according to a law, relatives of the director are not allowed to hold important management positions such as a head of the accounting & finance department). Although different in detail, this law is in a similar spirit to the 'law of avoidance' in the 19th century and earlier times and aimed to avoid nepotism. In the present case, it appeared, however, that as a brother of the director, Quan was able to exert a great deal of influence on the management of the enterprise, despite holding a minor management position.

This case also provided another example about formal rules and informal norms: that formal rules are not effective if they are not supported by the informal norms.

Opportunism

During interviews the author also found evidence about managers behaving opportunistic-ally. One obvious case was the actions of a manager in charge of a branch of the enterprise located in the central part of the country. The branch was responsible for assembling and delivering vacuum flasks to the region. Because the quality of the 'inside' part of a vacuum flask manufactured by the enterprise was much better and more expensive than that illegally imported from China, the manager decided to use the Chinese parts instead. He then sold the enterprise's parts to put the difference into his own pocket. The case was uncovered and the enterprise certainly suffered a loss of reputation (from an interview with Quan).

The author found similar perceptions opportunistic behaviour among other managers. Mr. Hoang, a personnel manager, told me in an interview about the buying activity of the enterprise:

> "I know exactly what they are doing and how much they 'earned' from transactions. It is a state enterprise! It is the same everywhere."

The garment enterprise

Opportunistic behaviour was also evident in the garment enterprise. The author observed an incident in which two managers and a subcontractor were having a 'row' over a contract. The story was as follows:

> The garment enterprise had obtained an export order (t-shirts) from an overseas company. The enterprise subcontracted this to a private company (sub-contractor). The sub-contractor had first to make sample products and then get the sample approved by the garment enterprise before it could start producing in large quantities. The sub-contractor produced a sample which was accepted by a manager in the trade department (the department in charge of certain trade areas). The manager said "go ahead" to the sub-contractor because, according to him, Ms. Huong, a

deputy director, had looked at the sample and said, "OK". After the sub-contractor started production, Mr. Van, a deputy head of the trade department, decided he did not agree with the sample. Van had been delegated by the director to take care of such activity, so thought he should have a say.

After the row had ended (inconclusively) Van said to me informally: "Did you know? They co-ti-nhe[*] with each other." When asked about the opportunistic behaviour in the enterprise, he said:

"With the current management of the state sector, if a director does not cheat then his subordinates will tell him to do so."

Another example concerned a seller who, according to the head of the administration & personnel department, was sent to Russia to promote and sell the enterprise's products there. The enterprise paid his expenses for everyday he stayed there so the seller tried to prolong his stay but do other things. The enterprise had to accept this because it did not have much information about the Russian market. The result was that all the money made from sales was just about enough to pay for his stay there.

9.3.3. Quantitative evidence

To try and increase the validity of the research in general and reduce the bias connected with the observation and interview methods, a questionnaire (Questionnaire I, see Appendix 2) was designed to get quantitative evidence. The data from the survey clearly supported our findings about opportunistic behaviour in the three case studies.

Question 18 in the questionnaire asked respondents whether they disagreed or agreed (on a five point scale from 1 to 5) with the statement: "Quite a few people from management in my enterprise use their power and position to 'earn' extra money (not in the book)." The result is not surprising. Table 9.1 shows the mean score and standard deviation from the survey sample.

Table 9.2. Perceptions of opportunistic behaviour
Mean and standard deviation (question 18)

	Mean	Std. deviation
Shoe enterprise (N=32)	4.13	0.94
Garment enterprise (N= 39)	3.67	1.06
Light bulb enterprise (N=20)	4.25	0.85
Overall (N=91)	3.96	1.11

1= strongly disagree, 2 = disagree, 3 = indifferent, 4 = agree, 5 = strongly agree.

157

The mean scores from individual enterprise samples and the overall sample are quite high. In the general sample, 63 out of 91 respondents (69.3%) strongly agreed or generally agreed with the statement. Only 8.8% did not agree with the statement. The mean score of the general sample (3.96) shows that nearly all respondents agreed with the statement. Although, the sample from the garment enterprise has the lowest mean score (3.67) among the three enterprises, the mean score and other statistical indicators still allow us to draw similar conclusions. Over 60% of the respondents (26 out of 39) agreed with the statement.

9.4. Other people's money: reconsidered

One of the conclusions we can draw from the above evidence is that opportunistic behaviour is not the exception, but a common occurrence in SOEs and state organisations in Vietnam. Other evidence from government sources also supports this conclusion. In fact, the government has realised this and has issued numerous regulations and circulars aiming at fighting this behaviour in SOEs and state organisations in general. One concerns 'avoidance' and does not permit close relatives (husbands, wives, father, mother, bothers and sisters) of the head and deputy head of state organisations to take management positions in the same organisation in the area of personnel, accounting-finance or buying-selling activities (Item10, Decision 64/1998/ND-CP).

Another example decrees that state organisations and SOEs buying equipment (e.g. computers and furniture) using state finance to the value of VND100 million (about USD7,000) or more must organise the purchase through an auction (Decision 20TC/KBNN, 1996).

That these 'avoidance' regulations did not work is clearly indicated in the cases of the shoe enterprise and the light bulb enterprise. The son of the director in the former was officially a normal employee, a seller, but was able to control sales activity. The requirement for auctions to take place when state organisations and enterprise buy equipment is interesting. Williamson (1975) argued that opportunism is associated with small-number bargaining conditions. He argued that firms try to avoid small-number bargaining conditions by deciding to 'make' instead of 'buy'. The situation in Vietnam is completely different, as state organisations and enterprises prefer small-number conditions! The regulation aims at *forcing* firms to take advantage of large-number conditions. Again, the regulation appeared to be very ineffective. In an interview, a manager in a private enterprise that supplies computers and software related a story about a large state organisation that had bought a number of computers from the enterprise. The manager revealed that the state organisation told the enterprise the price that would guarantee it got the contract. All the private enterprise had to do was follow the procedures and give a certain amount of money to the people involved. 'Fixing' in auctions is said to be common in Vietnam.

The above examples again prove that formal laws and regulations will be ineffective if they are not supported by cultural norms. Vietnamese often use the expression *cha* *chung khong ai khoc* (literally meaning 'nobody cries when a *common* father dies') to reflect the fact that people do not care about common things. The expression partly reflects the lack of co-operation amongst the Vietnamese and is rooted in the family context. In Vietnam, old people rely almost totally on their children who have a duty to take care of their parents. Some co-operation is needed amongst sons' families to take care of their 'shared' parents since there are examples of a lack of co-operation and even conflict amongst families about the 'parent matter'[*]. This social 'problem' has been featured in several Vietnamese novels, short stories, plays, dramas and films, and can be explained partly in term of poor living conditions. More importantly the lack of co-operation, as emphasised in the chapter of Vietnamese culture, originates from the family structure itself (e.g. non-blood relationships and the exogamous community family type). *Cha chung khong ai khoc* is now often used to explain the poor management of state assets in state organisations and SOEs.

Another interesting term widely used in business community is *tien chua*. *Tien chua* means literally money (*tien*) from pagoda (*chua*). The term is an extended meaning of *cua chua* (things or food from the pagoda). Children and poor people sometimes get free food (left by worshippers) from pagodas. Today, when people get something for free they often refer it as something from the pagoda. When students, for example, take a training course but do not pay a fee (often by cheating), they call it *hoc chua* (*hoc*-study). In interviews, three managers from the three SOEs (a deputy director of the shoe enterprise, head of administration & personnel department of the garment enterprise and a deputy head of the accounting & finance department of the light bulb enterprise) mentioned the term *tien chua* when they talked about their perceptions of people in their companies. A deputy director of the shoe enterprise said:

> "In Vietnam, many people consider money from SOEs or state organisations as tien chua, if they have the opportunities they would take it."

People consider the use of one's power or position to prosper their own family as normal or easy to understand. In Questionnaire I (question 20) we asked respondents their perception about the 'opportunism' problem in SOEs. It is interesting that 81 out of 91 respondents (89%) agreed that 'opportunism' in SOEs "is easy to understand". Only four respondents (4.4%) disagreed.

In question 21 we asked respondents a conditional question about whether they would undertake opportunistic activities if their position allowed them to do so. The question asked respondents whether they agreed or disagreed with the statement: "If I am in position where I can 'earn' extra money (not official salary), I believe I will find a way to earn more income". It is not surprising that 53 out of 91 respondents (58.2%) agreed with this statement. Only 18.7% of the respondents disagreed with it. The following discussion and Chapter 10 will examine in more detail key characteristics of the existing formal 'rules of the game', i.e. government policies, which either account for the above problems or make them worse. Suggestions will then be provided as to how to overcome those problems and improve the performance of the SOEs.

Discussion

The last three chapters presented our findings about the behaviour of one type of 'player', the Vietnamese SOEs, from which it emerged that SOEs have two dominant features: over-centralisation (structure) and *opportunism* (action). This section will first, briefly discuss the relationship between action and structure in the context of the Vietnamese SOEs with a reference to the *ideal type*, and second, place SOEs in the broad Vietnamese institutional context. This method will also confirm the guerilla capitalism thesis.

Action and structure

The classic problem of action and structure has long been a subject of major debates amongst social theorists. Attempts to resolve the problem in a single, consistent theory have often gone awry (Van de Ven and Poole, 1989). Social theorists have not been successful in developing a theory able to connect individual interests and social structure (Coleman, 1986; Van de Ven and Poole, 1989). This section will not discuss the action-structure debate but rather, provide some insights into the action-structure dichotomy within a particular context, that of the Vietnamese SOEs.

One of the key structural features of Vietnamese SOEs (both within the enterprise and between the enterprise and higher hierarchical levels) is *over-centralisation*. Centralisation is a product of, or associated with, Confucian cultural values and cognition in general and Vietnamese culture in particular. However, in the context of the Vietnamese SOEs we found that the SOEs were not only centralised, but *over-centralised*. The following throws some light on how this structure is produced.

As emerged in Chapter 5, one of the major aims of state enterprise reform in Vietnam is to decentralise the decision making autonomy to enterprise level. This objective has been achieved, but only to a limited degree. In Chapter 8 it became clear that SOEs are still, to a great extent, heavily dependent on and controlled by government organisations. The government does not trust the SOEs sufficiently to give them the authority to manage their (state) assets.

It is well-documented that in its corporatisation policy (Decision-90 and Decision-91), the Vietnamese government wanted a board-management structure of governance that could, in theory, run the business more efficiently. However, as the regulations concerning the management of state corporations demonstrate, the government did not trust the boards. The board members of Decision-91 corporations are appointed directly by the Prime Minister, the highest executive position in the country, the *Central Domain*. Ironically, the *boards (or the chairman) did not have the right to*

160

appoint the corporation's management team (the general director and deputy directors), the former also being appointed by the Prime Minister. The implicit assumption is that the government does not trust the board or the chairman of the corporation, despite their being government officials.

Another example of the government's limited trust is explicit in the regulations concerning the board and management team's overseas trips. According to Decision 39/CP (1995), any overseas trips (e.g. for business, study or visits) made by the chairman or general director of a corporation must be approved by the head of the government organisation that originally decided to establish the corporation (the Prime Minister for Decision-91 corporations). Overseas trips made by board members must be approved by the chairman. The rationale behind the regulation was that the government did not trust the people possessing important information about the state business corporations.

The fact that the government did not trust the boards or the director of state enterprises enough to delegate investment decisions down to the enterprise level is also well documented in several other regulations. The Circular 24/1998/TT-BTC dealing with compensation for inefficient investment decisions (see Chapter 8) is a clear example. The obvious consequence of this centralising policy in general, and the circular in particular, is to discourage risk-taking and entrepreneurial behaviour on the part of the enterprise. In an interview, the deputy director (in charge of production and quality) of the shoe enterprise said:

> "You need to be careful when making investment decisions yourself, it is OK if the investment project brings a profit or break-even. But if it results in a loss you will be in trouble, they (government officials) will charge you with lacking responsibility and mismanagement in using the state capital. You know that in a market economy, how can you be sure 100% or even 80% that an investment decision will bring a profit."

The analysis of certain actions (opportunistic behaviour) in Chapter 9 and of corruption in Chapter 6 has provided some justification for the government's policy that has led to the over-centralised structure of SOEs. Since opportunism is ubiquitous, it appears that centralisation and tightly controlled policy are the order of the day. In addition, the relative lack of co-operation amongst Vietnamese also partly explains the centralisation structures. Things often go wrong when people do not work together towards the same ends, and this justifies the need for a fair and discipline-dispensing figure at the top. This structural pattern pervades almost all social organisations ranging from the family to the nation, as the policy of rewarding discipline-dispensing family heads in traditional Vietnam (see Chapter 4) clearly indicated. The above analysis *partly* shows how certain actions (opportunistic behaviour and non-co-operation) produce a certain *structure* (centralisation and tight control from the top).

The 'corporatisation' policy (Decision-90 and Decision-91) which aimed at replacing the bureaucratic governance structure by one said to resemble that of Western corporations and the Korean *chaebol*, appears inappropriate. At this point, it is worth comparing the Vietnamese state corporations and the *chaebol*, since the people of Vietnam and Korea share many cultural traits (both countries are heavily influenced by Chinese culture). The key difference between the Korean *chaebol* and the Vietnamese state corporations is that the former is family owned and the latter are owned by the state. The board and key management positions in the *chaebol* are held by family members or close friends. As Biggart pointed out: "families not only own the *chaebol*, they typically run them" (Orru, Biggart & Hamilton, 1997, p.229). Thus, in the *chaebol*, the interests of the family are in line with those of the business, a crucial factor in their success. In contrast, the board members and executives of the Vietnamese corporations are not the owners of the business but state officials whose 'grace' and 'dignity' are to prosper their own family. Whenever there is conflict of interest between the family and the 'others' the family must come first, as has usually been the case throughout Vietnamese history.

The case of the shoe enterprise is a vivid example of family interest being placed above that of the enterprise. It is possible that if the enterprise had been owned by the director's family it would have performed much better, because then its profit would have officially belonged to her. She might then have tried to motivate employees to work toward the same end and Mr. Thong (mentioned in the case) could have officially and openly marketed and sold the firm's products at the market price.

It is widely accepted that large business organisations cannot operate effectively if they are over-centralised. Creativity and entrepreneurial skills are often wasted in such organisations, as demonstrated by the shoe enterprise where young and educated middle managers like Mr. Tuan and Mr. Hung had no opportunity to use and develop their management skills. On the other hand, in such organisations the director could be 'right' not to delegate decision making power to her subordinates, since she cannot really trust them. They are not related to her and may not be close friends. In addition, they may not co-operate with managers from other departments (this is true in the shoe enterprise, see Chapter 9), so forcing her to take control and keep track of everything herself.

The picture is somewhat different in private or family businesses. Private (family) businesses in Vietnam or other societies culturally connected with the Chinese are typically run by the owner's family or close friends, people who share the same interests, have similar responsibilities and work toward the same end. Family businesses in Vietnam are, therefore, sensitive and adaptive to the market and much more efficient than their SOE counterparts (in those areas where private and state businesses are being treated fairly equally) (Dapice, 1999). The case of the shoe enterprise provides insights into this. As Mr. Tuan (head of the production planning & materials department) pointed out, one of the reasons that the shoe enterprise performed better than many other SOEs in the industry was that the director and her son (Thong) ran the enterprise as if it was their family business. The two worked well together informally and adapted the company to market conditions, unlike many other SOEs that can appear inflexible and are burdened by huge amounts of unsold products (Dapice, 1999 and World Bank, 1999).

Transactions

Unlike small private businesses SOEs, especially medium- and large-size firms, cannot rely on informal methods (e.g. those based on network and trust) in carrying out transactions. They have to use formal institutions (e.g. the banking system) and legal systems (the court) which means that to a great extent, they cannot use methods such as network sanctions in handling business transactions, as pointed out by McMillan and Woodruff (1999a). Neither can they use private capital borrowed from family members and friends (self-financed) but must use the banking system. Since the banking system is highly inefficient, enterprises have to pay high interest rates on their borrowings (Fforde, 2001).

The ineffectiveness and inefficiency of formal institutions in Vietnam, as discussed in Chapter 6, are among the major reasons for the shortcomings of many SOEs. This was illustrated by the garment enterprise case where, in an interview, the head of administration & personnel complained that the enterprise found it difficult to get its money back (overdue payments) from domestic customers. The success of the enterprise was largely attributed to its subcontracted work to foreign companies (80% of the total revenue). Similarly, the light bulb enterprise also complained about their customers' overdue payments and 'cheating' (not following the terms of the sales contract). Since the courts are not able to enforce contracts, it is not surprising that many SOEs are now burdened by overdue debts from their business partners. At the same time better performing SOEs are being affected by poorly performing ones and subsequently, the whole sector is inefficient.

A banking system burdened by the debts of the SOEs, substantial overdue payment between SOEs (World Bank, 1999) and a huge amount of unsold stock in many SOEs (Dapice, 1999) provides vivid evidence of how inefficient the Vietnamese institutional matrix really is. In such an institutional environment, "large firms with substantial fixed capital will exist only under the umbrella of government protection with subsidies, tariff protection, and payoffs to the polity – a mixture hardly conductive to productive efficiency" (North, 1990, p.67).

These facts once again confirm our thesis about the existence of guerilla capitalism in Vietnam. Informal networking, personal trust, flexibility, and self-financing should be the order of the day.

Chapter 10: Embedded materialism – the limitation of the incentive structure in Vietnamese SOEs

This chapter deals with our findings about what we call 'embedded materialism' in general and how it finds expression in the current pay policy (one of the key components of the incentive structure in North's institutional framework) of the SOEs. 'Materialism' refers to the emphasis on materials (i.e. the quantity of products and how they are produced) rather than value (i.e. prices, make-ups). Materialism was rooted in Marx's labour theory of value and its practice in the Soviet-style economic system.

Chapter 8 presented an overall picture of industrial governance in the Vietnamese SOEs. A key finding was that SOEs are still, to a great extent, patrimonially dependent on the various government bureaux. To continue an analysis following North's institutional framework, this chapter focuses particularly on a major component of the formal side of institutions: the payment policy. In his theory of institutions, North emphasised the importance of an incentive structure that results from, or is associated with, the institutional matrix. Pay policy is an important and perhaps the most visible component of the incentive structure as a whole. In today's world, material rewards are undoubtedly one of the most (if not the most) important incentives for people working in almost every kind of organisations. Although lack of incentives is often singled out in the literature as one of the major reasons for the poor performance of SOEs in transitional countries in general and Vietnam in particular (see, for example, Nguyen Minh Tu, 1997; Shirley, 1997; and Pearce, Branyiczki & Bakacsi, 1994; and World Bank, 1995) no study has provided detailed information on the incentive system in the Vietnamese SOEs.

This section helps bridge this gap by presenting information on the Vietnam SOE payment system and its links to the problems of SOEs highlighted in previous chapters. Most of the data used in this chapter is taken from Vietnamese sources (e.g. various government decrees, regulations and laws) and from the three case studies, and has not been previously published in the West.

Any understanding of SOE pay policy in Vietnam must start with an examination of its history and ideological context. As noted earlier, the economic transformation must be seen as a process in which the old cannot be removed overnight, but is a path-dependence process. Borrowing Thomas Kuhn's terminology, Boisot (1996) has characterised the process of institution change from a planned to a market economy occurring in China and Vietnam as a "paradigm shift". He points out that the "old" paradigm (the Soviet-style model) still plays a significant part in today's Vietnam and China. Marx's labour theory of value, with its emphasis on materialism, was a building block of the old system that still exercises a great influence on Vietnam and China.

This chapter first briefly reviews some of the important points of Marx's labour theory of value, and then presents our findings on the payment system in the Vietnamese SOEs with reference to Marx and the prevailing socialist ideology in Vietnam. In the final part we will draw a link between materialism, the current payment policy and the performance of the SOEs in general, and more specifically the problems presented in Chapter 9.

10.1. Marx's labour theory of value

The theory of value is undoubtedly one of the major debates in economics and other social sciences. In common sense terms, the value of a product is often understood as its price. In economics, the concept of value has a long and distinguished history, with economists long attempting to capture the 'essence' of value. Modern economists contend that utility and scarcity determine value. Demand and supply, the expressions of utility and scarcity, are, in essence, major determinants of price and value. In the classical tradition, labour (not product price) is considered as the primary source of value. David Ricardo and Karl Marx also accepted labour as the central element in their theories of value but adopted a more radical approach by arguing that labour was also a measure of value.

For Marx, the value of "all commodities are only definite masses of congealed labour time" (Marx, 1970). The capitalist pays the worker an amount that is just enough for him to reproduce his labour. The difference between the exchange value of labour and the exchange value of its products is, according to Marx, the "surplus value", which the capitalist appropriates for him/ herself. 'Surplus value' is, thus, a measure of the degree of exploitation by which the capitalist exploits labour. Machines, equipment and other forms of 'capital' involved in the production process are, Marx argued, nothing but congealed labour – an accumulation of labour through time. Value is measured as the sum of congealed or dead labour (C), live labour (V) and surplus (M), hence the formula:

Value = C + V + M

From a capitalist point of view or at the micro level, the labour theory of value appears irrelevant. It plays down the role of entrepreneurs and management, which are not considered factors of production. Boisot (1996) pointed out that within the framework of the theory of value:

"The entrepreneur....claims no legitimate role, nor can he be remunerated in a world in which value is created by labour and by labour alone. He becomes an interloper who adds nothing to what is already produced by labour." (p.912)

165

Boisot also pointed out that unlike other theories of value (e.g. marginal utility and price theory of value) which are oriented towards alternative futures, Marx's labour theory of value is oriented towards a single past (present 'live' and past labour embedded in products).

Like many other social concepts, value is not a static or value-free concept. Marx developed the labour theory of value in order to demonstrate the exploitative nature of capitalism. Marx's concept of exploitation presupposed his labour theory of value (Zizek, 2002). He was concerned with the capitalist system as a whole, and not with a particular commodity or a capitalist firm at a specific time. Marx's theory of value was not a theory of price or markets. In it, "individual capitalists do not directly appreciate the surplus-value produced by 'their own workers'. Rather, the appropriation of surplus-value was conceived as a process of collective class exploitation, while the distribution of the aggregate (social) surplus-value amongst different capitals was seen as the effect of the inter-capitalist competition in the sphere of circulation" (Smith, 1996 p[8]). Marx's theory of value is, therefore, a theory of capitalism and not a theory of business or price determination in a particular market.

Despite its non-operational and non-practical nature, Marx's labour theory of value remains powerful, especially in countries that have attempted to put it into practice, as for example, Lenin and Stalin did in the former Soviet Union. The legacy of the Soviet-style model in Vietnam was reviewed at some length in Chapter 5. In the Soviet-style model, there was no exploitation at a class level and labour, especially direct labour, was highly appreciated. The management role was considered marginal. At its best, the Soviet-style system was an ideal social system in which there was no unemployment, equality was maintained and education and healthcare were free to everyone. The difference between the incomes of high rank officials and workers was marginal and the working class enjoyed the status that Marx would have wished for. Unfortunately, the Soviet-style system could not be sustained due, as detailed in Chapter 5, to two major reasons: information and lack of incentives for innovative and entrepreneurial activities.

One of the most important objectives of the SOE reform in Vietnam was to give SOEs more autonomy and incentives so that they could survive and compete successfully in a market economy. The next section presents our findings about the pay system in the reformed Vietnamese SOEs.

10.2. Payment practice in the Vietnamese SOEs

When it comes to payment practice, SOEs are under the control (both directly and indirectly) of their 'owner' ministry (the Ministry of Industry in the case of the three enterprises investigated) and two 'specialist' ministries (the Ministry of Finance and the Ministry of Labour, Invalids and Social Affairs). The two 'specialist' ministries, especially the Ministry of Labour, Invalids and Social Affairs, are responsible for drawing up regulations, checking and to some extent, taking care of employment

166

practices in SOEs. The reform process has seen a gradual transition from a direct intervention approach to indirect control through regulations and laws, especially two decrees:

> ➤ Decree 28/CP (28 March 1997) on the 'reform of salary and income management in state-owned enterprises'; and
> ➤ Decree 59/CP (3 October 1996) on the 'financial and accounting management mechanism to state-owned enterprises'.

These were introduced to clarify the 'principal/ agent' relationship in which the enterprise (the agent) is monitored and controlled through various regulations and motivated by the 'pay for performance' principle. Below are the major points of the incentive system in the Vietnamese SOEs.

10.2.1. The salary budget

The 'salary budget' (*qui luong*) is an important component of the incentive system in reformed SOEs and of the reform programme as a whole. The 'salary budget' (hereafter SB) is the amount that a state-owned enterprise is allowed to pay its total workforce in a given year, subject to the firm's performance.

At the beginning of each year, SOEs are required to prepare and submit a proposal for a planned SB to the relevant government bureaux for approval. In the case of the shoe enterprise, the company submits a planned SB to the Hanoi Industrial Bureau and the Hanoi Bureau of Labour, Invalids and Social Affairs. These bureaux consider and approve the amount, which will later be adjusted according to the firm's performance.

The calculation is based on a number of rules appearing in various government decrees, including the two mentioned above. The amount is a function of a number of variables so the calculation procedure is rather complicated. A shortened formula can be written as follows:

$$SB = L * k + O$$

In which:

L: is the number of labour hours converted from the quantity of products to be produced, (calculated following the industry-wide standard);
k: adjusted variable (which takes into account many factors such as the nature of the industry (i.e. heavy, light) different geographical areas (i.e. urban, rural) where the firm is based, regulated minimum wage level, and so on);
O: others (i.e., some special kinds of labour are not included in L).

It is clear from the above formula that the most important component of SB is the *quantity* of products produced. In the case of the shoe enterprise, for example, L is based on the total number of pairs of shoes the enterprise planned to produce. The number of pairs of shoe will then be converted into labour hours or labour.
A list specifies the 'standard' amount of direct labour (e.g. number of hours) needed

for an average worker to produce, for example, a pair of canvas shoes. This 'standard' amount is calculated by labour experts and approved by relevant government organisations. The list is applied to all state enterprises in the same industry, but it may well be outdated and too general. The shoe enterprise is currently using the list published in 1994, which does not specify different models or sizes of canvas shoes but only one category: *canvas shoes*. Box 10.1 shows a guideline for the calculation of the total labour hour for a product. The salary for indirect labour (including management) is often calculated as a proportion or percentage of direct labour. The ratio of indirect (including management)/ direct labour for a particular product is specified by the relevant government organisations.

At the end of the year, the enterprise and government bureau will review the enterprise's performance (i.e. whether or not the enterprise has met the year's plan) and decide the actual amount the enterprise can pay its workforce. The maximum amount the enterprise is allowed to pay its total workforce (the actual amount) and the SB could vary depending on how well the enterprise has fulfilled its annual plan. (i.e. the difference between actual and estimated revenues).

Box 10.1. A guideline for the calculation of total labour hour per product

TSP = Tcn + Tpv + Tql = Tsx + Tql (all-in labour hour).

In which:

➢   Tsp: total labour per product

➢   Tcn: direct production labour per product

➢   Tpv: support production labour per product

➢   Tsx: total production labour

➢   Tql: management labour per product (% of Tsx)

Source: Adapted from Decree 14/LDTBXH-TT (10-4-1997)

There are other constraints on the actual amount, for example on profit. In order to get the full amount possible for its workforce, the firm must meet the following criterion: its profit for the year must be higher than that of the year before. If the firm's profit is less than the year before, it can only pay its employees an amount less than the normal amount by the difference in profit of the two years. There are no such differences if it makes more profit than it did the year before. The government expects firms to perform better year after year (revenue and profit must be greater year after year). Another constraint is that the percentage increase in productivity must be higher than the percentage increase in salary.

10.2.2. Other regulations on payment

A number of other regulations concern payment policy in SOEs. One concerns the salary levels of different positions within the organisation, including the limit on the income of the enterprise's director. The decree 28 LB/TT states that "the income of the firm's directors (including salary and bonuses) must not exceed three times that of the average received by an employee". Other regulations concern salary the differentiation between different hierarchical positions.

Another regulation concerns the salary differences between SOEs operating in the same industry. According to Decree 28-CP/1997, the average salary per employee in one SOE (a successful one, for example) must not exceed twice the average salary per employee of the industry (e.g. the same types of products categorised by the government) as a whole. The industry-wide average salary per employee, is actually announced by the Ministry of Labour, Invalids and Social Affairs.

The enterprise has, *to some extent*, the discretion to pay its employees within the amount approved. It can draw up its own pay policy, but must follow government regulations and guidelines (e.g. the regulation that limits the income of the firm's director). It is common practice that for the purpose of payment, employees are often classified into two groups: direct and indirect labourers. The indirect labour group includes those people not physically involved in the production and transportation of the products (e.g. administrative staff, accountants, managers and director). The salary budget is accordingly divided into two parts, one for direct workers and the other for indirect. The payment of the second group, including the salary of the managers and the director, is dependent on the salary of the direct group.

So in the case of the garment enterprise, the enterprise paid 78% of the total payment package to its direct employee group and the remaining 22% to the indirect one. The light bulb enterprise set the average salary of a direct worker as a base to calculate the salary of the indirect group. The shoe enterprise paid indirect labourers the standard amount set by the government plus any bonus subject to the performance (productivity) of the direct group.

Direct workers are often paid on a piece-rate principle in which their salary is linked directly to the amount of work or number of products they produced. We found that all three enterprises applied the piece-rate system. The principle, according to Mr. Dung, personnel manager of the garment enterprise, was "to make it as clear as possible so that at the end of the day, workers should know approximately how much they would get from the day's work".

The indirect group is often paid following a government guideline which sets the salary scales for different jobs or positions. The difference in salary between staff working in a department and the head of that department (middle manager) is marginal. In the garment enterprise, for example, a salary scale specified the relative differences (points) between the salaries attached to different jobs and positions. In the personnel & administration department, for example, the scale ranged from 1.78 to 2.2 points with the head of the department (middle manager) given 2.2 points and the lowest position (most junior staff) 1.78 points. The majority of department staff got about 2.0 points. The difference in salary between the head of department and his staff is, therefore, marginal (2.2: 2.0). There is also not much difference in salary between an average worker and a middle manager. In 1998, the average salary of a worker was approximately VND1,200,000 a month and that of a middle manager VND1,320,000.

The shoe enterprise did not create its own salary scale, but followed the standard scale set by the government to make payments to its indirect group. Managers get the usual wage given to other staff of the same rank and an extra amount for management responsibility. The extra amount attached to a middle management position is about VND200,000 (in 1999), about 25% higher than he would get if he were not a manager. The difference in salary between a middle manager and a worker could be significant and surprising. Table 1 shows the salary of Mr. Tuan, head of the production & planning department and that of an average worker from the cutting-shop floor (one of the shop floors of the enterprise).

Table 10.1. Salary of a middle manager and a worker in 1999 (in VND)

Position	October	November	December
Head of the production & planning department	1,050,000	1,100,000	1,100,000
A worker	1,450,000	1,670,000	1,710,000

In 1999 VND100,00 was equivalent to USD7.2

The worker's salary is significantly higher than that of a middle manager (55% higher in December, 1999). When asked about the difference, Mr. Tuan said: "It is very common here for workers' salaries to be higher than managers like me, and some workers with high productivity are paid even more than the deputy directors. Workers' salaries are directly linked to their productivity, my salary is somewhat fixed. My salary can be higher at times when the enterprise operates at full capacity, but the difference is not significant."

10.3. Embedded materialism, incentive structures and the problems of Vietnamese SOEs

From the above survey of the Vietnamese SOE payment system we can draw a general conclusion that although there have been significant changes in the incentive system in Vietnamese SOEs, the system is still heavily influenced by Marx's labour theory of value and socialist ideology. This conclusion is drawn from two important characteristics of the system:

The payment system is still heavily labour based (materialism) rather than market based; and the socialist ideology of equality still dominates the system.

170

The rest of this chapter focuses on an analysis of the two points above and their links to the problems of SOEs including those highlighted in the last chapter.

Although there have been significant changes in the incentive structure, the strong influence of Marx's labour theory of value on current SOE payment systems is clear from the way the salary budget (SB) is calculated. As noted previously, the most important component of SB is the amount of labour (physical labour) spent on the products. Direct labour is considered as the root of the whole payment system and is at its 'centre', while management and other forms of indirect labour have become secondary and marginalised.

The embeddedness of the view that labour is a measure of value is also evident in the language used in various government documents. The use of the letter 'V' in various documents (e.g., decree 13/LDTBXH-TT) to denote 'salary' is one example. Marx used the letter 'V' as an abbreviation for 'live' labour in his formula of value: C + V + M. All these three letters C, V and M are the first letters of the German words for 'congealed' labour, 'live' labour and 'surplus' respectively. These abbreviations were kept in the Vietnamese translated version of Marxist texts. We also found these expressions used in interviews with some Vietnamese officials. For example, an official from the Ministry of Labour, Invalids and Social Affairs whose job was to design salary policies mentioned the letters C, V, M several times. He insisted that the "value of products equal to C + V + M" and "V must be calculated on the basis of the average amount of labour needed to produce the product". The embeddedness of the labour theory of value can also be found in the regulation restricting the rise in salary *vis à vis* the rise in productivity (percentage increase in salary must be smaller than percentage increase in productivity). This regulation, according to an official, is formulated in line with Marx's observation of the difference in trends of the increase in productivity and salary.

From the above evidence we can draw the conclusion that the payment system in the Vietnamese SOEs still, to a great extent, follows Marx's labour theory of value. The emphasis is placed on direct labour or ultimately on 'material', the latter part of the production process becoming the 'centre', and value marginalised. The 'materialist' orientation can also be found in other regulations affecting the operation of the Vietnamese SOEs. One of those regulations limits the amount an enterprise is allowed to spend on 'non-material' or 'market' activities including advertising, promotion, meetings, external affairs and so on. According to this regulation, the enterprise can only spend up to 7% of its total costs (Decree 59/CP) on market activities. The limit on this 'market associated' spending represents a limit on the autonomy of the firm in 'non-material' activities (e.g. advertising). It is therefore not surprising that most of SOEs have never advertised their products by using expensive media such as television.

Vietnamese SOEs, on the one hand, are for-profit entities. They have to compete in the marketplace and play by the market rules. On the other hand they are, as analysed above, constrained by various regulations that tend to limit their ability to act in response to the market. This conflict would inevitably result in some of the problems presented in Chapter 9.

The emphasis on the 'material' or 'physical' part of the production process institutionalised in the formal 'rules of the games' does not give the 'players' any incentive toward 'value' generation (i.e. seeking for high value products with high make-up, focusing on cost reduction, and so on). The evidence from the three cases, especially from the shoe enterprise, strongly supports this. In an interview, we asked a deputy director of the shoe enterprise to compare a SOE and an equitised enterprise to see which was more efficient and better suited to the market economy. He insisted that the equitised firm would be much better, and gave a number of examples to support his arguments.

> "You see, these people (he pointed to a number of his administrative staff) do not turn off the light in their offices when they go out for lunch. They see no benefit in it. I'm sure they would turn it off if they had worked for an equitised firm, because they would get a higher salary if the firm performed better."

He continued:

> "The same things happen on the shopfloor, workers here they only try to produce as fast as they can. There are no incentives for them to improve production methods that could reduce the amount of materials per product and eventually reduce costs. Their salaries and the salary of the enterprise as a whole depends on the number of pairs of shoes produced."

The director of the enterprise was also very disappointed by the current salary policy. She said: "The current salary policy is very unfair. Our enterprise has performed quite well (in terms of profit), but our salaries are very low." She believed strongly that the enterprise (enterprise's employees) deserved more. This was indicated in her opinions about the prospect of the enterprise being equitised:

> "Recently, the government has suggested we consider equitising the Enterprise, I said to them that we would agree, no problem, but they (the government) must pay us appropriately VND20 billion we have made over the last five to-seven years. At the time I was appointed as the director of the enterprise, it was nearly bankrupt. We started from scratch and now we have made a lot of money for the government, reinvested a lot but we only got a little of it."

The director also complained about the fact that the shoe industry was classified by the government as 'Class 3'. Currently, enterprises are classified into three categories (Class 1, 2 or 3) depending on the nature of work (i.e., heavy, light, safety and so on) of the industry they are operating on. Employees from Class 3 enterprises are often paid less than those from the other two classes. According to the director, the shoe industry should be in the Class 2 because "making shoes entails hard work, the production process involves substances like rubbers and chemicals which could be very harmful."

172

With the notion of embedded materialism, SOEs tend to place the emphasis on the amount of work done rather than its value. The make-ups or profits are not as important as the quantity sold. The quantity sold is important because it is linked directly to the amount of work and the pockets of the employees. This can partly explain the fact that the shoe enterprise did not focus on developing quality models with high value that were less labour intensive. The company relied on sub-contracting work from foreign agents with little profit. Marketing activities were not paid much attention. As we can see from its structure in Chapter 9, the enterprise does not have a marketing department or group specialising in marketing activities. According to the head of the import-export department, the enterprise did not need a marketing department. When asked whether it should have one, he explained with great confidence:

> "We do not need a marketing department, foreign agents will come to us and place orders, we just make shoes for them. We don't need to worry about the market, for the moment at least. Vietnamese shoes are competitively cheap and the demand for shoes in the world is great. So far workers here have had enough work to do."

The emphasis is placed on 'work to do'. The major objective, according to the leaders of the enterprise is not profit, although the government would not agree. As a deputy director said:

> "For SOEs, it's important to be 'stable', to have enough work and make no losses. The enterprise should make some profit. It is not necessary to make a lot of profit because if you do, many organisations will start to watch you. In addition, as you know, in Vietnam, they (the government) expect everything (i.e. financial ratios) higher this year than that of last year. So what would happen if you make a lot of profit this year but can't make the same or a higher figure next year? The enterprise's total salary budget will be deducted the difference between the profits of the two years!"

The government has always stressed the importance of profits, and expected SOEs to maximise their profits. These were expressed in the policy linking the enterprise's salary budget and its profits (as the deputy director mentioned: if the enterprise makes less profit this year than the year before, the enterprise's salary will be deducted an amount equal to the difference between profits of the two years). Far from its designed objective, the policy appears to have had little positive effect and even had adverse consequences. Firms tend to make or report just a little profit each year. In an interview Mr. Thang, an official involved in the implementation of the SOE reform programme said: "The general formula of the Vietnamese SOEs is to make a little profit every year and avoid losses."

Since profitability and efficiency are not a pressure, the management of SOEs like the shoe enterprise are able to take advantage and behave opportunistically. In the case of the shoe enterprise, although the director 'sold' the enterprise's products to her son at low prices, this was unlikely to have any significant impact on the pockets of the enterprise employees. This partly explains why pricing in the Vietnamese and Chinese SOEs, as found in Boisot (1996), is done in a very simple way: cost-plus pricing.

The same argument can be made about input prices and the inefficient use of materials. As the deputy director from the shoe enterprise implied in the above quotation, materials can be used more efficiently but the current payment system does not encourage the workers and the enterprise as a whole to do so. As the deputy director who is in charge of the production process pointed out:

> "The most important thing is that the shoe enterprise made some profit and workers had enough work to do. As long as a state enterprise does not make a loss in several consecutive years, its director's seat is unlikely to be challenged. As you may know, the government has put more pressure on directors of SOEs by issuing a decree that state that any director of a SOE making a loss in three consecutive years will likely be replaced. In reality the decree, as it was written, has not been effectively enforced)."

The 'materialism' in general and the current payment policy in particular may also account for the problem of overstocking in many SOEs. In order to ensure that employees have enough work and earn a reasonable income, many SOEs produce too many products, and still hold a large quantity of unsold products in stock (Dapice, 1999). Firms keep producing without any certainty that they can sell their products. The problem of overstocking has led to yet another common problem, that of *lai gia, lo that* (on paper enterprises make a profit, but actually they have made a loss). This is because it is unlikely that the firm can sell the stock (e.g. unsold shoes) at a price able to cover the cost of producing them whereas on paper, the stock is still valued as their production costs (congealed plus live labour).

The embedded materialism and prevailing socialist ideology of equality expressed in the payment policy of the Vietnamese SOEs also fuel problems presented in Chapter 9. Management is considered secondary to direct labour and managers (i.e. head of departments) are still considered as officials. They are undoubtedly underpaid. Despite the fact that they are part of a high power distance culture like Vietnam, the salary of a middle manager can be lower than that of an average worker. Since the importance of management is not formally and materially recognised and their responsibility is not clear, it is understandable that managers tend to behave opportunistically, as found in the shoe enterprise. As a production & planning manager in the shoe enterprise said frankly in an interview:

> "In fact, I don't care about salary, I don't even know how much I have received. It's about VND800,000 to VND900,000 a month I think. It's not significant. I think it's just enough to pay for my mobile phone and petrol (for my motorbike). I have to find out other ways to earn money."

He went on to talk about telephone expenses:

> "You see, a manager like me, because of the nature of the job, has to use a mobile phone frequently. It costs me about VND500,000 to VND600,000 a month. But the enterprise has only paid just over VND100,000 towards this sum. Even for a deputy director like Mr. Hung, the enterprise has only paid VND300,000 (a month) for his phone..."

In the past, the management role was primarily concerned with the implementation of plans set out by the government. The information-processing role was done by the government and managers did not have to make important decisions involving a great deal of information processing and judgement. The role of SOE managers is now significantly different. Their work involves 'market' activities. They have to make choices under conditions of uncertainty and with imperfect information. A decision made by the director of an enterprise like one of the three investigated could have a non-trivial impact on the lives of thousands of people. The current payment policy, which is largely inherited from the old system, appears irrelevant and irrational. The director of the shoe enterprise often worked, as she said, more than 12 hours a day but received a salary of less than USD200 a month. This amount was, she said, "lower than the salary of an accountant or a secretary working in a joint-venture, or even in many Vietnamese private companies in Hanoi".

Everyone in Vietnam would understand that a director deserves to get a higher salary and that he or she needs a greater amount to cover their living expenses. With this level of salary government bureaux, especially the ones that invented the payment policy, have *unofficially* accepted that directors and managers may get more income from unofficial sources. The current pay policy, an element of the formal 'rules of the game' has, to a certain extent, *legitimated* opportunistic behaviours. Such behaviour has become *socially* expected and natural. Those (managers and directors) who rely on their salary are often considered irrational. This partly explains why, despite being paid much less, many university graduates still prefer to work for state enterprises rather than joint-ventures or private firms. They could expect to get other sources of income if they work for state firms. Within an enterprise, it is difficult to prevent opportunistic behaviour or to create a healthy working environment if a majority of people see opportunistic behaviour as normal.

Materialism and the current payment policy also partially account for the problem of 'cooking the books', a widespread problem. Nguyen Minh Tu (1997) points out that the government "does not know whether enterprises are gaining interest or suffering losses" (p.6). Thus, it is not surprising that successful firms report a smaller profit and pay their employees an amount which is greater than that supposedly allowed. In an interview, a personnel manager from the light bulb enterprise revealed: "People here get much more than the salary figures from the book (the official figures reported to the government bureaux).' He further explained:

> "The enterprise is not allowed to pay high salaries to employees, so we must make the figures look .reasonable and find other ways to pay them more... Even if allowed to, it's unwise to keep the figures high. It's a sensitive issue. This enterprise is state owned, you see. The government does not want to see a big difference in salary amongst state firms... Also, if a salary is high they [the government] will start asking you why and they may start to make a reassessment of the labour/product and adjust the salary level."

Chapter 11: Policy implications

This monograph has attempted to construct a framework to explain the behaviour of the Vietnamese SOEs. The next section provides some suggestions as to how to improve the performance of the SOEs in general and in particular, to limit the problems presented in previous chapters. 'Performance' can, however, mean different things to different people and is linked to the firm's major objectives. For commercial SOEs these are, as laid down by the Vietnamese government, to survive and compete fairly and successfully in an open economy. The following suggestions concern the on-going, long-term survival of these enterprises in the context of markets, competition and globalisation. We believe that, given the unequal power relationship between the West, especially the USA, and the developing world, globalisation and 'capitalisation' seem unstoppable. Therefore Vietnamese enterprises, and Vietnam as a whole, must adapt if they are to survive in this hostile world.

In the process of SOE reform in Vietnam, no policy could be expected to please *everyone* involved. A policy designed to ensure the long-term survival of SOEs in the context of competition may not guarantee employment for everyone currently employed by those firms, hence the economic transition processes taking place in Vietnam, China and Eastern European countries have been described as "painful" (Harris, 1997).

To be consistent with the theoretical framework adopted in this work, the following suggestions are based directly on an analysis of the institutional matrix in Vietnam and cover both formal and informal characteristics. Two major groups of suggestions are proposed: privatisation, or the improvement of SOE performance without privatisation. The rest of the section is given over to a discussion of alternatives.

11.1. Privatisation / equitisation

Clearly, the Vietnamese culture (informal aspects) is most suited to family (owner-managed) businesses. Empirical evidence from the Overseas Chinese, who share many cultural traits with the Vietnamese, has strongly supported this argument. Westwood (1997) pointed out that owner-managed businesses were the core of industrial organisation in economies such as Singapore, Taiwan and Hong Kong. Drawing on others' work, Westwood (1997) also concluded that "the rationale for businesses in Southeast Asia is founded upon feministic considerations and the prime directive for enterprise owners is the inter-generational maintenance and perpetuation of the family's well-being, prestige and prosperity." (p.457). The success of these businesses must be connected to ownership.

176

SOEs appear foreign to Vietnamese cultural values and tradition. Therefore in order to take advantage of Vietnamese cultural values and traditions, privatisation appears an obvious reform measure. The owners of the privatised firms would be liberated from complicated and 'irrational' impositions from above and so be free to decide how to run the enterprise. Many positive Vietnamese cultural traits such as loyalty, reciprocity and harmony could then produce a better economic performance if placed in the right context: that of private owner-managed businesses. The owners of the privatised firms would try their best to improve their enterprise's performance because it was in line with their interests.

Over the last few decades, privatisation has become almost orthodox economic policy throughout much of the world (Megginson & Netter, 2001; and D'Souza, Megginson and Nash, 2001). It is widely agreed that privatisation can result in an increase in output, efficiency, profitability and an improvement in a firm's performance as a whole. Empirical studies have strongly supported the argument. Megginson and Netter (2001) and D'Souza, Megginson and Nash, (2001) have reviewed numerous recent studies about whether privatisation improves the firm's performance and concluded that "privatisation does work" (i.e. improves financial and operating efficiency). Reports on equitisation in Vietnam also show that equitised enterprises have subsequently improved their performance in terms of turnover and profits (Le Dang Doanh, 1995; and Dapice, 1999).

Evidence from empirical studies, especially from developing and transitional countries, has further supported this argument. In a review of recent privatisation studies Megginson and Netter (2001) and D'Souza, Megginson and Nash (2001) again concluded that "privatisation does work" (i.e. results in an increase in output, efficiency and profitability). Another important finding from these studies is that privatisation can also increase employment, which challenges the belief that privatisation results in layoffs and unemployment.

Reports on equitisation in Vietnam also reveal that those enterprises already equitised have subsequently improved their performance in terms of turnover, profits and employment (Le Dang Doanh, 1995; Dao Duy Tu, 1998 and Dapice, 1999). No-one from those equitised firms was laid off as a result of equitisation, in fact the firms expanded rapidly and employed more people because they had acquired more capital from shareholders.

It is important to note here that the suggestion that the Vietnamese policy makers should privatise SOEs does not imply that privatisation *always* works and that Vietnam should privatise *all* its SOEs. We are not suggesting that Vietnam should follow Eastern European countries and carry out a mass privatisation policy. It is important that the state remain in control of important, strategic industries so that it can effectively play a role in directing the country's development. If a large proportion of a country's wealth is in a few private hands, especially in countries where particularistic values dominate and the government is highly autocratic and corruption is widespread such as in those of Southeast Asia (Blunt, 1988; Richards,

1991; and Blunt, Richards & Wilson, 1989), then it is likely that those private hands will "corruptly run" the country. The government should, therefore, be cautious in designing its privatisation policy. However, we strongly urge Vietnam to speed up the privatisation of 'non-strategic' enterprises like those in the three case studies: there is no need for the state to run industries such as footwear and garments.

Some argue that privatisation could result in poorer services as a consequence of the greed of the private owners. If this is the case, we believe it would be more likely to happen after the privatisation of public sector industries like the railways. Customers are unlikely to suffer from the privatisation of very competitive consumer industries such as shoes and clothing.

Although privatisation/equitisation has been put on the agenda, the pace of equitisation has fallen short of the government's target (World Bank, 1999). The government should try to speed up privatisation, perhaps, concentrating first on small and medium enterprises in 'non-strategic' industries.

11.2. Further reform of the SOEs

In this section, we provide some suggestions as to how to improve the performance of SOEs without any change in ownership. Our previous suggestions were limited to the immediate privatisation of small and medium SOEs operating in 'non-strategic' industries. The immediate privatisation of large SOEs may not be practical, and needs to be considered carefully. Vietnam is still a very poor country with few, if any, families or individuals who can afford to buy all or the majority of shares in a large enterprise so as to be able to control and manage the enterprise like a family business. If shares are sold to many or several buyers so that no one person is able to take control of the firm, problems concerning the governance of the privatised firm could arise. Multiple-owner firms are clearly not family businesses, and the Vietnamese have no experience in running this kind of enterprise. In addition, the low trust and non-co-operation characteristics of the informal side of the institutional matrix in Vietnam would make it difficult to run such a multiple-owner enterprise, especially when market institutions (formal side) are still highly underdeveloped. The rest of this section provides a few suggestions on how to improve SOEs without privatisation.

From our analysis throughout this work, especially in chapters 5, 8, 9, 10, there are principal/ agent problems in the management of SOEs. It is important to note here that by principal/ agent, we do not follow the principal/ agent theory generally found in the literature and reviewed in Chapter 1 that treats the principal/ agent relationship at 'face-value', as the core block of explanation. In this work, principal/ agent problems are incorporated into a broader institutional framework and seen as a result of the institutional matrix.

11.2.1 Autonomy

As presented in Chapters 5 and 8, one of the difficulties in reforming the SOEs in Vietnam involves the governance structure, the relationship between the enterprise and government bureaux and the board of directors. The problem is that both the government bureaux and board of directors are not the 'real' owners of the enterprise. The government bureaux are not close enough to understand the business of the enterprise and their relationship with the enterprise, as pointed out in Chapter 8, is patrimonial. The idea of running SOEs using the Western board-executive model, with the board representing the government, is to ensure that the enterprise is closely monitored and supervised. The board of directors is supposed to understand the enterprise so that it can make strategic decisions but in reality, the roles of the board are not clear. The enterprise must still not only follow the many regulations issued by the government bureaux, but also report directly to them.

We suggest that a board of directors is necessary because the government bureaux are 'too far' from the business of the enterprise to understand them so in order for the board to have any real influence, it needs to be given sufficient autonomy. The board should decide the strategic direction of the enterprise and at least be given the autonomy to recruit and sign the enterprise director's contract. The board should decide on the salary of the director. It should be given the autonomy to set the firm's major objectives and review the performance of the director on the basis of the fulfilment of these objectives. Since the board is 'close' to the enterprise, it will be able to set realistic objectives based on the real capacity of the enterprise. The current method of setting the enterprise objectives is 'irrational' since it is not based on the real capacity of the enterprise or market conditions. The board should also be given the right to terminate the director's contract if he or she does not meet their expectations. The director's job is, therefore, not guaranteed even if the enterprise has made a profit. In return, directors should get what they deserve. The salary of a director could be ten times higher or more than that of a worker.

In order to fulfil this role satisfactorily, board members must be knowledgeable about the markets and businesses concerned. Currently, as a manager from the light bulb enterprise observed: "Board members, in general, are government officials who are about to retire... and they do not know anything about businesses." The government, he believed, should specify requirements for the job so that it could select "the right people".

The director should also be given more autonomy to run the enterprise. Directors should, for example, be allowed to make payment decisions, as these are one of the most, if not the most important tool in management. How can a director effectively run an enterprise if he or she is not allowed to use this tool? As a deputy director of the shoe enterprise complained when discussing the salaries of his subordinates (middle managers): "I know that people like Tuan and Hung deserve to get a much higher salary. They have worked here for 10 years and have very good knowledge of the shoe industry. Private shoemakers are willing to pay them two or three times higher than they get now. But we can't pay them more due to the government's salary policy. We are just waiting to see if there will be any change."

It is not the government, but the director of the enterprise who understands the business, and who knows more than anyone how to motivate his/ her subordinates (i.e. who should get what and why). But it is very unfortunate that they are not allowed to do very much. In addition, directors are not even allowed to choose their own deputies. They can suggest names but the final decision must come from government bureaux. This can result in internal conflicts in the management of the enterprise.

In summary, we propose that the government give more autonomy to the board of directors and the director of the enterprise. Autonomy alone is, however, insufficient to ensure better performance. As the board members in the Vietnamese SOE context are not owners, it could be unwise to give them a great deal of autonomy. They are not the 'real' principals like those in the context of the principal/ agent theory so board members may 'collude' with the director of the enterprise to get their own ends. Also, if a director is given a great deal of autonomy, he may use it to benefit him/ herself. Autonomy must, therefore, be accompanied by other reform measures. There must be a "panopticon" (Foucault, 1979 & 1980; and Bentham, 1962) or 'invisible principal' to watch over the board, the director and the managers and make them accountable. This will involve changes in the 'rules of the game' and is the subject of the following list of suggestions.

11.2.2. 'Normalisation' and the role of the market
Before suggesting ways of making the enterprise 'accountable' and 'manageable', it is worth mentioning Foucault's concept of governmentality. Foucault used the term "governmentality" in his study of the techniques used to manage and control populations (Gordon,1991; Townley, 1993). Governmentality, Foucault argued, was an "ensemble formed by the institutions, procedures, analyses and reflections, the calculations and tactics, that allow the exercise of a... very specific albeit complex form of power" (Foucault, 1979, p.20). One of the ideas behind the concept of governmentality is that before something can be governed, it must first be known. 'Government' is, therefore, dependent upon particular ways of knowing (Townley, 1993). Governing processes operate through regulatory controls that involve classifying and normalising the subject. So in the case of the Vietnamese SOEs, in order to 'control' or make them accountable, they must have been made 'known' and 'normalised'.

It is difficult to 'know' SOEs (i.e. whether they are profitable, whether they have used resources effectively and efficiently and so on) if they pursue different and divergent objectives. Materialism and the socialist ideology expressed in the payment policy have made it difficult to make the 'subject' (SOEs) *known* in a 'market' way. It is difficult to measure a director's performance if he/she has to pursue different objectives (i.e. profit, employment) at the same time. Although the Vietnamese government has stressed that 'profit' and 'efficiency' are *the most important objectives* of the SOEs, its regulations on the payment system have actually 'prevented' the enterprise from achieving these objectives. Since the Vietnamese government has expected SOEs to be 'efficient', 'profitable', 'competitive' and so on, it must regulate the SOEs in such a way that these objectives can be 'known'. If the government uses the language of the 'market' (profit, efficient and competitive) to talk about the performance of an enterprise, it must accept another set of 'market' language that includes the words layoff, labour market, unemployment, labour costs and so on. Materialism and value, efficiency and equality are mutually exclusive, so the government must abandon 'materialism' if it wants SOEs to be efficient, profitable and competitive in an open economy.

We suggest that the director should be allowed to decide on the enterprise's payment policy. Labour should be treated as a cost item, an input, and not a component or *proportion* of value. If labour is viewed as a cost item, it is likely that the director will seriously take into account information on the labour market in making decisions on hiring and rates of pay. The role of the government bureaux should be limited to the making and checking of regulations on general labour issues such as minimum wage, working condition standards, labour contracts and so on. They should not directly decide on the pay budget of every enterprise. Since the objectives (i.e. profitability and efficiency) are clear and measurable, the director can set targets and delegate a number of management decisions to middle managers. For example, if a middle manager like Mr. Tuan (head of the production and planning department in the shoe enterprise) were given clear and measurable objectives like material cost per product and product defect rate, he would focus his energy on achieving those objectives (i.e. selecting the right suppliers and reorganising production processes). The director does not need to make decisions on every lot of material supplied. As Tuan said: "If I were allowed to select suppliers, reorganise the production process and reward my workers, the production process would be much more efficient." Clear and measurable objectives can certainly help the enterprise to decentralise and release the potential of its managers, especially its middle managers.

If labour is viewed as a cost item in a production process aiming at efficiency and profitability, layoffs seem inevitable. Over-employment is a very common problem of SOEs in transitional countries and Vietnam is no exception. The problem of over-employment exists in all three cases investigated. In question 22 of the questionnaire we asked respondents whether their department had over employment (fewer people could perform the same job), most of the respondents (87%) agreed or strongly agreed. Fortunately, the problem of over-employment in the Vietnamese state sector in general is not as serious as that in China and some Eastern European countries (Dapice, 1999). This is because the level of industrialisation in Vietnam before the reform process was still very low compared to that of China and East European countries. The Vietnamese economy is still, to a great extent, agrarian. Dapice argued that Vietnam should have no difficulty in dealing with the problem of over-employment since it could use some part of the funds borrowed from the IMF and the World Bank to support redundant workers.

Promoting private businesses is another way of solving the problem of redundancy. Since the reforms began in 1986, private businesses have been playing an important role in job creation, and family businesses and private enterprises have absorbed a large number of redundant workers from the state sector (Vu Quang Viet, 1997). *Promoting private businesses is, therefore, an effective way of solving the problems of the SOEs.* Although the private sector has been playing a larger role in the Vietnamese economy since reform, the private sector has not been paid enough attention (Richards, Ha, Harvie, and Nguyen, 2002). As the World Bank has commented: "To date in Vietnam, the climate for the private sector has been grudging rather than supportive."

"Here, Vietnam differs markedly from China, where the private sector has been openly recognised as a key partner in the country's development." (World Bank, 2000). In designing reform programmes, policy makers must consider the economy as a whole, and the long-term impact SOEs may have on employment and the economy as a whole.

The very basic concept of equality needs to be reconsidered. The payment policy applied to SOEs was based on an outdated principle of materialism that was inappropriate in the context of a market economy. If Vietnam accepts the idea of the market, then it must play by the market's 'rules of the game'. That is, it must formally accept that a director or manager can earn much more than a worker. Not only SOEs but other types of enterprises (i.e., private, joint-venture and foreign enterprises) operate in Vietnam, so SOEs must play the market game if they are to compete with other types of businesses. Given the power of capitalism, of the market as expressed in the management practices of foreign and private businesses, 'equality' within the SOE sector alone would become an 'irrationality'.

If profitability and efficiency are the most important criteria by which to judge the board and director of an enterprise, then how do we know whether or not an enterprise is being efficient or profitable? And how much is a reasonable profit? The answer to these questions must involve 'classifying' and 'normalising' the subjects (SOEs). That is, there must be mechanisms and 'universal' criteria so that subjects can be measured and compared. The current assessment criteria applied are limited in the sense that they do not follow a mechanism in which firms are 'objectively' compared with each other. Government-imposed SOE targets (i.e. profit and revenues) are set and measured according to the principle of a percentage increase year after year, for example, 10% higher this year than last. An enterprise, therefore, is only compared with *itself*. They are not being 'known' universally and it is difficult to judge them. In the reform process, the government should use 'universal' criteria like 'return on investment' or profit rates to evaluate performance, and SOEs should be *universally* compared.

The availability of statistical data on various financial indicators to allow cross-comparison is very important. Government bureaux could take charge of regularly publishing statistical data on important financial indicators, and classifying SOEs based on those indicators. The board and the director could then be 'objectified', classified and judged on the basis of those indicators and classifications. Not only would SOEs be compared with other SOEs, they could also be compared with private and foreign enterprises operating in the same industry to allow the 'voice' of these enterprises to influence the reform of the state sector. SOEs could then be 'known' in a 'universal' way. The government bureaux could use public media like TV or newspapers to announce the information on classifications and assessments of the board and the director, and the enterprise as a whole. Operating in this way in a 'face' culture like Vietnam would be likely to have a certain impact on the behaviour of those in charge, who might try harder to avoid losing 'face'.

SOEs could also be made 'known' through market institutions such as banks and the stock market. Developing and improving the operation of the stock market in Vietnam would directly support the reform of SOEs. The stock market, however, is new in Vietnam and its development is a long-term project. We do not expect stock markets to play a key role in SOE reform in the very near future. *However, in the long-run, stock markets will certainly play an important role in the restructuring of the Vietnamese economy in general and the reform of SOEs in particular.*

In addition to stock market development, further reform of the banking system and accounting practices are required. Modern banking and accounting systems could certainly help ease some of the problems of the SOEs such as the 'bonus' phenomenon. The fact that in Vietnam, many transactions are still carried out in cash makes it more difficult for the government to check and control the business transactions of the SOEs.

In this chapter we have made various suggestions as to how to improve the performance of SOEs. These suggestions, bearing the ethos of market, capitalism and objectification, are directly based on our research findings about the working of SOEs in Vietnam. Given the current trend of the world economy and the power of capitalism and markets, we strongly believe that the Vietnamese economy in general, and its SOEs in particular, should begin to follow the 'the rules of the game' of the market and capitalism to some extent. These would naturally involve 'normalisation' and 'objectification' (i.e. board members and directors being 'universally' classified and measured). Transition is always a painful process!

Summary and conclusions

1. Summary

This study of SOEs in Vietnam has employed an embedded approach. The SOEs are not considered independent of their environments, but seen as embedded in them. We have employed an institutional approach to analyse the business environment in Vietnam in general, and SOE behaviour in particular. This institutional framework is seen as the rules of the game that provides incentive structures to the players (the business firms). The institutional approach employed in this research has allowed us to explain the various problems of the Vietnamese SOEs in the reform period. We have also given a number of suggestions for the reform of the SOEs in Vietnam.

Given the fact that Vietnam is in transition to a market economy while still pursuing a socialist ideology, formal rules that favour the development of capitalism are still, to a great extent, underdeveloped. The formal rules of the game were analysed at two levels: a general level (i.e. characteristics of the formal rules applied to the Vietnamese economy and society as a whole); and a specific level (i.e. current regulations and government policies applied to SOEs).

We have observed that, at a general level, formal institutions in Vietnam are characterised by (1) incompleteness, (2) lack of codification, and (3) weak enforcement. In addition, institutions such as the banking system and stock markets that are necessary to modern capitalism are underdeveloped or inefficient. The informal aspect of institutions is characterised by limited and bounded trust in economic transactions and corruption. These characteristics are deep-rooted in Vietnamese history and culture and stem from fundamental beliefs about the organisation and structure of the family, the village and government.

The nature of the institutional matrix in Vietnam, a combination of formal rules at the general level and informal norms resulting in insecure property rights and inefficient transaction costs is, it is argued, only suited to a special type of capitalism, guerilla capitalism. That is, capitalism characterised by economic firms (the ideal type) of small-scale, little fixed capital, a short-term orientation, and family controlled and managed. We have used the 'ideal type' as a 'base' from which to analyse and compare SOEs.

Most of the country's SOEs were established during the time that Vietnam was following the Soviet-style development model. They were products of an economic and social policy rather than established for the market, therefore they diverged

184

greatly from the ideal type. Through an investigation of three SOEs and evidence from other sources we have discovered (in Chapters 7 to 10), that SOEs are characterised by (1) over-centralised structures, (2) heavy dependence on government bureaux and (3) widespread problems of opportunism.

We have presented an in-depth case study of one SOE in which the director and her son used their power to gain their own ends at the expense of the enterprise's interest. Some of the problems of the SOEs arise from the lack of a *real* principal. There are ambiguities about who actually owns the enterprise, since government bureaux and the board of directors are not the real owners. The concept of industrial governance which is, to a great extent, still dominated by materialism and socialist ideology of equality, appears irrelevant in a market economy. This type of industrial governance, as was presented at some length in Chapter 10, has also caused many problems for SOEs. Under this governance structure, efficiency is not being paid enough attention and management expertise is under explored or wasted.

Drawing from the study, we have made a number of suggestions for improving the performance of the SOEs. The two major suggestions are (1) privatisation of small and non-strategic SOEs, and (2) improving the performance of SOEs without privatisation. We have proposed that SOEs should be given more autonomy by giving the board, the director and management of the enterprise the freedom to run the enterprise. The board, for example, should be allowed to appoint the director and sign his/ her contract, and we have also argued that decentralisation must be accompanied by clear, consistent and measurable objectives. In order to make the 'subject' (i.e. boards, directors, managers) accountable and manageable, it must first to be 'known'. This will inevitably involve a 'normalisation' process in which managers, directors and enterprises as a whole are classified, compared and judged based on 'universal' criteria (profit rates and return on investment). SOEs should follow the market rules of the game if they are to compete equally and successfully with other types of enterprises in an open economy.

2. Contribution of the research

The most important contribution of the present research is that (1) it provides an analysis of the business environment in Vietnam; (2) theoretically, the research is able to incorporate different factors (history, culture, institutions and politics) in a comprehensive theory of organisations and (3) methodologically, the research offers a unique approach to SOEs, reading SOEs through the language of the ideal type. Below we provide a brief discussion of these points.

The study provides a useful analysis of the business environment in Vietnam and here, it is important to note the difference between analysis and data. By analysis, we mean data that have been processed and codified into abstract concepts. There is currently a fair amount of data available about Vietnamese business and the economy, especially data from the World Bank, the IMF and other donor institutions. Those data are, to a great extent, still in the form of *raw materials* or collected according to pre-conceived frameworks or political propaganda. There is still little comprehensive literature on management and organisational behaviour in Vietnam. We have provided the following analysis of the Vietnamese business environment.

The overall business environment in Vietnam. We have examined both the informal and formal aspects of the business environment, analysing culture, history, tradition, and the recent development towards a market economy. To date, there are no other studies of the business environment in Vietnam that have taken such factors into account to the extent that this research study has done.

The nature of industrial governance in the SOEs during the reform period. In Chapters 7, 8 and 10 we extensively presented the nature of industrial governance in the Vietnamese SOEs. Although there are several studies (of a Western kind) of SOE reform in Vietnam like that of Fforde and de Vylder (1996), none of these provides a detailed analysis of the form and nature of industrial governance in Vietnam. We have also provided a great deal of information on regulations, decrees and policies concerning the management of SOEs in Vietnam which have not so far been made available in English or any other foreign language. The payment policy presented in Chapter 10 is such an example. This chapter not only provides an analysis of the payment system applied to the Vietnamese SOEs, but also explained the system through an analysis of its historical context.

The structure of the SOEs. Chapter 7 provided an analysis of the internal structure of the Vietnamese SOEs. Although it is often argued that organisations in high power distance and high collectivist cultures are characterised by authoritarian and highly centralised structures, no studies have provided empirical evidence in the Vietnamese case. In addition, centralisation and authoritarian structures are not the same everywhere in the world, they may take different forms in different countries or in different types of organisations. This work has provided empirical evidence on how and why the Vietnamese SOEs were structured.

The problems of the Vietnamese SOEs: we have constructed a framework to explain and provide empirical evidence on the problems of the Vietnamese SOEs. To date, no other studies have provided empirical evidence on these problems. Vietnamese SOEs are often described in the literature as having many problems such as inefficiency, but there are no studies that show how and why they are inefficient. Our study has provided information not only on the 'what' question (evidence about the problems), but also they 'why' and 'how' questions. We have taken into consideration both informal (i.e. cultural values) and formal aspects (the current policies and regulations concerning the management of SOEs) in our analyses and explanations of the problems of SOEs.

We have provided a number of suggestions for improving the performance of the SOEs, based directly on our research findings of the informal and formal aspects of the 'rules of the game'. We have given detailed analyses and explanations to justify these suggestions.

Theoretically, the present research has incorporated various societal aspects into a theory of organisations. There are many organisation theories, but most of them are concerned with only one level of analysis or a single-variable type of explanation. Many versions of cultural theory, for example, often over emphasise cultural values at the individual level (Hamilton and Biggart, 1988). Political theories over-emphasise the role of state and formal institutions. Economic theories over-emphasise self-interest and efficiency.

In this work we incorporated historical, cultural, economic and political aspects into a theory of organisations. Both the macro-level (politics and formal institutions) and the micro-level (interest and agency) were brought into this analysis. The institutional approach employed allowed us to incorporate a number of competing theoretical frameworks into one model of analysis, the institutional matrix. As emphasized, there are principal/agent problems in the management of the Vietnamese SOEs, but we do not take agency theory at 'face value', but have placed the principal/ agent problems in a broader institutional context. There are also problems of soft budget constraint (SBC) in the Vietnamese SOEs, but SBC cannot be *the cause* of the problems of SOEs. From our analysis, we can infer that SBC was likely to result from the prevailing socialist ideology, embedded materialism (formal) and the patrimonial nature of the Vietnamese society (informal). SBC is, therefore, not the cause of the SOE problems, but a consequence of the overall institutional matrix of Vietnam during the transitional period.

Any theory that took SBC at 'face value' to explain SOE behaviour would be too positive and repressive. Such a theory would not, for example, take into account cultural values and the history of the SOEs. Similarly, Child's C-space framework which took codification and diffusion of information as the centre of its explanation offers little information about the reality of the SOEs. It is true, as our analysis reveals, that uncodification is a characteristic of the Vietnamese institutions, but uncodification is a representation rather than a cause. 'Uncodification', as may be inferred, resulted partly from embedded materialism and the socialist ideology. Cultural theory alone is also unsatisfactory since it fails to include the distinguishing nature of the SOE legacy in transitional countries.

The institutional approach employed in this study has allowed all those competing theories (as reviewed in Chapter 1) to 'have their say' but not allowed them to act as the grand narrative in an explanation of the behaviour of the Vietnamese SOEs in transition. There is certainly no one truth and no one way of explaining this, but our framework has brought up different facets and 'voices' which would be silent in other concepts.

Methodologically, this work offers a unique approach to the study of SOEs in transitional countries. In studying the behaviour of the Vietnamese SOEs, we have gone back and forth from the specific to the general and vice versa. From an analysis of the specific features of the Vietnamese culture and general features of the formal institutions we have 'built' a general model, an 'ideal type' to capture the essential features of the Vietnamese institutional framework. We have then analysed the specific 'rules of the game' applied to the SOEs and explained their behaviour with reference to the general, the ideal type.

Although the ideal type methodology is a powerful tool to interpret and compare social phenomena, it has not been extended to the context of SOEs in traditional countries. In the present research, by using the ideal type, we were able to bring different types of concepts into a single unit of analysis. This method has allowed us to reconcile and incorporate the specific and the general in a relatively consistent way. The method has not been used in any study of the SOEs in transitional countries.

3. Limitations

As in any other qualitative research, there are always questions of bias and validity of the interpretations and theories generated. In the present research, we tried to ease the problem of validity by using data from multiple sources. Despite that, due to the limitations of time and resources, we cannot guarantee that the present research is completely free from such problems.

In using the ideal type methodology we have implicitly assumed that two constellations (the ideal type and the SOE in the present research) are comparable in terms of some features common to them both. Therefore there was a process of comparison and translation. Comparisons are always associated with the problem of loss of meaning and in addition, due to difficulties in gaining access to information, we were not able to investigate the three cases as deeply as we would wish in order to provide more specific solutions to SOE problems.

4. Further research

The present research is concerned mainly with one type of business in Vietnam, the SOE. Currently, there are other types of enterprises operating there including privatised firms, joint-ventures and foreign companies. The behaviour of, and strategies adapted by, these *players* to cope with the *rules of the game* in Vietnam are interesting areas for future research. Since privatisation is one of the major agendas for economic reform in Vietnam, studies of privatised firms could be useful to policy makers. Currently, privatised firms are not family businesses but are owned by various types of owners: employees, private, institutions and state. The state and state organisations still own a fair proportion of shares in many privatised firms. Given the fact that the Vietnamese have never experienced controlling and managing such large and multiple owner enterprises, the management behaviour of this type of firm is an interesting area to explore.

In addition, within the state sector, it would be interesting to discover how various government policies and practices (e.g. monopoly, protectionism, and subsidy) have a bearing on the performance of SOEs and their consequence for the private sector.

The other interesting area to explore would be political systems and formal institutions and their interactions with informal norms. Studies of the nature of different political structures and formal institutions employed in successful East Asian countries including Japan, South Korea, Taiwan, Hong Kong and Singapore, their interactions with informal norms there, and their bearing on economic organisations could provide useful guides for countries like Vietnam and mainland China.

APPENDICES

Appendix 1: List of decisions or responsibilities investigated (a replication of the Aston Studies)

Marketing

Introducing a new product
The price of products
Type of market to supply (type of outlets, type of customer)
The geographical spread of sales (in Vietnam, export, etc.)
The priorities of different product orders and deliveries.

Purchasing

The choice of suppliers of materials
The procedure for purchasing (e.g. whether to ask for several quotes. Order quantities, term of contract)

Production and work allocation

The overall production plan (annual) adopted
The scheduling of work (up to one month) against given plans
The allocation of work to be done amongst the available workers
Which machines or equipment to be used?
The methods of work to be used (not involving new expenditure)
When overtime will be work

Quality control

What items will be inspected (including what %) – inward supplies
What items will be inspected (including what %) completed product

Maintenance

The maintenance schedule or procedure
R&D What research and development work will be done (i.e. how much and what priority)

Investment and accounting

The level of expenditure on new capital equipment
The type or make of new capital equipment
What will be costed: to which items will the costing system be applied
What unbugeted money can spend on capital items?
What unbudgeted money can be spent on revenue/consumable items?

Staffing

Numbers of work group leaders/ supervisors
Appointing workers from outside the factory
Appointing supervisors from outside the factory
Appointing managers from outside the factory
The size of the total workforce
Total numbers of managers above workgroup leader level.
The salaries of production workers and management staff
The methods for selecting new workers and cadres

Discipline

Dismissing a worker
Dismissing or demoting a supervisor or manager

Training

The type of training offer

Organisation structure
Altering responsibilities/ areas of work of non-production departments
Altering responsibilities/ areas of work of production departments
Creating a new department
Creating a new non-production/new production job.

Office system
The design of office systems (including use of computers)

Representation of management
Who is the most junior person who can deputise for the director in his absence?

Appendix 2: Questionnaire I[*] – Perceptions about management in SOEs

This questionnaire was designed to ask managers and staff from the three case enterprises about their perceptions on management in their enterprise and SOEs in Vietnam in general.

Part 1: This part includes closed-ended questions with a five point scale:
1= strongly disagree; 2= disagree; 3=50-50; 4= agree; and 5= strongly agree

In general, it is the best performer who rises to the top of this organisation.

"Connection or who you know" is more important than job performance in getting ahead here.

Some departments in this organisation seem to care more about their own gain than the organisation as a whole.

Pay increases are based solely on job performance.

Promotion is based solely on job performance in this organisation.

It is standard practice in this organisation to use one's position to help friends or family.

Nepotism reduces this organisation's performance

In general, in this organisation the best performers are those who earn the most.

In general, in this organisation the pay policy does not encourage people to do their job effectively

Besides their salary, managers in this organisation have some additional source of income (not in the book)

In general, personnel policy encourages favouritism.

In general, personnel and payment policies seem to discourage co-ordination

Management practice (personnel and payment) here seems to create mistrust and resentment among employees.

My supervisor engages in favouritism.

I feel that my supervisor's treatment of employees has been biased.

192

Sometimes, my supervisor seems to lack confidence in his/her employees.

In general, some people in this organisation use their position and power (e.g. holding rather than sharing information) to obtain personal gain.

Quite a few people from management in my enterprise use their power and positions to "earn" extra money (not in the book).

In my opinon, in the SOE sector many managers (cadres) find the gaps in law and "earn" extra money.

In my opinion, the problem of opportunism in SOEs is quite easy to understand

If I were in the position that I could "earn" extra money (not official salary), I believe that I would find a way to get more income.

The work in my department could be better accomplished by fewer people if they were paid more.

Part 2: Respondents were asked to write down their perceptions about strong and weak points about management (1) of their enterprise and (2) of state enterprise in general.

Appendix 3: Questionnaire II - The 'bonus' phenomenon in economic transactions in Vietnam

1. Customers asking for a <u>personal</u> 'bonus' when they buy from the company:
   a. happens very often
   b. happens quite often
   c. rarely happens
   d. never happens

2. *SOE customers* asking for a <u>personal</u> 'bonus' when they buy from the company:
   a. happens very often
   b. happens quite often
   c. rarely happens
   d. never happens

3. *Private customers* asking for a <u>personal</u> 'bonus' when they buy from the company:
   a. happens very often
   b. happens quite often
   c. rarely happens
   d. never

4. When customers asked for a 'bonus', our company:
   a. usually gave a reasonable amount
   b. sometimes gave reasonable amount
   c. does not gave any amount
   Please, specify the average 'bonus' amount

5. Personal relationship with the buyers and the amount of 'bonus' is an important reason determining whether they buy from our company.
   a. strongly agree
   b. agree
   c. neither agree nor disagree

b. disagree

c. strongly disagree

6. In general, SOE customers will not buy our products if they do not get anything for themselves <u>personally</u>.

    a. strongly agree

    b. agree

    c. neither agree nor disagree

    d. disagree

    e. strongly disagree

7. In order to 'keep' the customers, giving presents or money <u>personally</u> to them in one way or another is very important:

    a) strongly agree

    b) agree

    c) neither agree nor disagree

    d) disagree

    e) strongly disagree

9. In Vietnam, giving money to SOE buyers <u>personally</u> in one way or another is very popular, an 'un-stated law' which need not be discussed

    a) strongly agree

    b) agree

    c) neither agree nor disagree

    d) disagree

    e) strongly disagree

Appendix 4: General information about the sample in the study of economic transactions (Questionnaire III)

Table 1: Ownership structure of the sample

Ownership type	Number of enterprises	Percentage
SOEs	13	40.6%
Private enterprises	14	43.8%
Others	5	15.6%
Total	32	100%

Table 2: Size of the sample's enterprises: capital

Capital (VND billion)	Number of enterprises	Percentage
Below VND1bn	4	12.5%
From VND1-5bn	6	18.8%
From VND5-10bn	7	21.9%
Above VND10b	12	37.5%
Total	32	100%

VND14bn=USD1m

Table 3: Size of the sample's enterprises: employment

Number of employees	Number of enterprises	Percentage
Under 100	16	50%
From 100-500	6	18.8%
More than 500	9	28.1%
N/A	1	3.1%
Total	32	100%

Bibliography

Alchian, A.A. & Demsetz, H. (1972) "Production, Information Costs, and Economic Organization", *American Economic Review*, 62, pp. 777-795.

Allison, G. T. (1971) The Essence of Decision: Explaining the Cuban Missile *Crisis*. Boston: Little, Brown.

Alvesson (1993), "The play of metaphors", in Hassard, J. & Parket, M. Postmodernism and Organizations (Eds.), London: Sage.

Armour, L. (1995) "Economics and social reality: professor O' Neil and the problem of culture", International Journal of Social Economics, 22 (9), pp. 79-87.

Arnold, N. S. (1994) The Philosophy and Economics of Market Socialism. New York: Oxford University Press.

Arrow, K. (1974) The Limits of Organization. New York: Norton.

Arthur, W. B. (1989) "Competing technologies, Increasing Returns, and Lock-In by Historical Events", Economic Journal, 99, pp. 116-131.

Barton, C. A. (1983) "Trust and Credit: Some Observations Regarding Business Strategies of Overseas Chinese Traders in South Vietnam," in, Linda Y.L. Lim and L. A. P. Gosling (eds.), The Chinese in Southeast Asia: Vol. 1, Ethnicity and Economic Activity. Singapore: Maruzen Asia, pp.46-64.

BBC (2000) Vietnamese official warns Politburo on corruption HTTP://NEWS.BBC.CO.UK/hi/english/world/asia-pacific/ newsid_894000/894134.stm.

Bechert, H. & Vu Duy-Tu. 1976. "Buddhism in Vietnam," in Dumoulin, H. & Maraldo, J.C. (Ed.) Buddhism in the Modern World. New York: Collier Books, pp. 186-193.

Bentham, J. (1962). *The works of Jeremy Bentham* (J. Bowring, ed.). New York: Russell and Russell.

Berger, P.L. & Luckmann, T. (1966) The Social Construction of Reality: A Treatise in the Sociology of Knowledge. Middlesex: Penguin Books.

197

Berger, P.L., Berger, B. & Kellner, H. (1973) *The Homeless Mind:* Modernisation and Consciousness. Penguin Books.

Berle, A. A. & Means, G. C. (1932) The Modern Corporation and Private *Property*. New York: Macmillan.

Blumer, H. (1962) "Society as Symbolic Interaction" In Rose, A. M. (ed.) Human Behaviour and Social Processes: An Interactionist Approach. London: Routledge & Kegan Paul.

Blunt, P. (1988) "Cultural Consequences for Organisation Change in a Southeast Asian State: Brunei", *Academy of Management Executive*, Vol2, No.3, pp235-240

Blunt, P. & Richards, D. (1993) (ed.) Readings in Management, Organisation & *Culture in East & South East Asia.* Darwin: Northern Territory University Press.

Blunt, P., Richards, D. & Wilson, J. (1989) "The 'Hidden-Hand' of Public Administration in Newly-Emerging States: A Theoretical and Empirical Analysis", *Journal of International Development,* 1(4), pp. 409-443.

Boisot, M. & Child, J. (1996) "From fiefs to clans and network capitalism: explaining China's emerging economic order", *Administrative Science Quarterly,* 41, pp. 600-628.

Boisot, M.(1996) "Institutionalising the Labour Theory of Value: Some Obstacles to Reform of State-owned Enterprises in China and Vietnam", *Organization Studies*, 17(6), pp. 909-928.

Boisot, M.H. & Child, J. (1988) "The iron law of fiefs: Bureaucratic failure and the problem of governance in the Chinese economic reforms", Administrative Science Quarterly, 33, pp. 507-527.

Boisot, M.H. & Child, J. (1990) Efficiency, ideology and tradition in the choice of transactions governance structures: the case of China as a modernising society, in Clegg. S.R. & Redding, S.G. (Eds.). *Capitalism in Contrasting Cultures.* Berlin: Walter de Gruyter, pp.281-314.

Boisot, M.H. & Child, J. (1999) "Organizations as Adaptive Systems in Complex Environments: The Case of China", *Organization Science,* 10(3), pp. 237-252.

Boisot, M.H. & Xing. G. (1992) "The Nature of Managerial Work in the Chinese Enterprise Reforms: A Study of Six Directors", *Organization Studies*, 13(2), Spring 1992, pp. 161-184.

Boisot, M.H. (1986) "Markets and Hierarchies in a Cultural Perspective", Organization Studies, 7(2), pp. 135-158.

Boisot, M.H. (1987) Information and Organization: The Manager as Anthropologist. London: HarperCollins.

Boisot, M.H. (1995) Information Space: A Framework for Learning in Organizations, Institutions and Culture. London: Routledge.

Bond, M.H. & Hwang, K. (1986) "The social psychology of Chinese people". In Bond, M.H. (ed.), The Psychology of the Chinese People. Hong Kong: Oxford University Press, pp. 213-266.

Bryman, A. (1988) "Introduction: Inside accounts and social research in organisations", in Bryman, A. (ed.), Doing Research in Organisations. London: Routledge, pp. 1-20.

Bryman, A. (1988) Quantity and Quality in Social Research. London: Unwin Hyman.

Burrell, G., & Morgan, G. (1979). Sociological Paradigms and Organizational Analysis. London: Gower.

Carmody, D. L. & Carmody, J. T. (1989) Eastern Ways to the Center: An Introduction to Asian Religions. Belmont, CA: Wadsworth.

Casson, M. & Lundan, S. M. (1999) "Explaining International Differences in Economic Institutions", International Studies of Management & Organization, 29(2), pp. 25-42.

Centre for International Economics (1997) "Viet Nam Enterprise Reform: T. A. No. 2696-VIE". Canberra & Sydney.

Chandler, A. D. (1962) Strategy and Structure: Chapters in the History of the American Industrial Enterprise. Cambridge, Mass.: The MIT Press.

Chandler, A. D. (1977) The Visible Hand: The Managerial Revolution in American Business. Cambridge, Mass.: The Belknap Press of Harvard University Press.

Chandler, A. D., Amatori, F. & Takashi, Hikino (eds.) (1997) Big Business and the Wealth of Nations. Cambridge: Cambridge University Press.

Chen, A. H. Y. (1999) "Rational law, economic development and the case of China" Social and Legal Studies, 8 (1), pp. 97-120.

Child, J. & Lu, Y. (1990) "Industrial Decision Making under China's Reforms

1985-1988", *Organization Studies,* 11(3), pp. 321-351.

Child, J. & Lu, Y. (1996) "Industrial Constraints on Economic Reform: The Case of Investment Decisions in China", *Organization Science,* 7(1), pp. 60-77.

Child, J. & Markoczy, L. (1993) "Host Country Managerial Behaviour and Learning in Chinese and Hungarian Joint Ventures", *Journal of Management Studies,* 30(4), 631-651.

Child, J. (1972) "Organisation structure and strategies of control: A replication of the Aston Study", *Administrative Science Quarterly,* 17, pp. 163-177.

Child, J. (1981) "Culture, Contingency and Capitalism in the Cross-National Study of Organizations", *Research in Organizational Behavior,* 3, pp. 303-356.

Child, J. (1990) "Introduction: The character of Chinese enterprise management", in Child, J. & Lockett, M. (eds.) *Reform Policy and the Chinese Enterprise.* London: JAI Press, pp. 137-152.

Child, J. (1994) Managing in China during the Age of Reform. Cambridge: Cambridge University Press.

Child, J. (1997) "Strategic Choice in the Analysis of Action, Structure, Organizations and Environment: Retrospect and Prospect", Organization Studies, 18(1), pp. 43-76.

Chu Thuong (1998) Thoi roi Chuong duong (That's it Chuong Duong), *Nguoi lao dong (Labourer)*, August, at http://www.fpt.vn/InfoStore/6B0B0001/1998/12/36752E0B.htm

Chu Thuong (2000) Con kien kien cu khoai (an ant sues a tuber of sweet potato), Bao lao dong (Labour Newspaper), May, at http://www.fpt.Vietnam/infoStore/6B0B0001/2000/05/392B6AA7.htm

Clegg, R. C & and Redding, S.G. (1990) Introduction: Capitalism in contrasting cultures, in Clegg. S.R. & Redding, S.G. (Eds.). Capitalism in Contrasting Cultures. Berlin: Walter de Gruyter, pp. 1-28.

Clegg, S. R., Dunphy, D. C. & Redding, S. G. (Eds.) (1986) The Enterprise and Management in East Asian. Hong Kong: University of Hong Kong.

Coase, R. H. (1937) "The Nature of the Firm", Economica, 4, pp. 386-405.

Coase, R.H. (1983) "The new institutional economics" Journal of Institutional and Theoretical economics 140: 229-231.

Cohen, B. (1991) The Vietnam Guidebook: The First Comprehensive New

Guide To Vietnam, With Angkor Wat. 2nd edition. California: Houghton Mifflin Company.

Cohen, J.A.(1990) China's influence on Vietnam's foreign business laws, China Business Review, 17(3), pp.43-45.

Cohen, M. L. (1976) House United, House Divided: The Chinese Family in Taiwan. New York: Columbia University Press.

Coleman, J. S. (1986) "Social Theory, Social Research, and a Theory of Action", American Journal of Sociology, 16, pp 1309-1335.

Coleman, R. (1990) Foundations of Social Theory. Cambridge, MA: Belknapp Press of Harvard University Press.

Commons, J. R. (1934) Institutional Economics. Madison: University of Wisconsin Press.

Contreras, G. (1995) "Teaching about Vietnamese Culture: Water Puppetry as the Soul of the Rice Fields", Social Studies, 86(1), pp. 25-28.

Cook, P. and Kirkpatrick, C. (1988), Privatisation in Less Developed Countries, Wheatsheaf Books.

Crozier, M. (1964) The Bureaucratic Phenomenon. Chicago: University of Chicago Press.

Cyert, R. & March, J. (1992) A Behavioural Theory of the Firm (2nd ed,). Oxford: Blackwell.

Dang Duc Dam (1997) Vietnam's Macro-Economy and Types of Enterprises. Hanoi: The Gioi Publishers.

Dang Nhu Van (2001) "Dau tu va tang truong: Du bao kinh te vi mo don gian cho giai doan" 2001-2010, pp.137-162 in Pham Do Chi & Tran Nam Binh (2001), Danh thuc con rong ngu quen: kinh te Vietnam di vao the ky 21, Ho Chi Minh City Publishing House.

Dapice, D.O. (1999) Kinh te Vietnam va cuoc khung hoang Chau A (Vietnamese economy and the Asian crisis), September, Harvard Institute for International Development.

David, P. A.(1985) "Clio and the Economics of QWERTY", American Economic Review, Vol 75 (2), pp 332-7 (May).

Denzin, N. K. (1978) The Research Act. (2nd edition), New York: McGraw-Hill Book.

Denzin, N.K. & Lincoln, Y.S (1998) Strategies of Research Inquiry (eds.), Thousand Oaks: Sage.

DiMaggio, P. & Powell, W. W. (1983) "The Iron Cage Revisited: Institutional Isomorphism and Collective Rationality in Organizational Fields", American Sociological Review, 82, pp. 147-160.

DiMaggio, P. (1988) Interest and Agency in Institutional Theory, in Lynne Zucker (Eds.): Institutional Patterns and Organizations: Culture and Environment. Cambridge: Ballinger, pp. 3-21.

DiMaggio, P. (1998) "The New Institutionalisms: Avenues of Collaboration", Journal of Institutional and Theoretical Economics, 154, pp. 696 – 705.

Donalson, L (1990) The Ethereal Hand: Organisational Economics and management theory, in Ott, J.S and Shafritz, J.M. (1996) Classics of Organization Theory (Eds.), 4th ed, Harcourt Brace, pp. 340-351.

Dore, R. (1983) "Goodwill and the spirit of market capitalism" The British Journal of Sociology, 34, pp.459-481.

Dore, R. (1987) Taking Japan Seriously: A Confucian Perspective on Leading Economic Issues. London: Athlone Press.

Douglas, M (1973), Rules and meanings: the anthropology of everyday knowledge. (ed). Penguin Books.

Douglas, M. (1987) How Institutions Think. London: Routledge and Kegan Paul.

D'Souza, J., Nash, R. & Megginson, W. (2001). Determinants of performance Improvements in Privatized Firms: The Role of Restructuring and Corporate Governance (Under journal review (March 2001) presented at 2001 American Finance Association 2001 annual meeting (New Orleans)

Durkheim, E. & Mauss, M. (1963) [1903] Primitive Classification. London: Cohen and West.

Durkheim, E. (1964) [1893] The Division of Labour in Society. New York: The Free Press.

Economist, The (1994) "A law unto themselves", Vol. 333, Issue 7886, October 22nd , p.41, London.

202

Economist, The (1995) "The Contradictions of Market Leninism". Vol. 336, Issue 7922, July 8th , pp. 6-10, London.

Economist, The (1997) "Nothing is really private in Vietnam". Vol. 343, Issue 8017, May 17th, pp. 45-7, London.

Economist, The (1999) "No trade", 353 (8142), October 23rd, p.48, London.

Economist, The (1999): "A cat to chase the giant rats". January 6th, pp. 66-67, London.

Economist, The (2000) "Goodnight Vietnam". Vol. 354, Issue 8152, pp.65-7, January 8th, London.

Eisenhardt, K. M. (1989) "Building Theories from Case Study Research", Academy of Management Review, 14(4), pp. 532-550.

Eisenheart, K. M. (1989) "Agency Theory: An Assessment and Review", Academy of Management Review, 14(1), pp. 57-74.

Evans-Pritchard, E.E (1937) Witchcraft, Oracles and Magic among the Azande. Faber and Faber, London.

Fforde, A. and de Vylder. S (1996) From Plan to Market: The Economic Transition in Vietnam. Boulder, CO: Westview Press.

Fforde, A (2001) Vietnam: Monthly Economic and Social Analysis, January. http://www.aduki.com.au/January%202001.htm.

Fligstein, N. (1985) "The Spread of the Multidivisional Form Among Large Firm, 1919-1979", American Sociological Review, 50, pp. 377-391.

Foss, N. J. (1999) "The Challenge of Business Systems and the Challenge to Business Systems", International Studies of Management & Organization, 29(2), pp. 9-24.

Foucault, M. (1979). Discipline & Punish: The birth of the prison. New York: Vintage Books.

Foucault, M. 1980. Power/knowledge: Selected interviews and other writings by Michel Foucault, 1972-77. (C. Gordon, Ed.). Brighton, England: Harvester.

French, J. R. & Raven, B. (1959) "The Base of Power", In Cartwright, D. (ed.) Studies in Social Power: University of Michigan, pp. 150-167.

Gardels, N. (1999) Looking Back 50 Years, Looking Forward, NPQ: New Perspectives Quarterly, 16(4), pp. 18-24.

General Statistical Office (2001), Statistical Yearbook 2000, Hanoi.

General Statistical Office (1999), Statistical Yearbook 1998, Hanoi.

Gerth, H.H & Mills, C.W (Eds.) (1948) From Max Weber: Essays in Sociology. London: Routledge

Geertz, C. (1973) The Interpretation of Cultures: Selected Essays. New York: Basic Books.

Ghoshal, S. & Insead, M. P. (1996) "Bad for Practice: A Critique of the Transaction Cost Theory", Academy of Management Review, 21(1), pp. 13-47.

Giddens, A. (1976) New Rules of Sociological Method. New York: Basic Books.

Giddens, A. (1990) The Consequences of Modernity. Cambridge: Polity Press.

Goenewegen, J. & Kerstholt, F. (1995) "On Integrating New and Old Institutionalism: Douglas North Building Bridges", Journal of Economic Issues, 29(2), pp. 467-475.

Goldstone, J. A. (1998) "Initial conditions, general laws, path dependence, and explanation in historical sociology", American Journal of Sociology, 104 (3), pp. 829- 445.

Gordon, C. 1991. Governmental rationality: An introduction. In G. Burchell, C. Gordon, & P. Miller (Eds.), The Foucault effect: Studies in governmentality: 1-52. London: Harvester Wheatsheaf.

Granovetter, M. (1985) "Economic Action and Social Structure: the Problem of Embeddedness", American Journal of Sociology, 91(3), pp. 481-510.

Greenwood, R. & Devine, K (1997) Inside Aston: A conversation with Derek Pugh, Journal of Management Inquiry, 6(3), pp.200-208.

Griffin, K. (1998) "The Management of Structural Adjustment and Macroeconomic Reform in Vietnam", Human Systems Management, 17(1), pp. 29-37.

Ha Van Tan (1983) "Co mot he thong chu Viet co thoi cac vua Hung", Bao anh Viet nam, No.291.

Haines, D. W. (1984) "Reflections of Kinship and Society under Vietnam's Le Dynasty", Journal of South East Asian Studies, 15(2), pp. 307-314.

Hall, E. (1976) Beyond Culture. New York: Doubleday.

Hall, R. H. & Xu, W. (1990) "Research note: run silent, run deep – cultural influences on organizations in the Far East", Organization Studies, 11(4), pp. 569- 576.

Hamilton, G. G. & Biggart, N. W. (1988) "Market, Culture, and Authority: A Comparative Analysis of Management and Organization in the Far East", American Journal of Sociology, 94 (supplement), pp. 52-94.

Hamilton, G. G. (1984) "Patriarchalism in Imperial China and Western Europe: A Revision of Weber's Sociology of Domination", Theory and Sociology, 13, pp. 393-425.

Hamilton, G.G., Zeile, W. & Kim, W.J. (1990) The network structures of East Asian Economies, in Clegg. S.R. & Redding, S.G. (Eds.). Capitalism in Contrasting Cultures. Berlin: Walter de Gruyter, pp.105-130.

Hampden-Turner, C. & Trompenaars, F. (1993) The Seven Cultures of Capitalism. Currency: Doubleday.

Harris, N. (1997) "Cities in a global economy: Structural change and policy reactions", Urban Studies, Vol.34, Issue 10, pp.1693-1703

Harold, C. (1996) "Taoism and Jung: Synchronicity and the Self", Philosophy East & West, 46(4), pp. 477-495.

Heller, F. A. and Bernhard, W (1981), Competence and Power in Management Decision Making: A Study of Senior Levels of Organisations in Eight Countries. Wiley.

Heller, F., Drenth, P., Koopman, P. & Rus, V. (1988) Decisions in Organizations: A three-country comparative study. London: Sage.

Heller, F.A. & Wang, Z.M. (1993) "Patterns of power distribution in managerial decision making in Chinese and British industrial organizations", international Journal of Human Resource Management, 4(1), pp.113-

Hickey, G. C. (1964) Village in Vietnam. New Haven: Yale University Press.
Hickson, D. J. & Pugh, D. S. (1995) Management Worldwide: The Impact of

Societal Culture on Organizations Around the Global. Penguin Books.

Hickson, D. J., Hining, C. R., Lee, C. A., Schneck, R. E. & Pennings, J. M. (1971) "A Strategic Contingencies' Theory of Interorganizational power", Administrative Science Quarterly, 16, pp. 216-229.

Hofstede, G. (1980) Culture's consequences: International differences in work related values, Beverly Hills CA: Sage.

Hofstede, G. (1991) Cultures and Organizations: Software of the Mind. London: McGraw-Hill.

Jamieson, N. L. (1984) "Towards a Paradigm for Paradox: Observation on the Study of Social Organization in Southern Asia", Journal of Southern Asian Studies, 15(2), pp. 320-329.

Jamieson, N.L. (1986) "The Traditional Vietnamese Village", Vietnam Forum, 7, Winter-Spring.

Jamieson, N.L. (1993) Understanding Vietnam. Berkeley and Los Angeles: University of California Press.

Jensen, M. & Meckling, W. (1976) "Theory of the Firm: Managerial Behaviour, Agency Costs, and Capital Structure" in Ott, J.S and Shafritz, J.M. (1996) Classics of Organization Theory (Ed.), 4th ed, Harcourt Brace, pp. 331-339.

Jensen, M. (1983) "Organization Theory and Methodology", Accounting Review, 56, 319-338.

Jung, C. G. (1940) The Integration of the Personality. London: Routledge and Kegan Paul.

Jung, C.G. (1969) Pshychology and Religion: West and East (2nd ed.) London Routledge & Kegan Paul.

Kerr, C., Dunlop, J. T., Harbison, F. H. & Myers, C. A. (1960) Industrialism and Industrial Man. Harmondsworth: Penguin Book.

Kirkbride, P.S. and Tang, S.F.Y. (1994) "From Kyoto to Kowloon: Cultural Barriers to the Transference of Quality Circles from Japan to Hong Kong", Asia-Pacific Journal of Human Resources, 32(2), pp.100-111.

Klostermaier, K. (1991), The nature of Buddhism, Asian Philosophy, 1991, 1(1), pp29-37.

206

Korczynski, M. (2000) "The Political Economy of Trust", Journal of Management Studies, 37 (1), pp. 1-21.

Kornai, J. (1980) The Economics of Shortage. Amsterdam: Nth-Holland.

Kornai, J. (1990) Vision and Reality, Market and State: New Studies on the Socialist Economy and Society. Hemel Hempstead: Harvester-Wheatsheaf.

Kornai, J.(1998), The place of the soft budget constraint syndrome in economic theory. Journal of Comparative Economics, 26(1), pp11-17.

Kroeber, A. & Kluckhohn, C. (1952) Culture: A Critical Review of Concepts and Definitions. Papers of the Peabody Museum of American Archaeology and Ethnology, Vol. 47. Cambridge, Mass.: Harvard University Press.

Kuhn, T. S. (1962) The Structure of Scientific Revolutions. Chicago: The University of Chicago Press.

Lawson, D. (1993) "Humanism in China", Humanist, 53(3), pp. 16-19.

Laycock, S. W. (1994) "The Vietnamese Mode of Self-Reference: A Model of Buddhist Egology", Asian Philosophy, 4(1), pp.53-69.

Le Anh Tu, P. (1997), "Vietnam's strong economic performance", Vital Speeches of the Day, 63(21), August 8th , pp.668-671.

Le Dang Doanh (1995) "Equitisation of state enterprises in Ho Chi Minh City: A positive contribution to the task of reforming state enterprises ", Report to a workshop on Equitisation in Ho Chi Minh City, August 3.

Li, D.D & Liang, M. (1998) Causes of the Soft Budget Constraint: Evidence on Three Explanations, Journal of Comparative Economics, 26 (1), pp.104-116.

Lucas, R. E. (1990) "Why Doesn't Capital Flow from Rich to Poor Countries?" American Economic Review, Vol.80(2), pp.92-96.

Luhmann, N. (1979) Trust and Power. Chichester: John Wiley.

Malesky, E., Hung, V.T., Dieu Anh, V.T. & Napier, N. (1998). The Model and the Reality: Assessment of Vietnamese SOE Reform–Implementation at the Firm Level. Working Paper No. 154, July. Ann Arbor, MI, William Davidson Institute, University of Michigan.

Megginson, W and Netter, J. (2001) From State to Market: A Survey of Empirical Studies on Privatization. Forthcoming, Journal of Economic Literature.

March, J. G. & Olsen, J. P. (1987) Rediscovering Institutions: The Organizational Basis of Politics. New York: The Free Press.

March, J. G. & Simon, H. A. (1958) Organizations. New York: John Wiley & Sons.

Marx, K. (1972) Capital: A Critique of Political Economy. London: Lawrence & Wishart.

McMillan, J. & Woodruff, C. (1999a) "Dispute Prevention without Courts in Vietnam," Journal of Law, Economics, and Organization, 15(3), p637-658.

McMillan, J. & Woodruff, C. (1999b) "Interfirm relationships and informal credit in Vietnam", Quarterly Journal of Economics, 114(4), pp. 1243-1284.

Mead, G. H. (1934) Mind, Self and Society: From the Standpoint of a Social Behaviourist. Chicago: The University of Chicago Press.

Ministry of Commerce (2000) "Vietnam is on the way reaching to the 21st Century, Hanoi: Hanoi Publisher.

Mintzberg, H. (1979) The Structuring of Organizations. Englewood Cliffs, N. J: Prentice-Hall.

Mirowski, P. (1989) More Heat than Light: Economics as Social Physics, Physics as Nature's Economics. Cambridge: Cambridge University Press.

Molyneux, I. (1995) The Vietnam Connection. Chippenham, Wiltshire: Antony Rowe.

Moore, M. (1998) Book reviews, Journal of Development Studies, 34(3). pp.147-150.

Morgan, G. (1986) Images of Organizations. Beverly Hills: Sage Publications.

MPI and ADB (1997) Enterprise Reform Project: Greater Equity Between Private and State Enterprises. October 1997. Hanoi: Raymond Mallon.MPI(*) (1997) Vietnam: A Medium Term Industrial Strategy. United Nations Industrial Development Organization (UNIDO) and Development Strategy Institute (DSI). September.

208

Mya Than & Joseph L. H. Tan (eds.) (1993) Vietnam's Dilemmas and Options: The Challenge of Economic Transition in the 1990s. Singapore: Singapore National Printers Pte Ltd.

Ralston, D. A., Nguyen V.T & Napier, N. K. (1999) "A Comparative Study of the Work Values of North and South Vietnamese Managers", Journal of International Business Studies, 30(4), pp. 655-672.

Needham, J (1956) Science and Civilisation in China, Cambridge: Cambridge University Press, Vol.2.

Nguoi Lao dong (1999) Tinh trang dung hoa don gia gia tang (the use of illegal accounting sheets has increased) at http://www.fpt.vn/infoStore/400D0001/09/37F131D7.htm.

Nguyen Khai (2001) "Dau tu truc tiep nuoc ngoai va phat trien kinh te, nhung bai hoc cho Vietnam" in Pham Do Chi & Tran Nam Binh (2001), Danh Thuc Con Rong Ngu Quen: kinh te Vietnam di vao the ky 21, Ho Chi Minh City Publishing House.

Nguyen Minh Tu (1997) "The reforms of state businesses", Vietnam's Socio-Economic Development, No. 12, Winter, pp. 3-12.

Nguyen Van Binh (1999) The nao la bat kha khang (what is a force majeure?), Lao Dong va Cong Doan (Labour and Trade Union magazine), October, p.29.

North, D. (1990) Institutions, Institutional Change and Economic Performance. Cambridge: Cambridge University Press.

North, D. C. (1986) "The New Institutional Economics", Journal of Institutional and Theoretical Economics, 142, pp. 230-237.

North, D. C. (1994) "Economic Performance Through Time", The American Economic Review, 84(3), pp. 359-368.

O' Neil, D. J. (1995) "Culture confronts Marx", International Journal of Social Economics, 22 (9).

Orru, M., Biggart, N. W. & Hamilton, G. G. (1997) The Economic Organisation of East Asian Capitalism. Thousand Oaks, CA: Sage.

Ouchi, W. (1980) "Markets, Bureaucracies and Clans", Administrative Science Quarterly, 25(1), pp. 129-141.

Parsons, T. (1951) The Social System. London: Routledge and Kegan Paul.

Pearce, J.L. and Xin, K. R. (1996) "Guanxi: connections as substitutes for formal institutional support", Academy of Management Journal, 39(6), pp.1641-1658.

Pearce, L.J.; Branyiczki, I. and Bakacsi, G. (1994) "Person-based reward systems: A theory of organisational reward practices in reform-communist organisations", Journal of Organisation Behaviour, Vol. 15, pp. 261-282.

Pejovich, S. (ed.) (1990) The Economics of Property Rights: Towards a Theory of Comparative Systems. Dordrecht: Kluwer Academic Publishers.

Perrow, C. (1986) Complex Organizations: A Critical Essay. 3rd edition. New York: McGraw-Hill.

Pettigrew, A. (1972) "Information Control as a Power Resource". Sociology, 16, pp. 187-204.

Pettigrew, A. (1973) Politics of Organizational Decision-Making. London: Tavistock.

Pfeffer, J. & Salancik, G. R. (1974) "Organizational Decision Making as a Political Process: The Case of a University Budget", Administrative Science Quarterly, 19, pp. 135-151.

Pfeffer, J. (1978) The External Control of Organizations: A Resource Dependency View. New York: Harper and Row.

Pfeffer, J. (1981) Power in Organizations. Cambridge, Mass.: Pitman.

Pfeffer, J. (1982) Organizations and Organization Theory. Cambridge, Mass.: Harper & Row.

Pfeffer, J. (1992), Managing with Power: Politics And Influence in Organisations, Boston, MA: Harvard Business School Press.

Pfeffer, J. (1997). New Directions for Organization Theory: Problems and Prospects. New York: Oxford University Press.

Pham Do Chi & Tran Nam Binh (2001), Danh thuc con rong ngu quen: kinh te Vietnam di vao the ky 21, Ho Chi Minh City Publishing House.

Pham Quyen & Pham Kim Oanh (1998) Luat ve doanh nghiep va nhung huong dan moi ban hanh (Enterprise Laws and New Guidelines), Hanoi: Statistics Publisher.

Pham Van Thuyet (1996) "Legal Framework and Private Sector Development in Transitional Economies: The Case of Vietnam", Georgetown International Law Review, 27, pp. 541-600.

Poole, M. S. & Van de Ven, A. H. (1989) "Using Paradox to Build Management and Organization Theories", Academy of Management Review, 14(4), pp. 562-578.

Popper, K. R. (1972) Objective Knowledge: An Evolutionary Approach. Oxford: The Clarendon Press.

Price Waterhouse (1996) Vietnam: A Guide for the Foreign Investor. (4th ed). January 1996.

Pugh, D. S. & Hinings, C. R. (1976) Organizational Structure Extensions and Replications: The Aston Programme II. Famborough: Saxon House.

Pugh, D. S., & Hickson, D. J. (1976) Organizational structure in its context: The Aston Programme I. London:Gower.

Redding, S.G. & Whitley, R.D. (1990) "Beyond bureaucracy: Towards a comparative analysis of forms of economic resource co-ordination and control", in Clegg. S.R. & Redding, S.G. (ed.). Capitalism in Contrasting Cultures. Berlin: Walter de Gruyter, pp.79-104.

Redding, S.G. (1980) "Cognition as an Aspect of Culture and its Relation to Management Processes: an Exploratory View of the Chinese Case", Journal of Management Studies, May, pp. 127-148.

Redding, S.G. (1993) The Spirit of Chinese Capitalism. Berlin/ New York: Walter de Gruyter.

Reed, M. (ed.) (1992) "Organizations and Modernity" In The Sociology of Organizations: Themes, Perspectives and Prospects. Harvester Wheatsheaf: Hertfordshire.

Richards (1996) "Does East Meet West? Perceptions of Dynamic Change in Vietnamese management Education", paper presented at the International Conference- higher Education in the 21st Century: Mission and Challenge in Developing Countries, May14-17th, Hanoi, Vietnam.

Richards, D (1991) "Flying against the wind"? Culture and management development in South East Asia, Journal of Management Development, 10(6), pp.7-21.

Richards, D., Ha, N., Harvie, C. and Nguyen, V.L. (2002). "The Predicament of the Limping Tiger: Difficulties in Transition for Small and Medium Sized Enterprises in Vietnam". In C. Harvie and B.C. Lee (Eds.), Small and Medium Sized Enterprises in East Asia. Cheltenham, Edward Elgar.

Rose, A. M. (Ed.) (1962) Human Behaviour and Social Processes: An Interactionist Approach. London: Routledge & Kegan Paul.

Saito, O. (1998) "Two kinds of stem-family system? Traditional Japan and Europe compared.", Continuity and Change, 13(1), pp. 167-186.

Saito, O. (2000) "Marriage, family labour and the stem family household: traditional Japan in a comparative perspective", Continuity and Change, 15(1), pp. 17-45.

Sartre, J.-P (1981) The Family Idiot: Gustave Flaubert, 1921-1857 (Vol. 1) Chicago: Chicago University Press

Sayer, A. (1984) Method in Social Science: A Realist Approach. London: Hutchinson.

Schein, E. (1992) Organizational Culture and Leadership. San Francisco: Jossey-Bass.

Schumpeter, J. A. (1942) Capitalism, Socialism, and Democracy. New York: Harper & Row.

Schumpeter, J. A. (1961) [1934] The Theory of Economic Development: An Inquiry into Profits, Capital, Credit, Interest and the Business Cycle. London: Oxford University Press.

Schutz, A. & Luckmann, T. (1974) The Structures of the Life-World. London: Heinemann.

Schutz, A. (1973) "The frame of unquestioned construct" in Douglas, M (1973), (ed). Rules and meanings: the anthropology of everyday knowledge. Penguin Books
Scott, W. R. (1987) "The Adolescence of Institutional Theory", Administrative Science Quarterly, 32(4), pp. 493-511.

Scott, W. R. (1995) Institutions and Organizations. Thousand Oaks: Sage.
Shirley, M. & Nellis, J. (1991) Public Enterprise Reform: The Lessons of Experience. Washington, D. C.: The World Bank.

Shirley, M. (1997) "The economics and politics of government ownership", Journal of International Development. 9:6, 849-64.

Shultz, C. J. & Andrey, W. J. (1997) "Asia's Next Tiger?", Marketing Management, 5(4), pp. 26-37.

Simon, H. A. (1982) Models of Bounded Rationality. 2 vols. Cambridge, Mass.: The MIT Press.

Smith, R. B. (1973) "The Cycle of Confucianism in Vietnam". In: Walter, V. (ed.) Aspects of Vietnamese History. Honolulu: University Press of Hawaii.

Smith, M.E.G (1996) "Understanding Marx's theory of value: An assessment of a controversy", Canadian Review of Sociology & Anthropology, Vol.33, Iss.3, pp357-376.

Steinberg, D.J. (1987) In Search of Southeast Asia: A Modern History. Ed. Honolulu: University of Hawaii Press.

Stiglitz, J. E. (1989) "Principal and Agent", in Eatwell, J.; Milgate, M. & Newman, P. (eds) Allocation, Information and Markets. The New Palgrave, London: Macmillan, pp. 241-253.

Strauss, A. & Corbin.J. (1998) Basics of Qualitative Research: Techniques and Procedures for Developing Grounded Theory. Thousand Oaks: Sage.

Strauss, A. (1987), Qualitative Analysis For Social Scientists, Cambridge: Cambridge University Press.

Strauss, A., Schatzman, L., Ehrlich, D., Bucher, R. & Sabshin, M. (1963) The hospital and its negotiated order, in Friedson, E. (ed.) The Hospital in Modern Society. New York: MacMillan.

Thanh nien (2000) Trao doi voi pho chu tich quoc hoi Mai Thuc Lan (conversation with National Assembly vice-chairman, Mai Thuc Lan) in http://www.vnn.vn.

Todd, E. (1985) The Explanation of Ideology: Family Structures and Social Systems. Oxford: Basil Blackwell.

Townley, B (1993) Foucault, power/knowledge, and its relevance for human resource management, Academy of Management Review, Vol. 18 Issue 3, p518-545.

Tran Ngoc Them (1997) Tim Ve Ban Sac Van Hoa Viet Nam (Discovering the Identity of Vietnamese Culture), Ho Chi Minh City Publisher.

Triandis, H. C. (1994) Culture and Social Behaviour, New York: McGraw Hill

Trompenaars, F. (1993) Riding the Waves of Culture: understanding cultural diversity in business, London: Nicholas Brealey Publishing.

Truong Giang (1999), Van ban nha nuoc va phap luat 1945-1998 (Law and legal documents 1945-1998), CD ROM

Truong Quang, Swierczek, F. W. & Dang Thi Kim Chi. (1998) "Effective Leadership in Joint Ventures in Vietnam: a Cross-Cultural Perspective", Journal of Organizational Change Management, 11(4), pp. 357-372.

UNIDO & DSI (1999) Tong quan ve canh tranh cong nghiep Vietnam (Overview of the Vietnamese industrial competitiveness). Hanoi: Nha xuat ban chinh tri quoc gia.

VASC (2000) "Sau nam thi hanh luat pha san doanh nghiep: co bao nhieu doanh nghiep can duoc tuyen bo pha san?" (how many enterprises should have declared bankrupt after six years since the Bankruptcy Law being in effect?), wysiwyg:/http://www.vnn.vn/tintuc/thoisu/tindadua.html

Vietnam Economic Times (1999) Hoa don bat hop phap (illegal VAT sheets), April 24th.

Vietnam Economic Times (2002) Kinh Te 2001-2002 (The Economy 2001-2002), pp1-102.

Vietnam Economic Times (2001) Kinh Te 2000-2001 (The Economy 2000-2001), pp1-102

Vu Quang Viet (1998) "State and private sectors in Vietnamese economy", Vietnam's Socio-Economic Development, No.13, Spring1998, pp.30-43

Vu Duy Thai (2002) Strengthening the Competitiveness of Enterprises In Need of Government Support http://www.worldbank.org.vn/partnerships/cg_meeting/strength_compet.pdf. Wang Z. M. & Heller, F. A. (1993) "Patterns of Power Distribution in Managerial Decision Making in Chinese and British Industrial Organizations", The International Journal of Human Resource Management, 4(1), pp. 113-128. Wang, C.K. (1964) "Introduction" in Weber, M, The Religion of China: Confucianism and Taoism. New York: The Free Press.

Weber, M. (1949) Methodology of the Social Sciences Glencoe: Free Press.

Weber, M (1951) The Religion of China: Confucianism and Taoism. New York: The Free Press.

Weber, M (1958) The Protestant Ethics and the Spirit of Capitalism. New York: Free Press.

Weber, M. (1968) Economy and Society. Roth, G. & Wittich, C. (eds.), Berkeley: University of California Press.

Westwood, R.I. (1997) "Harmony and patriarchy: the cultural basis for paternalistic headship' among the overseas Chinese", Organization studies, Vol.18, No.3, pp.445-480

Westwood, R. I. Tang, S. F. Y. & Kirkbride, P. S. (1992) "Chinese Conflict Behaviour: Cultural Antecedents and Behavioural Consequences", Organization Development Journal, 10(2), pp. 287-301.

Westwood, R.I & Kirkbride, P.S. (1998) International strategies of corporate culture change: emulation, consumption and hybridity, Journal of Organizational Change Management,11(6) pp. 554-577.

Whitley, R. (1992) Business Systems in East Asia: Firms, Markets and Societies. London: Sage Publications.

Whitley, R. (1999) "Competing Logics and Units of Analysis in the Comparative Study of Economic Organization", International Studies of Management & Organization, 29(2), pp. 113-126.

Whitley, R. (1999) "Firms, Institutions and Management Control: The Comparative Analysis of Coordination and Control Systems", Accounting, Organizations & Society, 24, pp. 507-524.

Wilkinson, B. (1996) "Culture, institutions and business in East Asia", Organization Studies, 17 (3), pp. 421- 447.

Williamson, O. E. (1975) Markets and Hierarchies: Analysis and Antitrust Implications. New York: The Free Press.

Williamson, O. E. (1985) The Economic Institutions of Capitalism: Firms, Markets, Rational Contracting. New York: The Free Press.

Williamson, O. E. (1991) "The Logic of Economic Organization", in Williamson, O. E. & Winter, S. (eds.) The Nature of the Firm: Origins, Evolution, and Development. New York: Oxford University Press.

Williamson, O. E. (1993) "Calculativeness, Trust, and Economic Organization", Journal of Law and Economics, 36, pp. 453-486.

215

Wollf, P. (1999) Vietnam – The Incomplete Transformation. London and Portland: Frank Cass.

Woodside, A. (1971) Vietnam and the Chinese Model: A Comparative Study of Nquyen and Ching Civil Government in the First Half of the Nineteenth Century. Cambridge, Mass: Harvard University Press.

Woodside, A. (1998) "Territorial order and collective-identity tensions in Confucian Asia: China, Vietnam, Korea", Daedalus, 127 (3), pp. 191-220.

World Bank (1992) Privatisation: The lessons of experience, World Bank, Washington D.C..

World Bank (1995) Bureaucrats in Business: The Economics and Politics of Government Ownership, World Bank, Washington D.C..

World Bank (1998) Vietnam: Rising to the Challenge. Economic Report of the World Bank Consultative Group Meeting for Vietnam, Hanoi, December 7th. New York: World Bank.

World Bank (1999) Vietnam: Preparing for Take-off? Informal Economic Report of the World Bank Consultative Group Meeting for Vietnam, Hanoi, December 14-15th. New York: World Bank.

World Bank (2000). Vietnam 2010: Entering the 21st Century Pillars of Development, Vietnam Development Report, December 14-15, 2000.

Yang, C.K. (1951) "Introduction" in Weber, M. (1951) Weber, M (1951) The Religion of China: Confucianism and Taoism. New York: The Free Press.

Yeh, R. & Lawrence, J. J. (1995) "Individualism and Confucian dynamism: a note on Hofstede's cultural root to economic growth", Journal of International Business Studies, 26(3), pp. 655-669.

Yin, R. K. (1994) Case Study Research: Design and Methods (2nd ed.). Thousand Oaks: Sage.

Zizek, S. (2002) "I am a Fighting Atheist: Interview with Slavoj Zizek" Interview by Doug Henwood, Intro by Charlie Bertsch. Bad Subjects, Iss. 59, February

Zucker, L. G. (1986) "Production of Trust". Research in Organizational Behaviour, 8, pp. 53-111.

Zucker, L. G. (1987) "Institutional Theories of Organization", Annual Review of

216

Sociology, 13, pp. 443-464.

Zucker, L. G. (ed.) (1988) Institutional Patterns and Organizations.
Cambridge, Mass.: Ballinder.

Index

A

agency theory, 2, 7, 8, 9, 34, 187
American-Vietnam War, 38
anchoretism, 63
Asian Development Bank, 5
Asian Financial Crisis, 89, 93
Aston Studies, 29, 31, 113, 114, 117, 118, 127

B

banking system, 14, 21, 96, 97, 163, 183, 184
Bankruptcy Law, 96
Barton, C.A., 103
Barton.C.A., 68
bat hieu, 67
Boisot, M.H., 2, 8, 9, 10, 11, 21, 55, 123, 164, 165, 166, 173
Bond, M, 13, 14, 66
bonus, 125, 137, 138, 140, 141, 142, 169, 183
bribery, 105, 137
bricoleur, 31
Buddha, 59, 60, 61
Buddhism, 44, 51, 59, 60, 61, 63, 206
bureaucracy, 9, 15, 53, 75
But, 59, See Phat

C

Cao Dai, 61
capitalisation, 176
capitalism, 3, 21, 22, 26, 27, 28, 49, 51, 52, 73, 79, 92, 99, 101, 106, 107, 111, 112, 166, 182, 183, 184
capitalist economies, 66
Carl Jung, 62, 64
Central Domain, 117, 118, 119, 120, 123, 124, 126, 160
Central Industrial Ministry, 128
central SOEs, 127, 128, 130
centrally-planned development model, 75
chaebol, 12, 13, 17, 21, 25, 85, 161, 162
Chandler, A.D., 15
Child, J, 2, 8, 9, 10, 11, 21, 33, 40, 55, 113, 114, 117, 118, 123, 128, 187, See Boisot, M.H and C-space
China-European Community Management Institute (Beijing), 9
Chinese Ch'ing dynasty, 42, 51
Chinese family businesses, 17, 18
Chinese Qing dynasty, 43
Chinese rule, 41, 42, 43, 44

Chinese SOEs, 8, 9, 10, 32, 55, 113, 117, 118, 128, 173
Chu Van An, 63
Chun Doo Hwan, 25
clan, 9, 46, 54
Coca-Cola Chuong Duong, 94
codification, 9, 10, 67, 93, 122, 123, 184, 187
cognitive aspects of culture, 63
collectivism, 12, 13, 68, 70
Commercial SOEs, 127
communism, 48, 55, 123
Communist Party, 26, 41, 42, 43, 50, 53, 65, 75, 104, 114, 123, 124, 125, 145
Communist Party Committee, 123, 124
Confucian culture, 152
Confucian dynamism, 12, 13, 14
Confucian education, 47
Confucian society, 24, 44, 100, 126
Confucian values, 24, 52, 69, 136, See Confucianism
Confucianism, 3, 13, 42, 43, 44, 45, 46, 48, 50, 51, 59, 60, 61, 62, 63, 64, 66, 70, 99, 101
Confucius, 44, 45, 46, 50, 51, 54, 61, 62
corporatisation, 84
corruption, 13, 25, 45, 89, 90, 104, 105, 106, 107, 109, 135, 161, 177, 184
Co-ti-nhe, 221
C-space, 2, 9, 10, 11, 187
culture dimensions, 2, 11, 12, 13, 14, 40

D

Dai cho, 103
Dapice, D.O., 84, 85, 162, 163, 174, 177, 181
de Vylder, S., 33, 41, 44, 74, 75, 78, 79, 80, 81, 82, 101, 106, 186
Decision-90, 84, 160, 161
Decision-91, 84, 85, 128, 130, 132, 160, 161
Deng Xiaoping, 92
dictatorship, 25
dishonesty, 103
distrust, 103
doi moi, 92
Donaldson, L., 8, 137
Dong chi, 65
Dong Yang, 93
Durkheim, E., 11, 30

E

economic development, 1, 5, 9, 24, 25, 26, 42, 72, 77, 86, 199
economic exchange, 19, 20
economic growth, 12, 13, 14, 25, 66, 82
Eisenhardt, K.M., 7, 8, 9, 92

embedded materialism, 3, 73, 112, 164, 170, 173, 174
embeddedness, 16, 21, 27, 110, 111, 171
entrepreneurial sprit, 58
equitisation, 83, 176, 177, 178
exogamous community family, 55, 69, 159

F

face, 10, 57, 70, 101, 153, 183
Feenstra, R.C., 26
fence breaking, 79
Fforde, A., 33, 41, 44, 74, 75, 78, 79, 80, 81, 82, 86, 90, 101, 106, 163, 186
fief, 9, 10
five Confucian virtues, 70
foreign direct investment, 89
foreign-owned enterprises, 86
formal rules, 18, 19, 22, 23, 24, 25, 26, 98, 107, 109, 156, 184
Foucault, M, 180
French colonialism, 59, 73, 74
French rule, 44, 73, 74

G

garment enterprise, 37, 38, 105, 115, 116, 121, 122, 124, 130, 131, 134, 135, 141, 156, 158, 159, 163, 169
GDP, 13, 85, 87, 88, 89
gentleman ideal, 45, 52
Giddens, A., 14, 26, 98, 99
globalisation, 21, 176
Granovetter, M, 16, 26, 98, 110, 111
guerila capitalism, 3, 107, 111, 160, 163, 184

H

Haiphong, 144, 147
Hamilton, G.G., 12, 13, 16, 17, 18, 21, 24, 25, 26, 27, 48, 49, 50, 67, 99, 111, 119, 162, 187, 205
Han, 51
Hanoi, 100, 140, 144, 148, 151, 175
Hanoi Bureau of Labour, Invalids and Social Affairs, 167
Hanoi Communist Party, 124
Hanoi Industrial Bureau, 153, 167
Hanoi Industrial Department, 124
Heller, F, 32
Hickey, G.C., 37, 40, 56, 58, 103
hierarchy, 16, 18, 46, 57, 58, 60, 66, 69, 70, 110, 138, 145
hieu, 48
Ho Chi Minh, 51, 60
Hoa Hao, 61
Hofstede, G., 2, 11, 12, 13, 14, 40, 66, 70, See culture dimensions
horoscopes, 64
household businesses, 86, 88
Hung kings, 41
Huynh Phu So, 61

I

IBM, 13
ideal type, 2, 3, 22, 28, 112
IMF, 5, 6, 35, 181, 185
individualism, 12
industrialisation, 181
informal norms, 19, 22, 98
institutional isomorphism, 26
institutional matrix, 3, 18, 19, 22, 23, 28, 37, 92, 107, 108, 110, 111, 163, 164, 176, 178, 184, 187
institutional theory, 2, 15, 26
institutional theory of organisation, 26

J

Japanese colonialism, 17
joint-ventures, 13, 86, 94, 104, 127, 175, 188
jokes, 58

K

Khuong Cong Phu, 44
kingdom of Aulac, 41
Kornai, J, 5, 6

L

Lao-Tze, 62
law enforcement, 90, 95, 96, 109
law of avoidance, 67
Law of Private Enterprise, 120
Law of State Enterprise, 120
Le dynasty, 42, 59
Le Loi, 42
Le Thanh Tong, 42
Lee Kuan Yew, 25
Lenin, 51, 166
Li Cam, 44
Li Tien, 44
light bulb enterprise, 37, 38, 116, 121, 130, 135, 155, 158, 159, 163, 169, 175, 179
local SOEs, 127, 129
Long An Mineral Water Joint-Venture, 96
Lu, Y., 33, 113, 117, 118, 128
luat (law), 138
Ly (1009-1225), 42
Ly dynasty, 59

M

Mai Thuc Lan, 104, 106
management behaviour, 5, 7, 9, 33, 188
Mao Tse-Tung, 92
market, 9
market economy, 1, 11, 28, 42, 92, 97, 106, 152, 161, 164, 166, 172, 182, 184, 185, 186
Marx, 48, 51, 165, 171
Marxism, 60, 64
Marx's labour theory of value, 3, 112, 164, 165, 166, 170, 171
materialism, 164, 165, 174, 175, 180, 181, 185
Mencius, 46, 53

M-form hypothesis, 16
Ministry of Commerce, 87, 105
Ministry of Finance, 128, 166
Ministry of Industry, 166
Ministry of Labour, Invalids and Social
    Affairs, 128, 132, 133, 143, 166, 169, 171
Ministry of Planning and Investment, 128
Ministry of Trade, 128
monopoly, 188
Mr. Cuong, 153, 155
Mr. Dung, 169
Mr. Hung, 151, 154, 174
Mr. Mai, 154
Mr. Minh, 148, 150, 152
Mr. Ngoc, 139
Mr. Nguyet, 153
Mr. Quan, 135, 155
Mr. Tan, 148, 149, 150
Mr. Than, 105
Mr. Thang, 173
Mr. Thong, 143, 144, 149, 150, 162
Mr. Tuan, 151, 153, 162, 170, 181
Mr. Van, 157
Mr. Vinh, 108, 109
Ms. Hong, 139
Ms. Tuan, 150
Ms.Trieu, 59

N

National Assembly, 104, 106
National Day, 135
neo-Confucianism, 45, 59, 66
Nguyen Binh Khiem, 63
Nguyen code, 92
Nguyen Cong Tru, 63
Nguyen dynasty, 42, 53
Nguyen Minh Tu, 133
Nobel Prize in Economics, 18
North Vietnam, 75
North, D., 2, 14, 16, 18, 19, 20, 21, 22, 23,
    25, 26, 27, 41, 42, 68, 72, 73, 75, 95, 97,
    98, 99, 109, 164, See institutional matrix

O

opportunism, 3, 10, 15, 98, 111, 134, 137,
    138, 140, 158, 159, 160, 161, 185
opportunistic behaviour, 175
organisational behaviour, 2, 3, 63, 186
organisational structure, 12, 13, 17
over-centralisation, 160
over-employment, 181
Overseas Chinese businesses, 103, 136
Overseas Chinese family businesses, 136

P

Park Chung Hee, 25
Parsons, T., 23, 24, 26, 210
path dependence, 73
patrilineal logic, 18
payment practice in SOEs, 166
Pettigrew, A, 29, 144
Pham The Duyet, 104
Phan Huy Ich, 63

Phat, 51, 59, 60, 61
post-Confucian, 25, 70, *See* neo-
    Confucianism
poverty, 25
principal/ agent theory, 7
private enterprises, 84, 86, 88, 96, 127, 182
privatisation, 5, 83, 176, 177, 178, 185, 188
protectionism, 188

Q

Quang Trung, 59

R

Red River, 52, 68
Redding, S.G., 12, 16, 17, 21, 24, 26, 45, 46,
    48, 49, 50, 51, 52, 61, 63, 65, 69, 70, 99,
    101, 108, 111, 136
religion, 50, 51, 60, 61, 62, 63, 64, 98
Ricardo, D., 165
rules of the game, 4, 18, 19, 25, 37, 92, 96,
    107, 108, 110, 112, 159, 175, 180, 182,
    183, 184, 185, 186, 188

S

salary budget (qui long), 132, 143, 167, 169,
    171, 173
SBC theory. *See* soft budget constraint
Scott, W.R, 23
Seventh Party Congress, 83
Shinto teachings, 70
shoe enterprise, 3, 29, 35, 36, 37, 38, 115,
    116, 118, 121, 122, 124, 125, 127, 130,
    133, 134, 137, 138, 143, 145, 146, 147,
    149, 151, 153, 154, 155, 158, 159, 161,
    162, 167, 168, 169, 170, 172, 173, 174,
    175, 179, 181
Silk Road, 68
Sixth Party Congress, 81
social rank, 58
social status, 57, 58
SOE behaviour, 2, 3, 22, 32, 184, 187, See
    SOEs
SOE pay policy, 164
SOE reform, 2, 73, 79, 82, 84, 90, 114, 127,
    166, 173, 176, 183, 186
SOEs, 1, 2, 3, 5, 6, 8, 21, 22, 29, 31, 32, 33,
    34, 36, 37, 73, 75, 78, 80, 81, 82, 83, 84,
    85, 86, 87, 96, 105, 112, 113, 114, 117,
    118, 120, 123, 127, 128, 133, 136, 138,
    143, 145, 153, 158, 159, 160, 161, 163,
    164, 165, 166, 167, 168, 170, 171, 173,
    174, 176, 178, 180, 181, 182, 184, 185,
    186, 187
soft budget constraint, 2, 5, 187, 207
soft taxation, 5
Soviet-style development model, 1, 73, 75,
    77, 92, 112, 184
Soviet-style development period, 77
Soviet-style economy, 76, 77, 78, 92, 97,
    101, 106, 123
Stalinist development model, 101
Standing Party Central Committee, 124
State Enterprise Law (1985), 84

State Enterprise Law(, 84
stock market, 21, 96, 97, 183
subsidy, 188
sun yung, 103
Sung, 51
surplus value, 165

T

Tao, 62
Taoism, 51, 62, 63, 214
Tay Son, 42, 59
Tet holiday, 135
Than, 60, 61
Thanh, 60
theory of human behaviour, 19
theory of transaction costs, 19
three pillars of institutions, 23
Three-Plan System, 79, 80, 82
tien chua, 159
Tienanmen Square, 67
Tokugawa village, 17
Trade Union Law, 125
Tran (1225-1400), 42
Tran Dang Khoa, 52
Tran dynasty, 59
Tran Ngoc Them, 41, 43, 51, 54, 57, 58, 60, 63, 100, 102, 106, 109
transaction costs, 3, 15, 16, 19, 20, 26, 28, 108, 109, 110, 111, 184
transaction-governance structures, 9, 10, 11
triangulation, 36
Trung sisters, 59

U

uncodification, 187
unemployment, 13, 25, 166, 177, 181

V

Van Lang, 41
VB Steel, 95
Vietnam Supreme Court, 96

W

Weber, M, 11, 22, 24, 26, 32, 43, 48, 50, 51, 58, 62, 90, 93, 98, 99, 102, 107, 136
Whitley, R, 12, 13, 16, 21, 24, 25, 27, 99, 101, 111
Williamson, O. E., 15, 16, 18, 20, 98, 110, 111, 137, 138, 158
Williamson's transaction cost theory of organisations, 15
World Bank, 5, 6, 35, 84, 86, 87, 88, 94, 97, 163, 164, 178, 181, 182, 185, 216

X

xiao, 48, 49, 119

Y

yin-yang, 30, 63, 68

Printed and bound by CPI Group (UK) Ltd, Croydon, CR0 4YY

08/05/2025

01864970-0001